FASHION SINCE 1900

JOHN PEACOCK

FASHION SINCE 1900
THE COMPLETE SOURCEBOOK

WITH A PREFACE BY CHRISTIAN LACROIX

1250 DETAILED ORIGINAL DRAWINGS IN COLOUR

Thames & Hudson

For Celia Rhoden

First published in the United Kingdom in 1993 by Thames & Hudson Ltd, 181A High Holborn, London WC1V 7QX

www.thamesandhudson.com

Previously published as *20th-Century Fashion*

Revised edition 2007

British Library Cataloguing-in-Publication Data
A catalogue record for this book is available from the British Library

ISBN-13:   978-0-500-51345-3
ISBN-10:   0-500-51345-7

Printed and bound in China by C.S. Graphics

Contents

Preface by Christian Lacroix

You have just opened a book which would have been one of the most wonderful gifts anyone could have given me when, as a child and a young man, I searched avidly for information about the fashions of the early twentieth century. The histories of costume that were available to me then simply glossed over those early decades, decades which are so important, so critical to an understanding of fashion's history. One had to turn instead to period magazines and films, or to family photograph albums, in order to travel back to those rich years in which the history of dress began its rush towards the dizzying kaleidoscope of styles which were to end in today's 'centrifugal fashion'.

In past centuries, the pace was slower; one moved gradually, subtly, from one fashion to another. When the nineteenth century gave birth to the twentieth, everything changed. There was a paroxysm of progress, speed, novelty.... Suddenly we could fly, we had telephones, we could record sound, we could capture life's images and project them onto a screen; strange machines shrank space and time with the speed of light. Art, politics, daily life – and therefore fashion – were also hooked into the rhythm of change. In fashion, change came virtually every year, even in the face of war, economic depression, existential crisis.

When I was young I sat day after day trying to analyze what Mr Peacock offers here – a kind of shop window in front of which one can go back in time: sleeves that were puffed and then narrowed, waistlines that rose and then fell, fabrics that were at first stiff and then soft, hats and hairstyles that went from the flamboyant to the minimalist and back again.

Studying the styles of the past was my favourite game and I would have liked it to have become my work: creating clothes for films, plays or operas, reconstructing this or that period. Such a talent is in fact typically English – or perhaps Italian: attention to detail, a gift for evoking the past, a sensitivity to documentary records. But the man or woman who undertakes research of this kind must tread warily: the more the century progresses, the greater is the gulf between magazine images of fashion and what is actually being worn on the street. There is no risk of that with this book, however. Here the everyday is patiently dissected side by side with fashion's idealized images.

Fashion Since 1900 presents us with a fresco that is all the more fascinating because it provides inspiration for the new fin-de-siècle – our own. In this panoramic assessment of the last one hundred years, what is still unseen is the inspiration we will draw from the clothes of today and tomorrow.

For if any theory is close to my heart – if only because it is proved every single day – it is that there is an almost Oedipal recycling of fashions: couturiers, who were all children once, have always been inspired by the past, first the distant past, then, increasingly, the more immediate past, until historical documents are replaced by the ever lingering memories of what one's mother wore. Just in this way did the fashion of the Belle Epoque (itself so spiced with 18th- and 19th-century quotations) inspire Christian Dior's New Look of 1947; the Directoire fashion of Paul Poiret, the 'sack' dresses of the fifties, even the 'crazy years' of the mid-twenties influenced the fashions of the early sixties, a decade which was to end, in complete thrall to the thirties, with the Retro/Biba look. Equally chronologically, it was during the seventies that Yves Saint Laurent made us look back at the forties with new respect (and the forties themselves were full of Victorian details). Throughout the eighties we went on exploring and re-exploring the fifties and sixties, and the nineties revisited the seventies.

The fashions of the present years are so diverse and contradictory that to understand them fully one would need another volume by Mr Peacock, just as rich, as detailed, and as comprehensive as this one. For our 21st-century fashion mixes not only all periods but also all countries, cultures, folklores and technologies, perhaps reflecting better than anything else the hope we all share of catching fleeting time.

Introduction by John Peacock

As dictated by the couturier, fashionable dress represents an ideal which few women attain but to which many aspire. This collection of drawings represents my impression of what that 'ideal' may have been from 1900 to the present day. This period has seen women's fashions undergo such a bewildering variety of changes that to do full justice to it would require a separate book for each decade. The transition from the tightly corseted and restricted 'lady' of 1900 to the tracksuited 'woman' of the 21st century has involved a rapidity of evolution unparalleled in any previous era.

This collection is divided into ten parts, each representing a decade and including a new part specially prepared for this edition, taking the reader right up until the present day. Each part begins with the work of leading couturiers (though since the 1960s it would perhaps be more accurate to describe these as 'designers') and continues with sections on Underwear, Leisure Wear, Day Wear, Evening Wear, Bridal Wear and Accessories. The division of each part into sections conforming to these headings is, of course, somewhat arbitrary and has been imposed in order to make a very complicated subject manageable within the aims of this book. For the same reason I have tended to simplify where necessary in order to help the non-specialist reader towards an understanding of the evolution of modern-day fashion.

An updated annotated chart at the end of the book depicts the fashionable outline in silhouette, and notes the principal changes in shape, length, colour, fabric, accessories, etc., for each five-year period. There is also a brief account of the working lives of those couturiers whose garments I have illustrated, as well as a select bibliography to assist those who may wish to take their studies further.

Vernon 1900

Maison Rouff 1901

Paquin 1903

Underwear 1900–1904

1900

1902

1904

1904

1901

1901

1902

1904

1904

1900

1901

1903

1903

1902

1903

1904

1901

1902

1902

1900

1902

1902

1903

1904

1904

1904

1904

1904

1902

1900

1903

1904

1900

1902

1904

1900

1900

1900

1901

1900

1901

1903

1903

1903

1903

1904

1903

1903

1904

1904

1904

1904

1903

Drécoll
1905

Worth 1905

Redfern 1908

Paquin 1909

1905

1906

1905

1906

1907

1908

1908

1909

1905

1906

1907

1907

1908

1909

1905

1905

1905

1905

1905

1906

1906

1907

1908

1908

1909

1909

Evening Wear 1905–1909

1905

1906

1908

1909

1905

1906

1909

1905

1908

1905

1905

1907

1905

1908

1907

1905

1906

1908

1908

1909

1909

1909

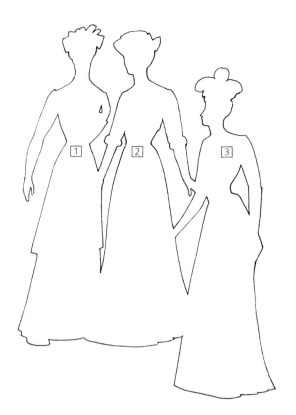

Couture Wear 1900–1903

1 Vernon 1900. Pink linen tailored suit with long fitted jacket; open side vents trimmed with silk braid and silk-covered buttons to match the detail on the slim fitted sleeves, bodice, mock waistcoat, side panels and hem of the flared skirt. Fine cream silk blouse with high stand collar and waterfall jabot. Cream straw hat with brim turned up at front and back and trimmed with stiffened silk ribbon and a silk posy. White kid gloves. 2 Maggy Rouff 1901. Pale green silk-velvet afternoon dress, fitted bodice with deep waistband, three-quarter-length sleeves gathered into narrow fur cuffs matching the asymmetric trimming on bodice and flared skirt. Mock blouse of striped silk with high stand collar. Heavy boldly patterned lace covering one shoulder, forming fitted undersleeves and trimming the skirt. Straw hat with brim turned up at each side, decorated with large green silk-taffeta bow and green curled ostrich feathers. 3 Paquin 1903. Cream wool day dress, fitted bodice with low V-shaped neckline and pale blue silk-satin infill which buttons through to high stand collar edged with narrow silk braid, long fitted sleeves trimmed at wrist with diagonally placed pale blue satin ribbon to match the banding on bodice and on hem of flared skirt. Small toque of swathed blue silk trimmed with cream ostrich feathers. Fur muff lined in blue silk.

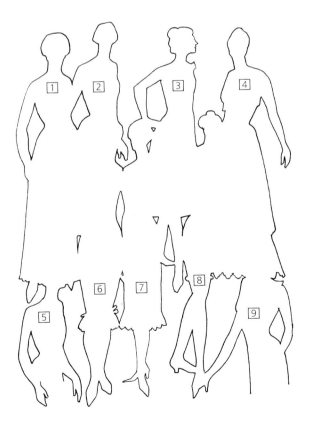

Underwear 1900–1904

1 1900. Striped nainsook petticoat, sleeveless bodice cut in one piece with ankle-length flared skirt; armholes, low neckline and pleated hemline trimmed with machine-made lace. 2 1902. Plain white cotton sleeveless camisole trimmed and edged with machine-made lace and satin ribbon, front fastening with hooks and eyes. 3 1904. Cream cotton bust improver/ brassiere, lightly boned and stitched, adjustable shoulder straps, satin ribbon trimming. Boned cotton-canvas waist corset with adjustable suspenders. 4 1904. Embroidered cotton corset heavily boned to give flat front and narrow waist, back lacing, front opening with hooks and bars, adjustable suspenders. 5 1901. Cream linen boned and stitched bust support, adjustable shoulder straps, side-front fastening at waist. 6 1901. White nainsook sleeveless camisole with low square neckline trimmed and edged with broderie anglaise, machine-made lace and ribbon; front fastening with tiny pearl buttons, taped and tied on waist over narrow hip basque. White cotton knee-length knickers trimmed with ribbon and lace. Black silk stockings. 7 1902. White nainsook combinations with high round neckline and short sleeves, trimmed to match the knee-length knickers with broderie anglaise, machine-made lace and embroidered ribbon. Black silk stockings. 8 1904. Cream ribbed-linen waist-length corset and bust support, low neckline trimmed with broderie anglaise and ribbon, adjustable shoulder straps, front fastening. Lightly boned ribbed-linen hip protector in matching cream, back lacing and front fastening, suspenders trimmed with ribbon. Purple silk stockings with clock embroidery at ankles. 9 1904. Heavy-rib cotton corset, heavily boned, whalebone front busk, back lacing and front fastening, suspenders covered with ruched ribbon. Waist-length nainsook camisole trimmed with broderie anglaise and threaded ribbon.

Leisure Wear 1900–1904

[1] 1900. Bicycling costume. Dark grey cotton bodice trimmed with large red satin bow at base of white cotton-piqué collar, matching white cotton cuffs. Leather belt with round brass buckle. Dark grey wool knickerbockers. Black wool stockings. Long brown leather lace-up boots. Small straw boater with ribbon trimming. [2] 1901. Riding costume. Dark green wool-serge tailored jacket with cut-away front, high button fastening, wide collar and revers, tight sleeves, flared skirt. Red wool waistcoat. White cotton shirt with high stand collar, turquoise silk necktie. Brown leather gloves and boots. Straw boater trimmed with ribbon. [3] 1903. Skating costume. Dark red velvet jacket and skirt; ermine fur trimming on the peter pan collar, the cape oversleeves, the wrists of the tight undersleeves and the hem of the flared skirt; matching ermine muff. Small hat covered with red velvet, black ribbon and feather trimming. [4] 1903. Tennis costume. Cream and beige striped cotton blouse and skirt, the top with mock-bolero effect buttoning to one side, the seaming continues through to the bishop sleeves. Leather belt with large silver buckle. Flared ankle-length skirt pleated at each side, sewn down from waist to hip-level. Cream canvas boots with low heels and pointed toes, side button fastening. [5] 1902. Bathing costume. Pale blue cotton top with square neckline, imitation strap opening and buttoned belt in white cotton, trimmed with a narrow red ribbon edging to match open skirt and hems of knee-length drawers. [6] 1903. Bathing costume. Navy blue cotton with white spots, trimmed with bands of plain red cotton; long sleeveless top with low round neckline, knee-length drawers. Rubber bathing shoes. [7] 1904. Bathing costume. Blue wool top with square neckline, cap sleeves and short split skirt edged with embroidered ribbon to match the top and the knee-length drawers. Blue wool turban.

Day Wear 1900–1902

[1] 1900. Turquoise wool day dress, cross-over bodice trimmed with fine looped braid to match hem of three-quarter-length sleeves and hem of flared skirt, smocked shoulder detail, finely tucked false front with high stand collar, lace trimming to match tight undersleeves, shaped belt with side button fastening. Hair dressed away from face over pads, large high bun. [2] 1901. Cream silk day dress with low scooped neckline, tucked collar and gathered tie, small brooch, short oversleeves, ruched belt, panelled skirt. Lace blouse with high stand collar and long fitted sleeves. [3] 1902. Knee-length red fox-fur coat with large collar and revers, wide sleeves with deep cuffs, edge-to-edge fastening, mock double-breasted button detail. Lace blouse with stand collar and jabot. Brown leather gloves. Hat with large brim, ostrich feather trim. [4] 1902. Long mid-grey wool-serge tailored travelling coat with small collar and revers, concealed front fastening; raglan sleeves with top-stitched wrist, strap, pockets and hem. Small brimless turban. [5] 1902. Light brown herringbone wool-tweed double-breasted tailored jacket, tight sleeves with shaped inset velvet cuffs matching the revers, buttons and hem of the flared skirt. White cotton shirt with high stand collar. Silk bow tie. Short leather gloves. Hat covered in brown silk with gathered crown and split brim bound with striped silk, matching bow, feather trim. [6] 1902. Lilac silk afternoon dress covered with white-spotted lilac chiffon, inserted shaped lace yoke edged with ruched silk, matching hip basque and insertions on the tucked pleated and gathered skirt, elbow-length pleated sleeves. Long-handled silk-covered parasol trimmed with lace. Long white kid gloves. Lilac straw hat with wide brim, ribbon and feather trimming.

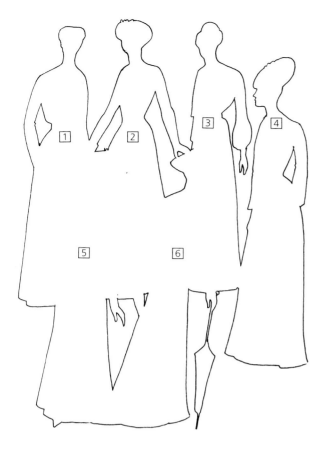

Day Wear 1903–1904

1 1903. Silk day dress, khaki and brown striped silk bodice with low square neckline edged with white silk collar, matching cuffs on long tucked and fitted sleeves, double-breasted button detail, brown velvet waistband, flared panelled skirt, button decoration at each side of front panel above the tucked hem. Lace infill with high stand collar. 2 1904. Pale green travelling costume, short bolero jacket with side button fastening, decorative buttoned-down shoulder straps, fitted inset sleeves with turned-back cuffs, princess-line skirt cut in one with the bodice. White kid gloves. Straw hat with upturned brim decorated with a silk posy and ribbon. 3 1904. Flower-sprigged silk-taffeta afternoon dress with lace insertions edged with plain brown silk ruching to match the hem of the three-quarter-length oversleeves and the trimming of the flared skirt. 4 1904. Dull yellow silk visiting costume; short pintucked jacket trimmed with guipure lace; flared skirt trimmed with matching lace, ribbon and braid. Pleated silk blouse with high stand collar. White gloves. Natural straw hat trimmed with lace and silk flowers. 5 1904. Short jacket of dyed musquash, peter pan collar, wide three-quarter-length sleeves with deep cuffs, edge-to-edge loop-and-button fastening, wide waistband. Flared skirt in blue striped wool. Long black leather gloves. Straw hat with wide flat brim and shallow crown bound and trimmed with ribbon and silk flowers. 6 1904. Pale cream cotton visiting costume, collarless bolero jacket with elbow-length sleeves gathered into wide cuffs, princess-line dress embroidered to match the bolero jacket. Long white kid gloves. Long-handled parasol. Natural straw hat with wide brim and small shallow crown covered in tiny silk flowers.

Evening Wear 1900–1904

1 1900. Pink silk ballgown with low neckline draped with lace from shoulders to centre front, ending in large bow and corsage of silk flowers; tightly fitted bodice with short lace-edged overbodice; draped cummerbund; flared skirt, the panel seams decorated with silk flowers and ribbon; four rows of pleated silk border the hem and train from each side of the front panel. Long white gloves. Double rope of pearls extending to waist, matching drop earrings. 2 1902. Pale turquoise silk ballgown, lace-edged off-the-shoulder neckline, wide ribbon straps, large puff sleeves with lace falls, fitted bodice, V-shaped pintucked panel emphasized by large silk flower, deep pleated cummerbund, flared skirt decorated with garlands of silk flowers and wide lace frill around hem. Long white gloves. Single strand of pearls, pearl drop earrings. Hair dressed with side parting and set in waves. 3 1903. Black silk dinner gown covered with spotted black chiffon; low scooped neckline edged with black and gold lace repeated on the hem and train of the skirt; the gathered sleeves, the sleeve frill and the bodice banded with insertions of gold lace; wide black velvet cummerbund. Corsage of flowers worn at waist and in hair. Long white gloves. Long rope of pearls knotted on bustline; necklace and pendent; small drop earrings. 4 1904. Cream lace evening gown mounted on cream silk, low neckline, short cap sleeve formed by scallop of lace continuing from overbodice, pale brown cummerbund, flared skirt dipping into long train at back. Long white kid gloves. Necklace set with stones, matching drop earrings. Hair dressed with thick plait of false hair.

Bridal Wear 1900–1904

1 1900. Cream silk wedding dress decorated with heavy boldly patterned off-white lace around the low V-shaped neckline, from shoulder to elbow of the fitted sleeves and in swags and bands circling the hem and long train of the flared skirt; pleated cummerbund; pintucked chiffon infill; high stand collar edged with lace. Long cream lace veil attached by small tiara of pearls. Double row of pearls at throat. 2 1902. Ivory silk-satin wedding gown with appliqué of embroidered lace on the shoulder, on the fitted bodice and on the panels, hem and train of the flared skirt; small lace-covered puff sleeves matching the front of the bodice and the frilled hemline of the skirt; horizontally tucked undersleeves end in a lace frill at wrist. Fine tulle veil sprigged with flowers covers the hair and is secured by narrow wreath of wax flowers. 3 1904. White silk-satin wedding gown trimmed with swathe of fine handmade lace across bustline, matching epaulettes and infill with high stand collar, a line of delicate beading and embroidery on the fitted bodice continues through to edge of overskirt and train, underskirt cut in flared panels. Silk-tulle veil spotted with tiny seed pearls. A posy of flowers held in a gathered fan of the dress fabric makes a small headdress.

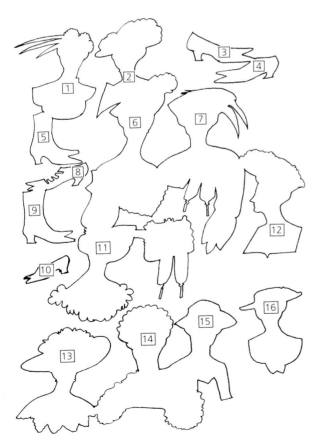

Accessories 1900–1904

1 1900. Small brimless fabric-covered hat decorated with three velvet flowers and three feathers. Small velvet shoulder cape. 2 1900. Hat covered with blue silk velvet, wide brim bound with red silk, blue ostrich feathers held by buckle and large red velvet bow. 3 1900. Grey leather shoes with openwork detail, trimmed with black leather, louis heels. 4 1901. Light brown suede shoes with high vamp, ribbon laces, pointed toes and stacked heels. 5 1901. High leather boots in two-tone grey, button fastening, high heels. 6 1903. Hat covered with silk, upturned brim trimmed with ostrich feathers and looped silk ribbon. Lace-trimmed tucked gathered and frilled blouse with high stand collar. Green velvet muff trimmed with velvet posy and large ribbon bow with tassled ends. 7 1904. Beige felt hat, upturned brim trimmed with two feathers and a silver brooch. Fox fur stole. 8 1903. Brown suede shoes with four cross straps, button fastenings, brown leather heels. 9 1903. High buttoned boots, grey canvas uppers, black patent-leather toecaps and heels. 10 1904. Brown suede shoes with louis heels, high vamp trimmed with ribbon bow. 11 1903. Headdress of tiny silk violets, Long rope of pearls looped three times around neck. Neckline edged with outsized silk flowers. 12 1904. Maroon velvet-covered hat with upturned brim, ostrich feather and satin bow trimming. 13 1903. Natural straw hat, crown covered with silk roses, single rose tucked under wide brim. Lace bertha collar, single strand of pearls and knotted gold chain. 14 1903. Hat brim covered with rows of gathered silk tulle. Peach-coloured feather boa. 15 1904. Masculine-style straw panama hat with upturned brim. 16 1904. Natural straw hat with asymmetric crown, swathed with spotted fabric, upturned brim. White shirt with eton collar, worn with short red tie.

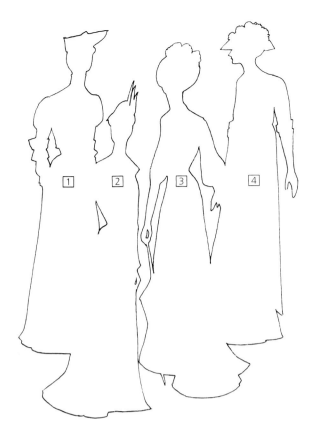

Couture Wear 1905–1909

1 Drécoll 1905. Pale blue wool winter costume trimmed with dark blue wool around neck, on turned-back cuffs of three-quarter-length sleeves and in centres of covered buttons; tight-fitting bodice open at front to reveal white silk false waistcost with double row of buttons; lace infill with stand collar matching gathered and frilled undersleeves; flared skirt with pleated side panels dipping to small train at back. Long white kid gloves. Felt hat with upturned brim. 2 Worth 1905. Deep purple panne-velvet visiting dress, fitted boned bodice with *ombré* beaded panel matching the detail on the wrists of the fitted sleeves and on the panel of silk tulle at each side of the flared skirt which dips into long train at back, cummerbund trimmed with fringed beaded motif, high neckband and jabot of fine lace. Small lacquered straw hat with narrow brim turned up at back, trimmed with ribbon, braid and bird-of-paradise feathers. 3 Redfern 1908. Cream silk princess-line visiting dress decorated with embroidered openwork flowers and leaves, fitted bodice with stand collar, decorative shoulder straps with beaded tassel ends, three-quarter-length sleeves narrow into fitted grown-on cuffs, flared skirt with long train. Long white kid gloves. Long-handled silk-covered parasol. Beige silk-covered hat with wide upturned brim decorated with cream ostrich feathers. 4 Paquin 1909. Pink silk and silk-chiffon afternoon dress, high waist, chiffon overbodice with inset bands of fine lace, asymmetric swathe of ribbon-trimmed chiffon ending with silk posy, three-quarter-length sleeves with double cuffs, silk underskirt, middle skirt of fine lace, overskirt hem cut into uneven points trimmed with rectangles of silk ribbon. Long white gloves. Natural straw hat with turned-down brim, wide shallow crown covered with silk flowers.

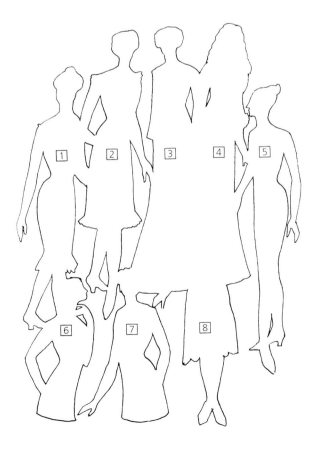

Underwear 1905–1909

1 1905. White nainsook sleeveless combinations with low neckline, fitted bodice with V-shaped lace insertions, front fastening with covered buttons, wide knee-length open-crotch knickers trimmed with machine-made lace. Black silk stockings. 2 1906. Stiffened cotton camisole, front fastening, taped waist, worn over short sleeveless fine lawn chemise trimmed with broderie anglaise and satin ribbon, open french knickers trimmed with bands and insertions of machine-made lace. Black silk stockings. 3 1905. Apple green wool housecoat; front edges, high waistbelt, shawl collar and wide sleeve cuffs decorated with appliqué of pink and cream satin leaves. 4 1906. Pink velvet housecoat trimmed from neck to hem and around the flared sleeves with bright pink curled feathers, fastening with velvet rouleau looped around large mock self-fabric buttons. 5 1907. Heavily boned and stitched cotton corset, back lacing, front fastening with hooks and bars, adjustable suspenders. Waist-length nainsook chemise with scalloped edge, wide shoulder straps, wide lace trim. White silk stockings. 6 1908. Heavy-duty cotton corset and bust support cut in one piece, heavily stitched and boned, wide shoulder straps, back lacing and front opening. 7 1908. Stiffened cotton corset, cut high under bust, boned to shape waist and with extra-long front busk to flatten stomach. White lawn chemise trimmed with broderie anglaise and satin ribbon. 8 1909. Pink cotton-satin corset, heavily stitched and boned, trimmed with ribbon bow and deep band of lace, back lacing and front fastening with hooks and bars. Knee-length nainsook sleeveless petticoat with low neckline, trimmed with ribbon and lace to match scalloped hemline. Black silk stockings.

Leisure Wear 1905–1909

1 1905. Dark cream cavalry-twill motoring coat with large double-cape under-collar, top-stitched collar and wide revers, tailored bodice and flared skirt, sloping hip-level pockets, long fitted sleeves, all edges top-stitched. Brown leather gloves. Natural straw hat trimmed with large bow and two feathers, hat secured with long cream gauze veil worn over hat and tied under chin. 2 1906. Fur-lined dark pink three-quarter-length double-breasted ski coat with large fur collar; revers, pockets, cuffs and covered buttons in dark plum-coloured velvet matching the wide binding on hem of flared tweed skirt. Leather gloves. Knitted red wool scarf with fringed hems. Fur hat covering head, ears and chin. 3 1907. Tennis costume. White shirt with stiff collar and cuffs, worn with blue wool necktie. Knitted cream wool collarless cardigan, button fastening, large patch pockets. Ankle-length flared beige wool skirt. White canvas lace-up shoes with round toes and flat heels. 4 1907. Golfing costume. Olive green wool-tweed tailored suit, Norfolk-style jacket with pleats running from shoulder to hem, wide buckled belt, high buttoned fastening, narrow collar and revers, inset sleeves with shaped cuff, ankle-length panelled flared skirt, scalloped border on hemline. Brown leather gloves. Brown leather lace-up boots with flat heels and pointed toes. Green wool-tweed peaked cap. 5 1908. Sailing costume. Blue wool-gabardine hip-length double-breasted jacket bound with red braid, trimmed with gold anchor motifs on collar and cuffs, shiny gold buttons, ankle-length pleated skirt. White leather lace-up boots with grey leather pointed toecaps and flat heels. Blue brimless hat trimmed with red ribbon, bow and pompon. 6 1909. Riding costume. Green and grey striped long tailored jacket, high single-breasted fastening, narrow revers, dark green velvet collar and cuffs, flap pockets placed low on hips, narrow ankle-length skirt with large box pleat at back. Leather gloves and riding boots. Black bowler hat with veil covering face.

Day Wear 1905–1906

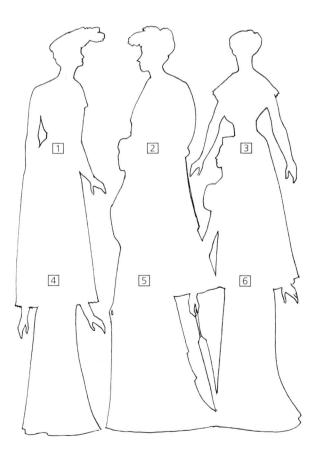

1 1905. Pink silk visiting costume trimmed with bands of guipure lace, short bolero jacket with long narrow collar, fitted inset sleeves with shaped cuffs, flared skirt trimmed with dark red silk pleating to match cummerbund and jacket lining. Cream chiffon blouse with high stand collar embroidered at edge, finely pleated jabot. Cream straw hat trimmed with feathers. 2 1905. Three-quarter-length dyed-musquash coat, edge-to-edge clasp fastening under bust, wide three-quarter-length sleeves edged at wrist with fur dyed deep red to match large tail-trimmed collar. Long white gloves. Beige felt hat with upturned brim, blue ostrich feather trim. 3 1905. Pale olive-green afternoon dress, fitted undersleeves, three-quarter-length pleated oversleeves; pleated cape-effect, with frilled edge, caught into wide cummerbund; high stand collar and outline of bodice edged with embroidered braid and trimmed with small rosettes; hem of flared skirt banded with scallops of ribbon and braid and tipped with rosettes. Hair side-parted and set into waves. 4 1905. Light green wool day dress with cross-over effect bodice, edged with lace and ending in two large bows at front above waistband, full sleeves gathered into band at elbow, two tiers of lace frills to match infill at neck, flared skirt dips into back train. 5 1905. Lilac silk afternoon dress, draped cross-over bodice, matching short oversleeves, purple velvet bow trim, matching cummerbund, three-tier skirt banded with fine pintucks and embroidered flowers echoed on bodice and sleeves. 6 1906. Striped cloth visiting costume, V-shaped neckline detail edged with scalloped and embroidered white silk collar and infilled with ruched silk, cummerbund and sleeve cuffs in striped silk matching piping on flared skirt. Leather gloves. Long-handled umbrella. Small brimless hat trimmed with three feathers.

Day Wear 1906–1909

1 1906. Peach pink spotted cotton day dress and short sleeveless bolero jacket, fitted dress bodice with shaped yoke of fine lace, imitation button strap opening, flared skirt trimmed with ribbons and rosettes above hemline, white cotton-lawn oversleeves with frilled edges. Hat with upturned brim, worn at an angle, trimmed with fabric roses and ostrich feathers. 2 1907. Red velvet afternoon pinafore dress with low V-shaped neckline open to above waistband, gathered epaulettes, flared skirt with frilled hem decorated with bows. White lawn blouse, finely pintucked stand collar and inset yoke with embroidered edge, two-tier broderie-anglaise gathered oversleeves, fitted undersleeves. Straw hat with wide brim, shallow crown covered with gathered fabric and trimmed with feathers. 3 1908. Mustard-yellow tailored wool suit, long close-fitting jacket, low neckline, embroidered revers, matching sleeve cuffs, inverted box-pleated skirt. Long narrow fur stole. White leather gloves. Natural straw hat with wide turned-down brim and shallow crown trimmed with a bundle of pheasant feathers. 4 1908. Lilac and purple pin-striped tailored suit, long fitted jacket cut into long point at front, front-button fastening in sets of two, large fur collar and and matching muff, inverted box-pleated skirt. Straw hat with bound edge trimmed with looped ribbon and ostrich feathers. 5 1909. Pink silk-satin formal afternoon dress, princess-line fitted bodice and narrow skirt, embroidered yoke to under bust, elbow-length horizontally tucked oversleeves, lace infill with high neck and matching undersleeves. Long-handled silk-covered parasol. Hat with outsized brim, shallow crown covered with ostrich feathers. 6 1909. Princess-line afternoon dress, high waist effect with embroidered braid placed under bust, matching braid on scooped neckline and elbow-length sleeves, split overskirt matches fabric of bodice, lace infill. Long white gloves. Straw hat with narrow brim and wide deep crown banded with ribbon and trimmed with fabric roses.

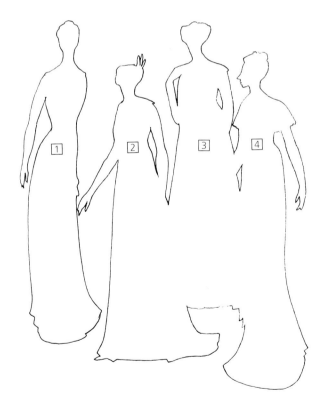

Evening Wear 1905–1909

1 1905. Evening gown of grey silk chiffon mounted over dark blue silk, fitted bodice, low scooped neckline, short pleated chiffon cap sleeves, narrow black velvet cummerbund, flared skirt with long back train, hem bound with black velvet and embroidered above with beaded flowers and leaves to match front panels of bodice. Long black gloves. Double pearl necklace, matching earrings. 2 1906. Pale green, pink and silver beaded ballgown, underbodice held under bust with wide cummerbund, upperbodice wraps over at front, short sleeves of unmounted beaded chiffon, skirt raised at each side to reveal underskirt. Long white kid gloves. Pearl necklace and matching earrings. Hair decorated with three pale green feathers. 3 1908. Pink silk evening gown with high waistline, low scooped neckline, infill of white tucked and gathered lace to match short cap sleeves, overskirt cut into handkerchief points and banded with embroidered braid to match straight hem of underskirt. Long white kid gloves. Silk posy at bosom. Necklace of pearls and pink stones, matching earrings. Hair dressed in centre parting and set in waves. 4 1909. Black lace dinner gown, high waist position marked with black silk cummerbund, low neckline edged with cape-effect draped collar, corsage of flowers at bosom and in hair, short tiered black lace sleeves, skirt of tiered lace, long train. Long gloves. Necklace and earrings of pearls and emeralds.

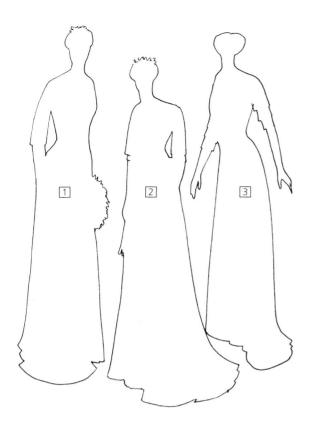

Bridal Wear 1905–1909

1 1905. Cream satin wedding dress; fitted bodice tucked, braided and tassled at each side of the front insert of finely pleated chiffon and decorated down centre front with row of tassels; high stand collar; long inset sleeves tucked horizontally to the elbow, tassel trim; narrow tucked cummerbund with short sporran of tassels; flared skirt with tucked and braided hem. Delicate silk veil falling from headdress of wax flowers and leaves. 2 1906. Ivory white satin wedding dress, low scooped neckline edged with beaded and embroidered braid, matching curved high waistbelt, neck infill of gathered and tucked lace to match undersleeves and hem of underskirt, two-tier elbow-length oversleeves, open overskirt forms long train. Crescent-shaped headdress of wax and silk flowers, fine silk-tulle veil. 3 1909. Pale cream fine silk-ottoman princess-line wedding gown, fitted bodice with panel of fine handmade lace, high stand collar, matching fitted undersleeves, inset tiered elbow-length oversleeves, seamline from shoulder to hem emphasized with fine scalloped lace ribbon. Long handmade lace veil attached to hair at back.

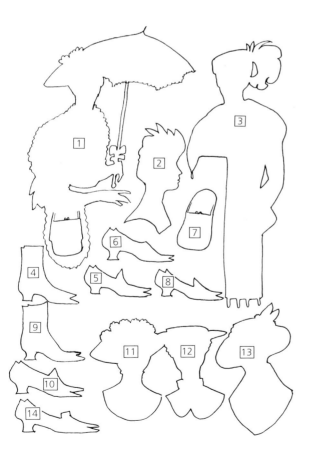

Accessories 1905–1909

1 1905. Large natural straw hat with wide brim, crown covered with silk flowers. Lace jabot attached to high stand collar. Boa of curled feathers. Long white kid gloves. Cloth bag with pleated detail, metal frame and clasp, chain handle. Lace-edged silk-covered parasol with long handle. 2 1905. Small brimless feather-covered and trimmed hat. 3 1908. Feather-covered brimless hat trimmed with a bird of paradise. Long ermine stole and matching muff. 4 1905. Grey leather lace-up boots with thick heels and pointed toecaps. 5 1908. Suede shoes with high tongue, grosgrain bow decoration, louis heels and pointed toes. 6 1905. Lace-up leather shoes with high louis heels and pointed toes. 7 1907. Embroidered cloth bag, metal frame, chain handle. 8 1907. Canvas shoes with leather heels and pointed toecaps, ribbon laces. 9 1906. High buttoned boots, grey canvas upper part, black patent-leather body, louis heels. 10 1908. Black patent-leather shoes with red leather piping and heels, cut metal buckles. 11 1908. Fabric-covered hat, wide brim with bound edge, wide shallow crown covered with silk flowers. Pleated and tucked blouse with high stand collar, small gold brooch worn at throat, long rope of pearls. 12 1909. Lacquered straw boater with wide shallow crown trimmed with petersham ribbon, flat stiff brim. 13 1909. Hat with large crown swathed with velvet, silk rosette detail, fur-covered brim, matching fur collar. 14 1909. Suede shoes with louis heels, pointed toes and cut-metal buckle trim.

Paul Poiret 1910

Jean Patou 1913

Drécoll 1913

1910

1911

1912

1910

1914

1914

1914

1910

1911

1912

1913

1914

1910

1910

1911

1911

1912

1912

1913

1913

1914

1914

Evening Wear 1910–1914

1910

1911

1912

1913

1914

1912

1910

1914

Stein & Blaine 1914

Bergdorf Goodman 1916

Paquin 1919

Underwear 1915–1919

1915

1915

1915

1917

1919

1919

1917

1915

1916

1918

1919

1919

1915

1916

1915

1916

1917

1917

1919

1918

1918

1919

1915

1918

1919

1915

1915

1917

1919

1915

1915

1915

1915

1916

1917

1917

1917

1919

1919

1918

1919

1917

1918

1919

1916

1917

1917

1919

1919

1918

1919

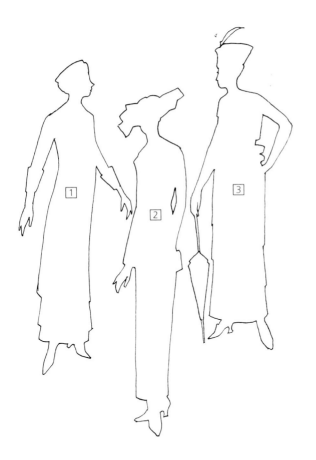

Couture Wear 1910–1913

1 Paul Poiret 1910. Red velvet suit. Seven-eighths-length high-waisted fitted jacket, edge-to-edge fastening under the bust, bracelet-length inset sleeves with deep flared multi-coloured brocade cuffs, matching shoulder-wide shawl collar and turned-back facings; fitted velvet dress with high round neckline and narrow keyhole, wrist-length fitted sleeves; narrow two-tiered skirt, top tier with button detail at each side of the panel seam above the hem. Brimless velvet and brocade hat, half rosette trim. Black leather shoes with large buckle trim, pointed toecaps and louis heels. 2 Jean Patou 1913. Brownish-pink tailored wool-serge suit, jacket with high waistband, wide revers, narrow velvet collar, inset sleeves decorated at wrists with three pearl buttons, vertical pockets on natural waist position, narrow ankle-length skirt. Cream silk blouse with high round neckline, gold and amber brooch worn at throat. Straw hat with wide upturned brim and large crown draped with brown silk to match outsize bow trimming. Small suede envelope purse. Suede shoes with wide instep straps, pointed toecaps and louis heels. 3 Drécoll 1913. Afternoon dress. High-waisted ankle-length black silk dress topped with dress of fine white voile, trimmed and edged with scalloped embroidered lace around neckline, around high-waisted overbodice and around cap sleeves, also banding the hems of the uneven tiered skirts; high waist emphasized by wide black silk belt tied into bow at back and trimmed at front with red silk flower. Natural straw hat with wide upturned brim, black feather trimming. Pearl necklace. Long white fabric gloves. Black leather shoes with buckle trimming, pleated tongues, pointed toes, high louis heels.

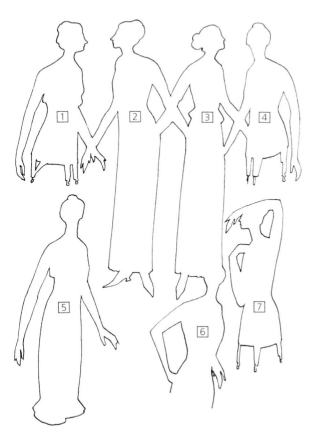

Underwear 1910–1914

1 1910. Long-line flesh-coloured woven satinized-cotton corset, boned and stitched, long front busk, broderie-anglaise trimming, front opening and back lacing, elasticated suspenders. Sleeveless white lawn chemise, low neckline, lace edging. 2 1910. Ankle-length high-waisted white nainsook petticoat, wide straps, decorative lace insertions on bodice and around hem of narrow skirt. Black silk stockings. Red velvet mules with bow trimming, pointed toes and low louis heels. 3 1911. White lawn chemise, elbow-length sleeves, low square neckline, trimmed and edged with insertions of machine-made lace and pink ribbon. Cotton petticoat with narrow pleated hemline, trimmed with two bands of pintucks and pink ribbon bows. White silk stockings. Brown velvet slippers. 4 1912. Flesh-coloured elasticated-cotton corset, lightly boned, front busk, front hook and bar fastening, front lacing below waist, back lacing, adjustable suspenders. White nainsook chemise with double shoulder straps, trimmed with broderie anglaise and insertions of pintucks and lace ribbon. 5 1914. White nainsook combinations, high-waisted bodice with front opening and narrow shoulder straps, trimmed with threaded ribbon and machine-made lace to match knicker legs. 6 1914. Sleeveless white cotton brassiere, low neckline and armholes edged with lace, adjustable button fastening on front waistband, front bodice decorated with openwork embroidery 7 1914. Flesh-coloured cotton-net brassiere, lace-trimmed neckline, short inset sleeves, front button strap opening and waistband. Elasticated cotton waist-girdle, front panel of criss-cross firm cotton ribbon, right side opening, adjustable suspenders.

Leisure Wear 1910–1914

1 1910. Knitted blue striped wool sleeveless swimsuit, thigh-length fitted maillot with cross-over bodice to side waist, narrow self-fabric belt with silver clasp fastening, knitted plain blue tights. Blue cotton headscarf, tied at back of head. Black rubber shoes. 2 1911. One-piece multi-colour striped cotton swimsuit, button fastening from low round neckline to below waist-level, short sleeves, knee-length drawers. Matching striped cotton turban. Black rubber shoes. 3 1912. Sleeveless hip-length maillot in dark blue knitted cotton spotted with yellow stars, low neckline and armholes bound with plain blue knitted cotton to match the narrow waistbelt gathered into a large brass ring, knee-length drawers. Matching star-spotted cotton turban.
4 1913. Golfing costume. Knitted green and brown wool waistcoat. White cotton shirt worn with striped silk tie. Ankle-length brown wool-tweed skirt, button detail on curved side hem. Light brown felt hat with large crown and curled brim. Brown leather flat-heeled golfing shoes with pointed toecaps and fringed turned-down tongues. 5 1914. Bicycling costume. Yellow linen hip-length jacket with white cotton collar and revers, matching cuffs on raglan sleeves, inverted box pleats from high yoke seam to belted waist. White cotton blouse with cuffed sleeves. Tan linen ankle-length flared skirt. Pale green fet hat with large crown and wide turned-down brim. Flat-heeled brown leather shoes, large buckle trim, pointed toecaps.

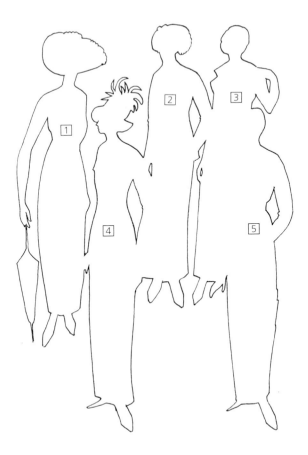

Day Wear 1910–1912

1 1910. Fine pale grey silk dress, deep V-shaped neckline bound with black silk to match cuffs on three-quarter-length dolman-style sleeves and pleated cummerbund, ankle-length skirt split from hem to short horizontal knee-level gathered seam which forms low side panniers. Large black velvet hat with wide brim trimmed with ostrich feathers. Jet bead necklace and earrings. Long black fabric gloves. Long-handled parasol. Black leather shoes with wide ribbon ties and pointed toes. 2 1911. Orange checked wool tailored suit, fitted jacket with edge-to-edge hook and bar fastening, button decoration, large broderie-anglaise collar matching cuffs of three-quarter-length inset sleeves, narrow ankle-length skirt with channel seams and button trimming. Rust-coloured hat with narrow upturned brim, feather and flower trimming. Long beige leather gloves. Brown leather shoes with three buttoned straps and pointed toes. 3 1911. Lilac and white striped cotton day dress with asymmetric neckline; covered buttons, cuffs of three-quarter-length sleeves, and high waistbelt covered with grey cotton satin to match the bound seams and hemline of narrow skirt; machine-made lace undersleeves, neckline and small skirt panels. 4 1910. Green wool tailored suit; fitted hip-length jacket with top-stitched seams and decorative panels on the hipline, on the hem of the fitted inset sleeves and on the side hem of the narrow ankle-length skirt. Light brown felt hat with upturned brim and high crown banded with petersham ribbon and topped with cock feathers. Light brown leather shoes with small bead trim and pointed toes. 5 1912. Cream silk button-through day dress, yellow silk-velvet dolman-style sleeves forming a bolero-effect matching high waistbelt and banded hem of narrow panniered skirt. Yellow felt and brimless hat with buttoned flap detail. Leather shoes with punched double straps and pointed toecaps.

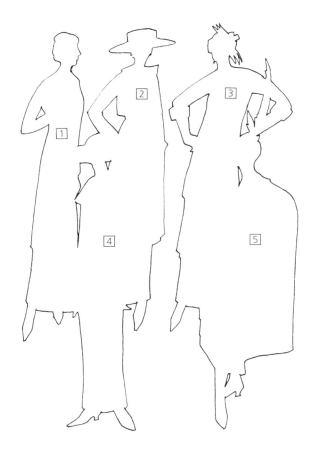

Day Wear 1912–1914

1 1912. Pale turquoise cotton day costume, yoked and belted jacket with imitation button fastening to low hipline, fitted inset sleeves with buttoned strap cuffs, matching ankle-length skirt. Mid-calf-length pink and red printed-cotton blouse with high round neckline, covered buttons from neck to waist. 2 1913. Summer costume, short blue cotton bolero jacket with three-quarter-length inset sleeves, yellow revers and jacket linings, pointed hem, appliqué flower motif; blue striped cotton dress, long sleeves with pleated cuffs, matching wrapover neckline, wide blue cotton waistband, gathered knee-length overskirt, narrow ankle-length underskirt banded at knee-level with appliqué flower motif. Natural straw boater with stiff brim, flat top crown banded with blue ribbon and a pleated bow. Black leather shoes with three straps and pointed toes. 3 1914. Brown silk suit; unfitted hip-length jacket with three-quarter-length inset cuffed sleeves bound with brown velvet, braided and embroidered to match the crossover revers, curved hip-level pockets and lowset three button fastening; ankle-length skirt with apron-effect overskirt. Beige felt hat with upturned brim and tall crown, large ribbon rosette and red feather trimming. Brown and cream leather button boots with pointed toes. 4 1913. Pink silk suit with lilac satin bindings; high-waisted collarless wrapover jacket; short embroidered oversleeves, matching high waistbelt, patch pockets and godets in front of narrow ankle-length skirt; inset undersleeve trimmed with fur, lace blouse with V-shaped neckline, waterfall of matching lace at each side of the belt to hipline. Natural straw hat with wide brim, large domed crown banded with lilac silk and trimmed with large bow. Silk-covered shoes with fine cross straps and pointed toes. 5 1914. Cream linen suit with buttoned high waistbelt; wing collar, edge-to-edge fastening and three-quarter-length sleeves trimmed with narrow black braid; ankle-length draped wrapover skirt. Black velvet cape lined with red satin, matching black velvet hat trimmed with red ribbon and black feathers. Long cream gloves. Black leather shoes, silver buckles, red piping and matching heels.

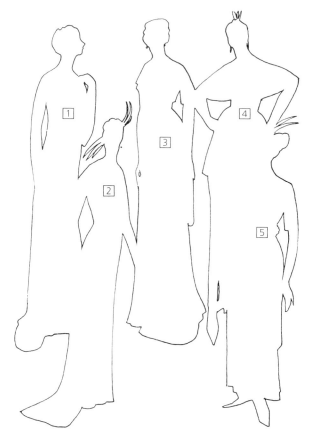

Evening Wear 1910–1914

1 1910. Purple panne-velvet dinner dress, pink beaded and embroidered silk chiffon yoke, satin-bound elbow-length dolman sleeves and fringed underskirt, high waistbelt, flower embroidered bodice to match wide band on the narrow skirt at knee-level, open side and train trimmed with white fur. Ruched silk headband decorated with small rosettes. Glass bead necklace and matching earrings. Long white gloves. 2 1911. Gold-coloured silk-satin ball dress, underbodice gathered onto silk-chiffon yoke, short inset sleeves decorated with ropes of glass beads, asymmetric beaded and fringed chiffon shawl worn over one shoulder, narrow skirt with long train. Hair decorated with bird-of-paradise plumes. Amber drop earrings and necklace. Long white kid gloves. 3 1912. Pink silk-satin evening gown, high waist emphasized by cream silk cummerbund and rosette with long end ribbons, matching embroidered and beaded floating front panel, ruched bodice, embroidered cap sleeves with handkerchief points, skirt gathered at each side of front panel to form low panniers, long train. Small tiara set with stones; pearl necklace and drop earrings. Long white kid gloves. 4 1913. Green silk-organdie evening gown, high waist banded by bright green satin cummerbund, wrapover bodice forms elbow-length sleeves, hip-length overskirt trimmed with cream lace to match neckline and sleeve hems, wrapover draped skirt. Small tiara edged with *diamanté* stones and decorated with central bird-of-paradise feathers. Drop earrings and matching jet bead necklace. Long black gloves. Black satin shoes, buckle trim, pointed toes and louis heels. 5 1914. Evening dress; light purple silk underbodice with high waist, narrow skirt and uneven hemline; lilac silk-chiffon overbodice, short dolman sleeves decorated with bead-embroidered bow motif, purple silk-satin cummerbund, matching bound hems. Jewelled tiara trimmed with long bird-of-paradise feathers. Long crystal drop earrings and matching necklace. Silk posy on cummerbund. Long cream satin gloves. Black silk stockings. Black satin shoes with cross straps, pointed toes and louis heels.

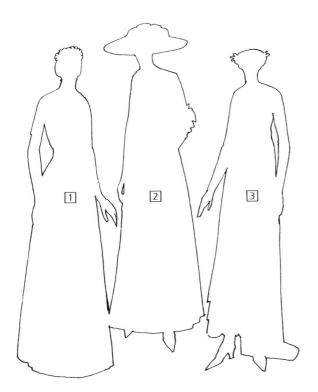

Bridal Wear 1910–1914

[1] 1910. Pale cream silk-satin wedding dress with high-waisted fitted bodice, deep V-shaped neckline infilled with lace and pleated silk, high stand collar with lace frilled edge, short tucked oversleeves, fitted finely tucked undersleeves with lace cuffs, tucked cummerbund, full-length flared skirt with inserts of tucked silk from high waist to hem, decorated with self-fabric covered buttons and silk cord frogging. Headdress of white and cream flowers, hip-length silk-gauze veil. Short cream kid gloves. [2] 1912. Lightweight blue wool wedding dress finely striped with pink, pink silk collar edged with lace to match the wrapover cuffs of the long fitted inset sleeves and the centre-front button strap opening, bodice gathered from high yoke seam to high waist, self-fabric cummerbund, flared panelled skirt off the ground. Hat with wide brim covered with pleated pink silk, crown draped with blue silk. White kid gloves. Blue leather shoes with pointed toes. [3] 1914. Ankle-length white lace wedding dress mounted on white silk crepe, V-shaped neckline edged with crystal bugle beads matching scalloped edges of short cap sleeves and hems of tiered skirts, wide white silk-crepe sash tied at front to form floating panel, beaded and embroidered above the pointed hem with a spray of stylized flowers, long detachable back train. Headdress of pearls and wax flowers, hip-length silk-gauze veil. Long white kid gloves. White satin shoes with round buckle trim, pointed toes and louis heels.

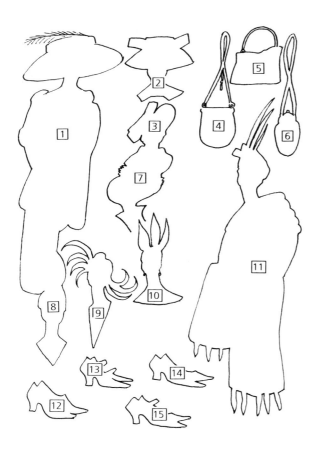

Accessories 1910–1914

[1] 1910. Natural straw hat with large crown trimmed with blue ribbon band, silk flowers and large blue feather, shoulder-wide brim. Long fox-fur-and-ermine wrap and matching muff. Long white kid gloves. [2] 1911. Natural straw hat with high crown banded with wide blue silk ribbon, knotted in front to form large bow, wide turned-down brim. [3] 1912. Brown felt hat with shaped upturned brim; outsized wired silk-taffeta bow trimming. [4] 1912. Suede leather bag with long knotted cord handle, tassel trim, embroidered chrysanthemum motif below metal clasp. [5] 1910. Metal-framed leather bag, bakelite clasp and fluted asymmetric detail, embossed wreath of leaves in centre of bag. [6] 1911. Beige leather bag with long handle, bakelite clasp and trim. [7] 1913. Black felt hat with wide brim turned up at one side, trimmed with large feather pompons. [8] 1912. Silk turban, fan of feathers threaded through a ring covered with silk and edged with fine pleating. [9] 1913. Bird-of-paradise feather hair ornament attached to back of head with clasp. Long glass drop earrings and matching bead necklace. [10] 1914. Three feather and brooch hair ornaments. Crystal and jet drop earrings and matching necklaces. [11] 1914. Beige felt hat with asymmetric upturned brim, trimmed with three long feathers and silk bow. Banded fur wrap trimmed with tails, matching muff banded with contrast colour fur. Leather bag with long handle, asymmetric envelope-flap opening. [12] 1910. Black leather shoes with round buckle trimming, pointed toes, red louis heels and linings. [13] 1912. Snakeskin shoes with double buttoned instep strap, pointed toecaps and louis heels. [14] 1914. Brown and cream two-tone leather shoes, wide instep strap, pointed toecaps and louis heels. [15] 1914. Pale blue silk evening shoes, single instep strap, high heels and pointed toes covered with blue and silver brocade.

Couture Wear 1914–1919

1 Stein & Blaine 1914. White tailored broadcloth suit, fitted hip-length jacket with long inset sleeves, shaped fur-trimmed cuffs, matching high stand collar and side tie-belt, covered button fastening from side of high collar to jacket hem and through to hem of the straight ankle-length skirt. Hat with fur-trimmed brim, large cream straw crown banded with black silk, small single-feather decoration at one side. Short white cotton gloves. Black leather shoes with pointed toes and louis heels, worn with white cloth spats. 2 Bergdorf Goodman 1916. Pale blue wool-jersey walking suit, hip-length jacket with high waist, buttoned belt, buttoned-down patch pockets, long raglan sleeves with narrow wrist cuffs, wide shawl collar, top-sewn detail, flared ankle-length skirt. Yellow lacquered straw hat with wide turned-down brim, high crown, white petersham band and silk flowers. Long cream lace-up boots, pointed toes and louis heels. 3 Paquin 1919. Off-white and blue dress and coat, shawl collar and hem of overbodice trimmed with black monkey fur, three-quarter-length coat with inset sleeves and narrow turned-back cuffs, open panel seams from below bustline to hem held in place by narrow buttoned-down belt. White straw hat, wide wired brim, high wide crown with pointed top, banded with black silk ribbon. White silk stockings. Black leather shoes with oblong buckle trim, edges piped in white, pointed toes and louis heels.

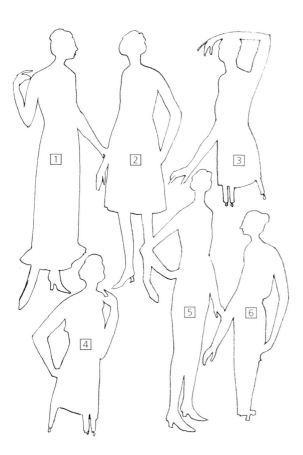

Underwear 1915–1919

1 1915. White nainsook petticoat with high waistline, cross-over bodice, low neckline; bodice and hem of the flared and frilled skirt decorated with diamond-shaped insertions of machine-made lace. Black silk stockings. Velvet house shoes. 2 1915. Peach coloured sleeveless knee-length step-in chemise, patterned with sprigs of flowers; low neckline, armholes and hemline edged with narrow lace; buttoned flap between the legs from back to front forming knickers. Black silk stockings. Red velvet mules trimmed with small round silver buckles; pointed toes and louis heels. 3 1915. Pink cotton boned corset with elasticated panels at hip-level, front hook and bar fastening, back lacing, adjustable suspenders, lace trimming. White embroidered silk chemise, low neckline with scalloped edge. 4 1917. Black cotton-satin high-waisted corset, long bones from under bust to low hipline, front hook and bar fastening to low hipline and laced through to hem, adjustable suspenders, black lace and red satin bow trimming. White silk chemise trimmed with black lace ribbon. 5 1919. Waist-length pink silk and lace chemise, decorated with rows of vertical pintucks and ribbon; peach-coloured elasticated cotton corset, elastic waistband, light boning over hips and either side of the front hook and bar fastening; adjustable satin ribbon suspenders with small satin ribbon rosettes. Cream silk stockings. Peach-coloured velvet mules with bow trim, pointed toes and louis heels. 6 1919. White knitted wool sleeveless all-in-one combinations, low scooped neckline trimmed with blue satin bow, threaded elastic waistline, knee-length drawers elasticated at knee, bow trim.

Leisure Wear 1915–1919

1 1915. Golfing costume. Hip-length beige serge top with deep slashed neckline, turned-back revers, short raglan oversleeves, fitted undersleeves, wide buttoned belt, pockets inset into curved panel seam on hipline, ankle-length skirt with centre-front inverted box pleat. Beige felt hat with high wide crown trimmed with band of pink silk, turned-down brim. Light brown flat-heeled leather shoes with pointed toes and long fringed tongues. 2 1916. Golfing costume. Hip-length brown linen jacket, edge-to-edge fastening with buttoned belt on waist and matching belt under bust, large flap pockets with three-button decoration on inside edge, top-stitched seams and edges; cream linen blouse with large peter pan collar; ankle-length cream linen flared skirt. Brown felt hat trimmed with wide cream petersham band. Cream cotton stockings. Brown and cream flat-heeled leather shoes with pointed toecaps and fringed tongues. 3 1917. Black checked taffeta bathing dress, low V-shaped neckline bound with white checked taffeta to match cuffs on the short dolman sleeves and the narrow shaped waistband, bias-cut skirt with handkerchief points, knee-length drawers, matching taffeta headscarf. 4 1918. Golfing costume. Hip-length green knitted wool jacket, wide off-white shawl collar matching turned-back cuffs of raglan sleeves, mid-calf-length cream linen skirt. Knitted cream wool brimless hat. Cream cotton stockings. Flat-heeled shoes with pointed toecaps and fringed tongues. 5 1919. Golfing costume. Yellow knitted-silk hip-length unfitted top, white knitted shawl collar and matching waist sash with tassled ends, high yoke seam, inset shirt sleeves; flared white linen ankle-length skirt. Natural straw hat with wired brim, high crown trimmed with wide petersham band. Grey stockings. Cream flat-heeled lace-up leather shoes with brown trimmings. 6 1919. Knitted blue wool bathing costume, low scooped neckline, short dolman sleeves, decorative side lacing from hip to waist. Blue towelling turban.

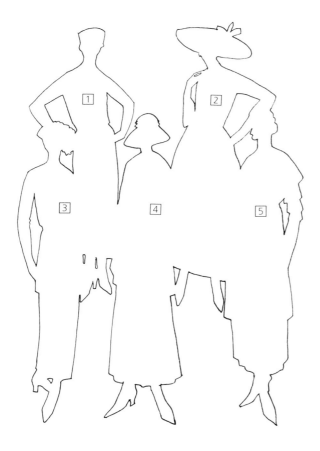

Day Wear 1915–1917

1 1915. Blue/grey wool day dress, fur-trimmed waist-length shawl collar edged with satin ribbon and silk tassel fringe matching the three-quarter-length inset sleeves and the two diagonal seams across the straight ankle-length skirt. Blue brimless felt hat. Grey silk stockings. Black leather lace-up shoes with pointed toecaps and high louis heels. 2 1916. Pale cream afternoon dress with waist-length fur-covered shawl collar matching trimming on the short open overskirt, long dolman-style sleeves with deep shaped buttoned cuffs, ankle-length full skirt with wide knee-level inserted embroidered band. Large natural straw hat with wide wired brim, shallow crown trimmed with striped ribbon and small feather. Brown and cream button boots with pointed toes. 3 1915. Ankle-length lilac and white striped cotton dress, hip-length plum-coloured cotton top with shawl collar trimmed with white piqué buttoned-on detachable collar, three-quarter-length inset sleeves, button trim to match bodice above and below low-slung tie-belt. Plum-coloured felt hat, upturned brim, large blue ostrich feather trim. Black leather shoes with small buckle trim, pointed toes and low louis heels. 4 1916. Green linen tailored suit, collarless hip-length jacket, decorative buttoned strap fastening to match waistbelt and cuffs of inset sleeves, ankle-length panelled skirt. Brown felt hat with turned-down brim, small crown decorated with green and brown cut felt petals. Tan leather gloves. Tan leather and beige canvas button boots, pointed toecaps and high louis heels. 5 1917. High-waisted printed-cotton top with large cap sleeves and detachable white piqué shawl collar, wide purple cotton pleated cummerbund, lilac cotton dress with three-quarter-length tiered sleeves and full ankle-length skirt. Waved short-cropped hair. Pale grey stockings. Black leather shoes, pointed toes, high shaped tongues, high heels.

Day Wear 1917–1919

1 1917. Camel-coloured wool suit, three-quarter-length jacket with highwayman collar, buttoned yoke with top-stitching to match the hip-level slanting pockets, inset sleeves with buttoned cuffs, wide threaded buttoned belt, ankle-length full skirt. Brimless brown felt hat trimmed with silk ribbon and bow. Leather gloves. Silk stockings. Brown leather shoes, buckle trim, pointed toes and louis heels. 2 1919. White silk afternoon dress banded with blue silk on the boat-shaped neckline, the short kimono-sleeve hems, and the hem of the ankle-length skirt; matching high-waisted threaded belt. Short waved hair with side parting. Large pearl earrings. Pale grey silk stockings. Grey suede shoes, pointed toes, low louis heels. 3 1918. Three-quarter-length ponyskin coat trimmed with large fox fur collar, elbow-length cuffs and matching brimless hat, three-button side fastening, pocket sets into side panel seams, button detail above hem, low-placed suede and leather belt. Tan leather gloves. Brown and white leather button boots, pointed toecaps, low louis heels. 4 1918. Mid-calf-length white silk dress, hip-length red linen edge-to-edge jacket fastened with wide buttoned belt threaded through large metal buckle, white shawl collar matching the large patch-pocket flaps and the cuffs of the fitted inset sleeves. Large straw boater banded with red and blue silk ribbon. Large glass bead drop earrings and three-tier necklace. White silk stockings. Black leather court shoes, tiny buckle trim, pointed toes, louis heels. 5 1919. White silk afternoon dress trimmed with black silk on edge of collarless wrapover bloused bodice, on hems of three-tier overskirt and on neck infill; buttoned waistband, inset sleeves with buttoned cuffs, mid-calf-length underskirt. Straw hat with asymmetric brim, large crown swathed with black silk. White silk stockings. Black leather shoes, buckle trim, pointed toes, louis heels.

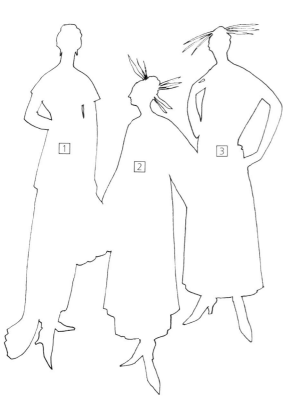

Evening Wear 1915–1919

1 1915. Cream silk-satin crepe evening dress, low V-shaped neckline front and back, edges decorated with gold-and-green beaded and sequined flower motifs matching the looped-up back train, short cap sleeves cut in one with the high-waisted bodice, wide belt under bust, draped ankle-length skirt wraps over at back. Waved hair dressed into long flat bun at back. Long jet drop earrings. Long cream kid gloves. Dyed ostrich feather, folding fan. Cream silk stockings. Gold brocade shoes, two-buttoned instep straps, pointed toes, louis heels. 2 1918. White silk-satin evening coat lined with red silk panne velvet, matching ankle-length dress; coat has wide shawl collar, wrapover front from side seam to side seam, held with self-fabric tassled tie-belt on hipline; wide wrist-length sleeves, open underarm seam, beaded with shiny red and dull black plastic sequins to match the neckline and hem of the dress. Hair dressed into waves and curls, decorated with three sprays of bird-of-paradise feathers. Grey silk stockings. Red leather shoes, diamond-shaped buckles, pointed toes, louis heels. 3 1919. Mid-calf-length black silk underdress. Ankle-length black silk-net beaded overdress, wrapover front, wide dolman sleeves narrow to wrist, black silk-chiffon side and back panels gathered into ruched hipband. Hair waved and dressed into bun, bird-of-paradise feather decoration. Black silk stockings. Black satin shoes, wide instep straps and pointed toes embroidered with bugle beads, louis heels.

Bridal Wear 1915–1919

1 1915. Pale cream duchesse-satin wedding dress, V-shaped neckline to high-waisted cummerbund and large bow, short dolman sleeves; hip-length top tier of narrow skirt curves up to centre front, middle tier dips at front and back; ankle-length straight underskirt; long detachable train falls from back of cummerbund. Beaded headband decorated at each side with looped ribbons, bows and wax flowers; hip-length fine silk net veil. Long white fabric gloves. White silk stockings. White kid shoes, pointed tongues, pointed toes, high heels. 2 1915. Cream silk-crepe wedding dress, hip-length wrapover lace top has short cap sleeves with scalloped edges to match hem; underdress with bishop sleeves, cuffs trimmed with lace, high stand collar, ankle-length skirt trimmed with embroidered and beaded ribbon, matching high waistbelt, large bow motif of bugle beads above hem on left-hand side. Headdress of wax and silk flowers, cream waist-length net veil. Cream silk stockings. Cream kid shoes, tiny buckle trim, pointed toes, louis heels. 3 1917. Cream tussore-silk wedding suit, jacket with high-waisted inset belt, single off-centre button fastening, wide shawl collar, three-quarter-length inset sleeves with deep cuffs, ankle-length flared skirt, hem embroidered with row of silk knots. Cream straw hat with wide brim and large crown trimmed with band of pink silk roses. Cream silk stockings. Cream leather shoes, silver buckle trim, pointed toes, louis heels. 4 1919. Cream fine silk wedding dress, straight unfitted bodice, high round neckline, long inset sleeves with flap detail falling from elbow to wrist, trimmed on the point with a silk-covered ring; bodice, sleeve hems and underskirt trimmed with silver thread embroidered lace. Headdress of wax flowers, mid-calf-length fine silk veil. Cream satin shoes trimmed with bows, pointed toes, louis heels.

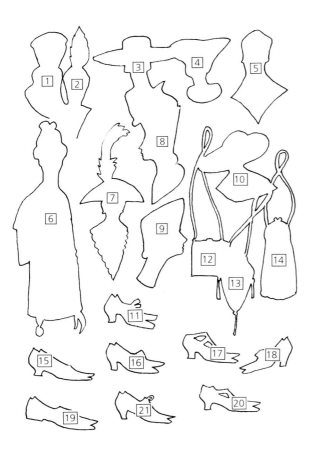

Accessories 1915–1919

1 1915. Fine beige wool draped turban, oval silver buckle trimming. 2 1915. Brimless pale blue felt hat with flared crown, bird-of-paradise feather trim. 3 1915. Natural straw hat, wide straight brim, large crown draped with pink silk. 4 1916. Pale grey astrakhan hat, white ermine trim. 5 1917. Black felt hat with deep turned-back brim and high domed crown, banded and piped with white silk. 6 1918. Hip-length knitted yellow silk sweater, large sailor collar banded in orange to match the inset sleeve cuffs, the hem, and the pompons on the tie-belt, neckties and crown of the matching hat. 7 1919. Brown felt bicorne hat, red petersham rosette and yellow feather trim. 8 1917. Draped red silk-velvet toque. 9 1919. Beige fet toque trimmed with black cord. 10 1919. Green and red striped cotton hat, wide wired brim and close-fitting sectioned crown. 11 1919. Blue silk evening shoes, blue and pink brocade medium-high heels and bow fastening, square toes. 12 1917. Beige suede bag, long handle, silver frame and clasp fastening. 13 1918. Black velvet evening bag; beaded design in pink, black and pale blue; black beaded tassel trimming. 14 1919. Pink silk evening bag, central motif of multi-coloured beads, matching fringe, long handle, silver frame and clasp. 15 1916. Brown leather shoes, petersham bow trim, pointed toes, louis heels. 16 1917. Black leather shoes, pleated tongues, silver buckles, pointed toes, louis heels. 17 1919. Silver satin evening shoes, double T-straps embroidered with crystal beads, pointed toes, louis heels. 18 1919. Beige suede shoes, wide instep straps with punched detail matching the pointed toes, high heels. 19 1917. Pale red leather golfing shoes, flat heels, pointed toecaps and slashed tongues in dark red leather. 20 1918. Cream canvas lace-up shoes with pointed toecaps, louis heels. 21 1919. Pale grey evening shoes, T-straps, cut-out shapes on sides and front, pointed toes, louis heels.

Worth 1923

Chanel 1920

Jeanne Lanvin 1924

Callot Soeurs 1924

Underwear 1920–1924

1920

1920

1923

1924

1921

1924

1924

1920

1921

1922

1924

1921

1922

1923

Day Wear 1920–1923

1920

1920

1921

1922

1923

1923

1924

1923

1923

1924

Evening Wear 1920–1924

1921

1920

1924

1922

1923

1920

1921

1922

1923

1924

1920

1920

1920

1921

1922

1920

1921

1921

1922

1920

1923

1920

1923

1920

1922

1924

1923

1920

1921

1923

1924

1921

1924

1922

1923

1924

1922

1924

1922

1923

1923

1924

Jean Patou 1925

Henri 1927

Chanel 1928

Redfern 1929

1925

1925

1926

1926

1928

1927

1929

1925

1926

1928

1928

1927

1929

1929

1925

1925

1925

1926

1926

1927

1928

1929

1928

1927

1927

1929

1925

1925

1928

1929

1926

1927

1925

1926

1929

1927

Couture Wear 1920–1924

1 Chanel 1920. Pale grey crepe-de-chine cape suit, hip-length cape hem trimmed with wide band of dark flying-squirrel fur, matching high stand collar, dress with round neckline, low-slung narrow tie-belt, band of slashed self-fabric fringing around hips and above hem of narrow ankle-length skirt. Brown felt hat with deep crown and upturned brim, trimmed with brown dyed ostrich feather. Single row of large colourless glass beads with matching drop earrings. Pale grey silk stockings. Brown leather shoes with high tongues, buckle decoration, pointed toes and high heels. 2 Worth 1923. Light brown wool-crepe dress, U-shaped neckline edged with band of white silk, bib-shaped fringe of beads trimming lower outer edge and above wide silk-covered turned-back cuffs of inset sleeves, straight hip-length bodice bloused across front and caught with two white discs at each side, straight ankle-length skirt. Brown felt hat with deep crown and wide upturned brim. Short brown leather gloves. Beige silk stockings. Brown leather shoes with cut-out detail, pointed toes and louis heels. 3 Jeanne Lanvin 1924. Black crepe-georgette dress with high stand collar; inset bishop sleeves slashed into long points above wrist, infilled and cuffed with layers of white silk chiffon; straight hip-length bodice decorated from high neck down to and around low waistline with steel disc buttons; mid-calf-length straight skirt. Black silk-covered brimless cloche hat, large feather trimming at one side. Grey silk stockings. Black leather shoes with T-straps, pointed toes and high heels. 4 Callot Soeurs 1924. Red crepe-georgette dress with V-shaped neckline, straight-cut bodice bloused on hipline, finely ruched and braided hip decoration repeated on tiered hems of tight inset sleeves, mid-calf-length gathered skirt. Red straw hat with narrow upturned brim, petersham band and bow decoration. Gold hoop earrings. Flesh-coloured silk stockings. Black leather shoes with T-straps, net side infill, pointed toes and high waisted heels.

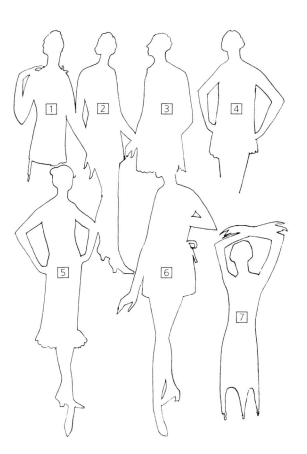

Underwear 1920–1924

1 1920. Pink cotton corset, spiral wire supports, reinforced cross-over straps, front hook and bar fastening, back lacing, six adjustable suspenders, broderie anglaise trimming. White cotton chemise with ribbon shoulder straps. 2 1920. White cotton-drill corset, reinforced with panels of stitching, laced on each side with elastic cord, buttoned-down shoulder straps, detachable elastic suspenders. Pale grey silk stockings. Court shoes with pointed toes and low louis heels. 3 1923. Sleeveless pale pink sprigged voile camisole, centre-front button opening, V-shaped neckline edged with white broderie anglaise, repeated on the hems of the wide thigh-length knickers, pink ribbon trimming. 4 1924. White cotton-voile combinations, wide blue ribbon shoulder straps and threaded waistline, scalloped edges to neck and hemlines, embroidered flower motifs below shoulder straps and at side of the short split on outside seam of knicker legs. 5 1921. Waist-length sleeveless striped cotton brassiere with low round neckline edged with narrow lace to match the armhole, front button opening, matching knee-length knickers trimmed with wide lace frill around hems, elasticated waistband. Grey silk stockings. Black mules with purple pompons, pointed toes and low louis heels. 6 1924. Pale blue crepe-de-chine step-in camiknickers trimmed across straight neckline and around short knicker legs with beige machine-made lace, matching shoulder straps. Short hair styled into tight waves. Flesh-coloured silk stockings. Blue shoes with instep straps, pointed toes and low louis heels. 7 1924. Pink cotton corselette, narrow elasticated shoulder straps, knitted elastic band around bust and side-hip panels, adjustable elastic suspenders.

Leisure Wear 1920–1924

1 1920. Bicycling costume. Knee-length grey checked wool coat, buttoned from inset waistbelt to high round collar, two-welt breast pockets with single-button trim, two large flapped pockets set at hip-level, long inset sleeves, knee-length breeches in matching fabric. Large grey wool cap with wide peak. Short brown leather gloves. Knitted green wool stockings. Brown leather lace-up brogues with flat heels. 2 1921. Blue linen pin-striped sports jacket, long collar and revers, low fastening with two brass buttons repeated on wrists of inset sleeves, patch pockets. White cotton tennis dress with low V-shaped neckline and collar, red cotton tie, mid-calf-length flared skirt. Straw boater trimmed with red petersham band and bow. White cotton stockings. White canvas shoes with flat heels and ribbon laces. 3 1922. Riding costume. Fine cream wool short-sleeved shirt, peter pan collar, wide tucks from shoulder to waist, knitted wool necktie. Cavalry-twill jodhpurs, bound pockets, buttoned side seams. Brown leather hat with wide peak. Brown wool stockings. Brown leather lace-up shoes with flat heels and pointed toes. 4 1924. Tennis costume. Mid-calf-length white ribbed-cotton wrapover dress, shawl collar, inset buttoned belt, raglan sleeves cut in one with the shaped yoke, flared buttoned double cuffs. Wide headband. 5 1921. Bathing costume. Hip-length green cotton shift; low square neckline banded with red and white cotton ribbon, repeated on the edges of the short sleeves, around the hem of the skirt and matching the buttoned low-set waistbelt; short gathered knickers in matching cotton. 6 1922. Hip-length blue striped cotton bathing costume with plain white sailor collar, sleeve cuffs, low-set belt and hem binding. Turban in matching fabric. 7 1923. Knitted blue wool one-piece bathing costume, the edges of the low V-shaped neckline, infill, short sleeves, knicker legs and tie-belt bound with yellow wool to match the seams; button opening on the shoulder seams. Straw hat with upturned brim, black plastic hatpin. Large pleated parasol.

Day Wear 1920–1923

1 1920. Hip-length cream wool jacket with wide collar and revers, single-button fastening, deep inset wrist-length sleeves with wide turn-back cuffs, decorative top-stitched front panel seams incorporating pockets with three-button trimming. Mid-calf-length striped wool straight skirt. Brimless red velvet turban style hat. Brown leather shoes with round buckle trim and pointed toes. 2 1920. Patterned lilac rayon mid-calf-length day dress with wide bias-cut collar edged with plain lilac rayon to match the straight neck edge, the cuffs of the three-quarter-length inset sleeves, the low-placed draped cummerbund and the hem of the knee-length open overskirt. Hat with wide brim and high crown covered with lilac fabric, draped with fine scalloped lace and trimmed with silk flowers. Glass bead necklace. Black leather shoes with wide buttoned straps, pointed toes and low shaped heels. 3 1921. Unfitted mid-calf-length cream wool flannel coat, the edge of the wide collar decorated with top-stitching to match the turned-back cuffs of the inset sleeves and the bottom inside edge of the L-shaped top-stitched side panels; two-button fastening. Outsized stiffened felt beret, trimmed with large feather. Short brown leather gloves, matching shoes with high tongues, pointed toes and low shaped heels. 4 1922. White spotted cream voile day dress, wide boat-shaped neckline edged with embroidery to match the hems of the three-quarter-length inset sleeves and at each side of the hip-length unfitted bodice, gathered skirt. Large straw hat with wide brim and deep petersham band around high crown. Leather shoes with cross-over straps, pointed toes and low shaped heels. 5 1923. Ankle-length brown striped silk day dress, collarless high round neckline, inset bishop sleeves gathered into brown velvet buttoned cuffs matching the draped buckled hip-belt and the straight underskirt visible through the side split of the silk overskirt. Brimless brown felt cloche hat trimmed with two black feather pompons. Black jet beads. Black leather shoes with wide buttoned straps, pointed toes and low heels.

Day Wear 1923–1924

1 1923. Ankle-length dark pink crushed-velvet coat, inset sleeves trimmed with fur at wrists to match high collar and hemline, side button fastening to low hip seam, gently flaring skirt. Brimless grey straw cloche hat. Short grey leather gloves. Grey silk stockings. Black leather shoes with strap and button fastening and pointed toes. 2 1923. Mid-calf-length blue cotton day dress with blue-and-white checked cotton-gingham cap-sleeved bodice, uneven crenellated hip seam, flared skirt. Short permed hair with side parting, set into formal waves, hairslide. Pale grey silk stockings. Blue leather court shoes with pointed toes. 3 1923. Red worsted wool suit, three-quarter-length unfitted jacket, wide collar and revers bound with black braid, set-in shoulder cape over tightly fitted wrist-length sleeves, centre-front fastening with tiny buttons, bound pockets at hip-level, mid-calf-length matching straight skirt. White silk shirt worn with narrow black necktie and black jet cufflinks. Red felt hat with wide split upturned brim, button trim and black braid binding. Short black leather gloves, matching shoes with red leather tongues, pointed toes and high heels. 4 1924. Mid-calf-length flower printed pink silk afternoon dress with wide pintucked boat-shaped neckline piped top and bottom, short three-tier sleeves matching the detail around hipline. Hair cropped short at the back, long side curls, side parting. Flesh-coloured silk stockings. Black leather court shoes with pointed toes and high heels. 5 1924. Three-quarter-length brown silk tunic dress with bishop sleeves gathered into long grey silk cuffs matching the collar on the high round neckline, the wide hip-level buckled belt, the wide central panel and the mid-calf-length narrow underskirt. Black felt hat with wide divided brim, crown trimmed with narrow petersham ribbon. Long black jet beads. Pale grey silk stockings. Black leather court shoes, pointed toes, high straight heels.

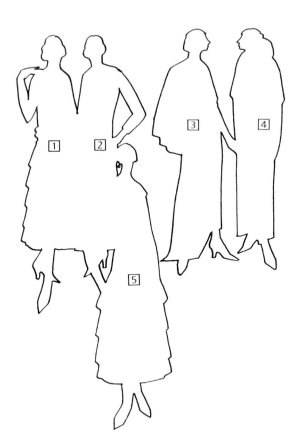

Evening Wear 1920–1924

1 1920. Sleeveless pink satin evening dress, low scooped neckline, straight tubular hip-length bodice, draped dark pink velvet cummerbund above pintucked yoke decorated on one side with corsage of silk flowers, mid-calf-length gathered tiered skirt. Short permed hair, set into formal waves and side parting. Pearl necklace. Flesh-coloured silk stockings. Dark pink satin shoes with narrow cross straps, pointed toes and low louis heels. 2 1921. Ankle-length red satin evening dress, long fitted red chiffon inset sleeves, collarless wrapover bodice fastening on side hip, beaded and embroidered outsized multi-coloured flower motif, ankle-length skirt hem edged with tiny glass beads to match other edges. Short permed hair, set into formal waves and side parting. Silk stockings. Black satin shoes with pointed toes and high red leather heels. 3 1922. Black velvet ankle-length tubular-shaped evening dress, bias-cut hip-length grey silk-chiffon cape attached to narrow beaded ribbon shoulder straps, beading repeated on V-shaped hip yoke and on edges of short straight train. Short straight hair cut with fringe. Grey silk stockings. Black satin court shoes, pointed toes and low louis heels. 4 1923. Ankle-length edge-to-edge red panne-velvet evening cape, large feather collar, deep yoke of boldly patterned multi-coloured printed panne velvet. Short permed hair, set into formal waves and fringe. Silk stockings. Black satin shoes trimmed with silver buckles, pointed toes and high shaped heels. 5 1924. Blue silk evening dress, unfitted hip-length tubular-shaped bodice, low scooped neckline, short sleeves, silver lace sleeveless overbodice with slashed V-shaped neckline to hip-level at front and back, trimmed on the centre front with ribbon rosette and streamers, mid-calf-length gathered tiered skirt trimmed with small ribbon posies. Short straight hair with heavy fringe. Long glass drop earrings. Flesh-coloured silk stockings. Silver kid shoes with cross-over straps and pointed toes.

Bridal Wear 1920–1924

1 1920. Ankle-length cream silk-taffeta wedding dress, round neckline edged with pearls, short inset sleeves edged with frills of machine-made lace over matching scalloped tiers to elbow level and short apron front, bodice with high waistline, embroidered motif of leaves and rosebuds, panniers of tiered frills of taffeta at each side, ending above hemline. Silk-tulle veil, headdress of silk flowers. Long gloves. Silk stockings. Satin shoes, bar straps, pointed toes. 2 1921. Ankle-length lace wedding dress mounted over pale pink silk, hip-length bodice gathered from low round neckline, scalloped hemline, edge-to-edge white silk-satin coat, dolman-style sleeves with deep scallop infilled with lace godet, edges embroidered and beaded, hip-belt fastening at one side with silk posy. Long silk-tulle veil, headdress of silk and wax flowers. Long kid gloves. Silk stockings. Satin shoes, rosettes, pointed toes, louis heels. 3 1922. Wedding dress of ivory silk-crepe-georgette with pale pink all-over pattern of small squares; wrapover neckline open to low waist position, bound with self-fabric; embroidered infill, matching detail on pointed hem of swathed hip-sash; long narrow inset sleeves. Large straw hat trimmed with pink silk roses. Silk stockings. Satin T-strap shoes, pointed toes, louis heels. 4 1923. Mid-calf-length white lace wedding dress mounted over white silk dress with flesh-coloured silk-chiffon yoke and sleeves, lace overdress with V-shaped scalloped neckline, matching sleeve and hem detail, low white silk ribbon belt fastened with posy at hip to match trimming on brimless felt cloche hat. Silk stockings. Silk shoes, low louis heels. 5 1924. Ankle-length gold and cream wedding gown, low round neckline bordered with embroidery and beading to match hems of flared inset sleeves, low-slung tied hip-belt and edges of long train. Square silk-chiffon veil, wide hem decorated with tiny seed pearls, headdress of wax flowers. Pearl drop earrings and necklace. Silk stockings. Gold and cream silk-brocade shoes trimmed with gold kid, pointed toes, louis heels.

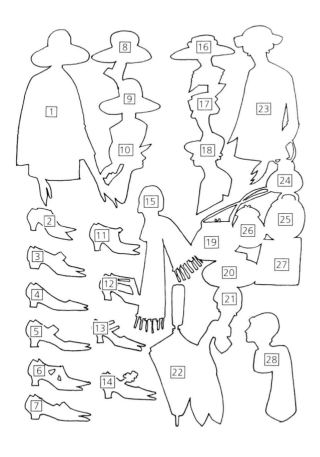

Accessories 1920–1924

1 1920. Cream artificial-silk blouse trimmed and edged with embroidered braid. Straw hat, wide brim, large crown banded with wide ribbon. 2 1920. Pale blue leather shoes, cut-out cross-over detail, side button fastening, pointed toes, waisted heels. 3 1920. Brown leather lace-up brogues, pointed toes, thick stacked heels. 4 1921. Black kid shoes, red kid trimming and waisted heels. 5 1921. Blue suede shoes, wide bar straps, pointed toes, louis heels. 6 1922. Cream leather shoes, T-straps and cross-over bars, pointed toes, waisted heels. 7 1922. Black leather shoes, shaped pintucked inset tongues, pointed toes, low heels. 8 1920. Cream straw hat, wide turned-down brim banded with red silk ribbon. 9 1920. Grey straw hat, wide wired brim, large crown trimmed with velvet ribbon band and bow. 10 1920. Brown straw hat, large crown trimmed with striped silk. 11 1922. Brown leather shoes, top-stitched openwork detail, ribbon bow fastening, pointed toes, high heels. 12 1923. Grey leather shoes, T-straps, cut-away sides, pointed toes, high waisted heels. 13 1924. Brown leather shoes, double bar straps, pointed toecaps, louis heels. 14 1924. Black leather shoes, bar straps decorated with rosettes, pointed toes, high heels. 15 1923. Red felt cloche hat, turned-back asymmetric brim pinned with small bow-shaped brooch. Long multi-coloured knitted scarf, fringed ends. 16 1921. Straw hat trimmed with ribbon and silk flowers. 17 1921. Straw hat, wide upturned brim edged with silk flowers, large ribbon bow. 18 1922. Hat covered with yellow and white spotted fabric, trimmed with artificial fruits. 19 1920. Pink silk embroidered evening bag, long handle. 20 1923. Blue velvet evening bag, silver frame. 21 1923. Felt beret, top-stitched detail on crown. Red silk scarf, white satin lining. 22 1923. Striped silk umbrella, thick carved-ivory handle. 23 1922. Red artificial-silk blouse trimmed with blue and white ribbon. White straw hat, wide upturned brim edged with red ribbon. 24 1923. Red velvet evening bag, gold metal frame and chain handle. 25 1924. Embroidered bag, shallow plastic handle. 26 1920. Green silk bag embroidered with flowers. 27 1924. Patchwork leather bag, long handle, metal frame. 28 1924. Yellow felt cloche hat, narrow upturned brim, trimmed with large felt flower. Fur scarf.

Couture Wear 1925–1929

1 Jean Patou 1925. Straight hip-length light green knitted wool sweater with high round neckline, pink designer initials incorporated into the asymmetric sunray decoration on one shoulder and above the bands of blue and pink on hipline, repeated on the hems of long scarf; knee-length box-pleated wool skirt. Pink linen knee-length edge-to-edge unfitted coat with stand collar, inset sleeves with deep cuffs and decorative elbow-length buttoned straps, echoed in the detail at base of large patch pockets. Natural straw cloche hat with narrow upturned brim, brown band. Beige leather gloves. Flesh-coloured silk stockings. Two-tone leather shoes, pointed toecaps, low stacked heels. 2 Henri 1927. Hip-length double-breasted blue hopsack tailored jacket, wide collar and revers, fitted inset sleeves, brass button trimming on outside of wrist to match jacket fastening. White crepe-de-chine blouse, buttoned-down collar. Blue and grey checked necktie. Straight knee-length grey wool skirt with wide flat cuffed hem. Grey straw cloche hat, narrow upturned brim, blue petersham band. Short grey leather gloves. Pale grey silk stockings. Black leather shoes trimmed with blue leather around instep strap, opening and pointed toecaps, low stacked heels. 3 Chanel 1928. Two-piece suit in pale green silk jersey with brown zig-zag stripes. Fingertip-length edge-to-edge jacket, cuffed raglan sleeves, tie neckline; dress with V-shaped neckline edged with narrow white silk collar and trimmed with large bow, repeated on low side-hip seam; knee-length skirt, side panel of pressed knife pleats; hip-level white silk tailored belt. Green cloche hat, narrow upturned brim, brown ribbon band. Flesh-coloured silk stockings. Brown leather shoes, pointed toes and medium high heels. 4 Redfern 1929. Panne-velvet two-piece suit. Edge-to-edge jacket, stand collar, tie fastening, fitted inset sleeves trimmed at elbow-length with black monkey fur to match uneven hem; dress with V-shaped neckline, intricate seaming on low waist and hiplines, bias-cut skirt dipping to front and back. Black lacquered straw hat with wide brim and deep crown. Pale grey silk stockings. Black leather T-strap shoes, pointed toes and high heels.

Underwear 1925–1929

1 1925. Knee-length patterned crepe-de-chine slip trimmed with bands of ribbon and insertions of machine-made lace around the straight neckline, across the bust and repeated at hip-level. Short permed hair dressed into formal waves. 2 1925. Waist-length elasticated cotton bust-flattener brassiere, wide adjustable shoulder straps, centre-front securing strap, wide elastic side panels; hip-girdle in matching fabric, cut in panels, front hook and bar fastening plus lacing from hip-level to hem, six adjustable suspenders. 3 1926. Knee-length satin slip banded around the neck and hemline of the half-circle skirt with machine-made lace. Short permed hair with side parting, set in formal waves. Green velvet mules, pointed toes, medium-high louis heels. 4 1926. Cream silk-satin brassiere, ruched in centre front and darted under arms, narrow rouleau shoulder straps, back fastening. Panelled hip-girdle in dark cream patterned cotton twill, shaped front panel with hook and bar fastening, lacing on each side from hem to low hipline, adjustable suspenders. Dark flesh-coloured stockings. Brown kid mules trimmed with cream, pointed toes, low heels. 5 1927. Pink and beige cotton corset and bust-flattener, elastic bust gussets and hip panels, wide shoulder straps and adjustable suspenders, back opening. Short-cropped hair, slide decoration. 6 1928. Pink crepe-de-chine brassiere with darted cups, narrow shoulder straps, back fastening, machine-made lace trimming repeated on hem of the short knickers. 7 1929. Elasticated cotton corset and brassiere, darted bodice, wide shoulder straps, shaped neckline and hem edged with machine-made elastic welt, double front panel to hip-level, back and side fastenings with hooks and bars, adjustable suspenders. Short permed hair, parted in centre, set into formal waves and into curls over the ears.

Leisure Wear 1925–1929

[1] 1925. Tennis outfit. White linen two-piece suit, hip-length collarless top with cap sleeves, belted on low waistline, fastening with buttoned straps, top-stitched darts open from below the bust to hipline; knee-length knife-pleated skirt. White headband and visor. Straight short-cropped hair. White cotton ribbed stockings. White canvas lace-up shoes with flat heels. [2] 1926. Tennis outfit. Sleeveless white cotton dress with square neckline, unfitted bodice with vertical inset panels which continue onto the hipline of the knee-length knife-pleated skirt, narrow hip-belt. White cotton headband. White cotton stockings. White canvas lace-up shoes with flat heels. [3] 1928. Bathing costume. Sleeveless hip-length turquoise knitted cotton top with all-over jacquard pattern, plain brown binding around low neckline, hip-belt and hemline in matching fabric, plain turquoise knitted cotton shorts. Tightly fitting rubber bathing cap with chin strap. [4] 1927. Beach wear. Sleeveless cream linen top with boat-shaped neckline bound in navy blue, matching U-shaped decoration and flared linen shorts. Rubber bathing cap with chin strap. [5] 1928. Golfing costume. Beige knitted wool three-piece suit, hip-length edge-to-edge jacket, bands of brown and orange down each side of the front and hem, around the hems of the inset sleeves, and repeated on the straight neckline and in three rows around the hipline of the unfitted sweater; knee-length skirt, knife pleats at each side of the wide central box pleat. Light brown lacquered straw hat with large crown and wide brim, orange petersham band. Flesh-coloured silk stockings. Brown and cream leather lace-up brogues with flat heels. [6] 1929. Bathing costume. One-piece white knitted wool sleeveless top banded around hem with red and white design, narrow waistbelt with oval buckle, short knickers. Blue wool beret. Blue silk scarf edged with red. [7] 1929. Beach wear. Hip-length cream linen top, wrist-length flared inset sleeves, wide collar and revers, high yoke seam, tie fastening on side hip, trousers in matching fabric with wide flare from knee to hem and inset pleated godets. Striped cotton blouse. Light brown straw hat with large crown and wide unwired brim. Large amber bead necklace. Linen shoes decorated with embroidered raffia flowers, flat heels.

Day Wear 1925–1927

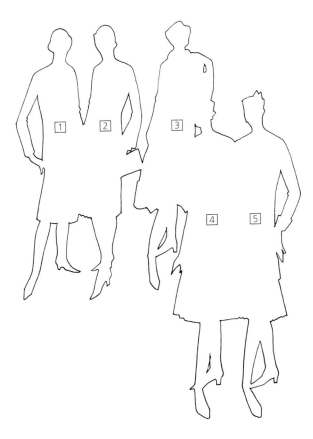

[1] 1925. Pink herringbone wool-tweed suit, hip-length unfitted jacket, high round neckline with double collar, silk scarf tied into large bow, inset sleeves with strap detail at wrists, side/front button fastening, low buckled belt, straight knee-length skirt, short inverted box pleats in side seams. Lacquered straw cloche hat. Flesh-coloured silk stockings. Leather shoes with wide cross straps, pointed toes, low thick heels. [2] 1925. Green wool crepe suit, hip-length unfitted jacket, long pointed collar and waist-length strap opening in contrasting green wool crepe to match cuffs of fake undersleeves, semi-inset sleeves split from wrist to elbow, button trimming to match detail on bodice seaming above waistline, straight knee-length skirt with knife-pleated front panel. Green felt cloche hat, top-stitched crown, narrow split upturned brim. Green leather clutch bag. Matching leather shoes with double cross straps, pointed toes, medium high heels. [3] 1926. Knee-length yellow wool edge-to-edge coat trimmed with fur; wide inset sleeves, narrowed by large single pleat at wrists, trimmed with covered buttons. Pale yellow patterned rayon day dress, wide neckline bound with self-fabric and tied into bow at front, fake front button fastening edged at each side with pintucks, low yellow leather belt with large round buckle, bias-cut skirt with uneven pointed hemline. Brown straw cloche hat. Flesh-coloured silk stockings. Brown leather shoes, wide cross straps, cut-out detail on each side front, pointed toes, high heels. [4] 1926. Knee-length edge-to-edge black wool crepe coat, wide revers and front edges bound with strips of red and white wool crepe, narrow hip-level self-fabric buckled belt, knee-length straight skirt. Hip-length white pleated-silk blouse, high round neckline bound with red and white silk. Black straw cloche hat, red petersham trimming. Black leather T-strap shoes, pointed toes, high heels. [5] 1927. Hip-length red silk jacket, cut-away front fastening under the high collar and on the hipline with a swathed buckled basque, inset sleeves with wide turned-back cuffs trimmed with white to match the collar and buttons. Pleated blue silk dress, tiered knee-length skirt. Red lacquered straw cloche hat. Blue leather shoes with narrow cross straps, pointed toes, high heels.

Day Wear 1927–1929

1 1927. Knee-length striped silk day dress, long inset sleeves with bias-cut wristbands matching straps from shoulders to hip-belt, wide collar and revers, buttoned strap opening, flared skirt with inverted box pleats. Short hair with straight fringe. Silk stockings. Black leather court shoes, pointed toes, high heels. 2 1927. Cream wool suit, hip-length top with high round neckline bound with self-fabric and tied into large bow at one side, unfitted bodice split to below bust, decorated with shaped pintucked panel matching the cuffs on inset sleeves and the small panels on knee-length flared skirt. Brown straw cloche hat, wide petersham band. Silk stockings. White leather shoes, brown toecaps, high heels, trimming. 3 1928. Checked wool suit. Long unfitted edge-to-edge collarless jacket, edges bound with plain wool to match the hems of semi-inset sleeves and patch pockets; dress in matching fabric, square neckline, inset band across bustline, low hip-belt, knee-length box-pleated skirt. Brimless pink velvet hat gathered onto wide headband. Amber beads and earrings. Short leather gloves. Brown leather shoes with T-straps, pointed toes, high heels. 4 1928. Unfitted green herringbone tweed coat; raglan sleeves flaring out from wrists to elbows, trimmed with small buttons; tailored collar and revers, side button fastening on low waistline, shaped top-stitched panel seams. Blue felt cloche hat, green petersham band. Blue and green striped silk scarf. Blue and black leather clutch bag. Silk stockings. Black leather court shoes, pointed toes, high heels. 5 1929. Knee-length grey fur coat, large wrapover shawl collar, raglan sleeves with decorative band of fur running from shoulder to wrist repeated on centre front from above bust to hemline. Brimless purple felt cloche hat. Short leather gloves. Purple leather clutch bag with black plastic trimming. Silk stockings. Black leather shoes, wide cross straps, pointed toes, high shaped heels. 6 1929. Knee-length ribbed turquoise silk coat; inset sleeves; flared elbow-length double cuffs edged with fur to match shawl collar, edges and hems; side wrapover front fastening with self-fabric belt tied into large bow. Turquoise silk turban-style hat. Short leather gloves. Silk stockings. Black leather shoes, three cross straps, pointed toes, high heels.

Evening Wear 1925–1929

1 1925. Knee-length sleeveless tubular-shaped beaded chiffon evening dress, waist-length V-shaped back neckline piped with gold tissue and infilled with flesh-coloured matt chiffon; handkerchief godets at each side of hip, dipping below hemline. Short straight hair. Glass bead necklace and bangle. Silk stockings. Gold kid shoes with narrow cross straps, pointed toes and high louis heels. 2 1925. Tubular-shaped beaded chiffon evening dress with wide shoulder straps, piped with fine silk velvet, matching bands around bust and hiplines, knee-length skirt with scalloped hem. Short straight hair. Gold hoop earrings. Gold brocade shoes with pointed toes. 3 1926. Sleeveless tubular-shaped white silk evening dress, boat-shaped neckline edged with rows of red and white plastic beads matching the armholes of the bead-striped bodice and the patterned band around hips, knee-length gathered skirt. Short permed hair set into formal waves and side parting. Red plastic earrings and bangles. Silk stockings. Red leather shoes with narrow cross straps, pointed toes and high heels. 4 1927. Sleeveless tubular-shaped chiffon evening dress, beaded all over with metallic grey sequins; low V-shaped neckline, armholes, low uneven waist seam and irregular hem bordered with gold and bronze sequins. Short hair with side parting. Long drop earrings, matching bangle. Silk stockings. Black satin shoes edged with gold kid, pointed toes and low louis heels. 5 1928. Blue silk crepe-de-chine evening dress suspended from flesh-coloured chiffon yoke, pleated hip detail echoed on wide V-shaped neckline, bias-cut skirt with irregular hemline. Short permed hair set into formal waves. Silk stockings. Blue satin shoes with *diamanté*-studded T-straps, pointed toes and high heels. 6 1929. Brown lace mounted over brown silk ankle-length tubular-shaped dress with low V-shaped back neckline, bound to match the infill and armholes in brown silk satin; asymmetric waterfall of lace topped with satin flowers on one hip. Short-cropped hair with side parting. Long drop earrings and matching bangles. Pale silk stockings. Brown satin shoes, cross straps, pointed toes and louis heels.

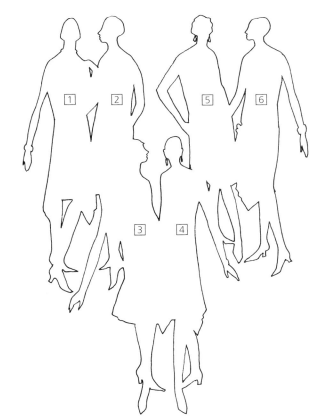

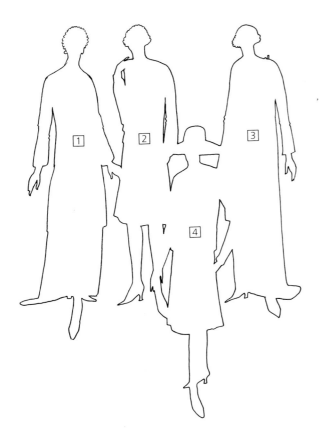

Bridal Wear 1925–1929

[1] 1925. Pale pink crepe-de-chine wedding dress, boat-shaped neckline edged with rows of three pearls to match the deep armholes, the three diagonal bands and the cuffs of the inset bishop-style sleeves, around the scalloped hip seam and hemline of the knee-length gathered skirt; long train falling from shoulders also edged with pearls. Wired organza headdress decorated with pearls, square silk-chiffon veil. Pale silk stockings. Pale pink silk shoes, pearl trimming, pointed toes and high shaped heels. [2] 1926. Pale cream georgette wedding dress, deep boat-shaped neckline edged with pearls, hip-length tubular-shaped bodice embroidered with stylized flower design of silver and crystal beads, repeated around the cuffs of the inset bishop-style sleeves, knee-length flared skirt. Machine embroidered silk-tulle veil, headdress of tiny wax flowers. Pale cream silk stockings. Cream silk shoes with pointed toes and high shaped heels. [3] 1927. Pale cream georgette over pale pink crepe-de-chine wedding dress and long train, low wide scooped neckline edged with tiny pearls to match detail on the open inset sleeves, hip-length tubular-shaped bodice embroidered with pearls and crystal beads, knee-length gathered skirt with beaded and scalloped hemline. Machine embroidered veil with scalloped edges, pinned into hair under posies of wax flowers, matching corsage on one shoulder. Pale silk stockings. White satin shoes, bar straps, pointed toes and high shaped heels. [4] 1929. Pale cream silk wedding dress, low U-shaped neckline bound with ivory silk and edged with decorative saddle stitching to match hems and button fastenings of the inset sleeves, hip band and apron panel worn over the knee-length knife-pleated skirt. Large pale cream straw hat, high crown with wide band of pleated ivory silk. Pale silk stockings. Ivory kid shoes, open punchwork decoration, bar straps, pointed toes and high shaped heels.

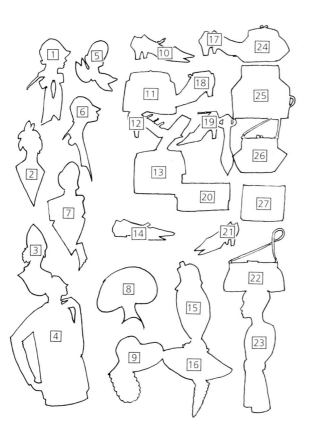

Accessories 1925–1929

[1] 1925. Beige felt cloche hat, narrow brim turned up at back, petersham ribbon band and bow. Red silk scarf tied into large bow. [2] 1926. Cloche hat covered with felt leaves, decorated on one side with wired felt leaves. [3] 1927. Felt cloche hat, pointed upturned peak, feather trimming. Glass beads and earrings. [4] 1927. Knitted lilac wool V-neck sweater, buckled hip-belt, purple pleated-silk scarf. [5] 1925. Felt cloche hat, buckled petersham band. Striped silk-taffeta scarf. [6] 1926. Straw cloche hat, narrow turned-down brim, petersham band. Large silk flower pinned to shawl collar. [7] 1927. Cloche hat, turned-down brim, petersham band. Long spotted silk scarf. [8] 1928. Straw hat, oval-shaped brim, shallow crown banded with pink ribbon tied into formal wired bow at back. [9] 1928. White straw hat, wide wired brim bound with blue ribbon to match the twisted band around deep crown. [10] 1925. Silver kid evening shoes, beaded bar straps, pointed toes, high heels. [11] 1926. Blue silk evening bag, silver frame, jewelled clasp. [12] 1926. Brocade evening shoe, four bar straps, pointed toes, high shaped heels. [13] 1926. Canvas bag, threaded leather strap and handle. [14] 1929. Crocodile leather shoes, bar straps, pointed toes, flat heels. [15] 1928. Felt cloche hat, narrow turned-down brim, inset band and pintucked panel, decorated with wired strips of felt. Large fur collar. [16] 1929. Pink silk organdie hat, wide wired brim, shallow crown decorated with silk flowers. Long bead necklace. [17] 1926. Brown leather shoes edged with grey scalloped leather, pointed toes, high heels. [18] 1926. Two-tone lace-up leather shoes, pointed toes, high thick heels. [19] 1927. Blue silk shoes, ankle straps, rouleau ribbon decoration, pointed toes, high shaped heels. [20] 1927. Silk clutch bag embroidered with stars. [21] 1929. Black and white leather shoes, pointed toes, high thick heels. [22] 1928. Leather bag, inset leather bow motif, long handle, silver frame. [23] 1929. Felt cloche hat, upturned brim, punchwork decoration. Amber earrings and necklace. Fur scarf. [24] 1926. Patchwork bag, metal clasp and frame. [25] 1926. Crocodile leather bag, solid plastic handle and clasp. [26] 1928. Tapestry embroidered bag, triangular side gussets, long handle, metal frame. [27] 1929. Leather bag, envelope-shaped flap, press-stud fastening.

Norman Hartnell 1930

Jacques Heim 1931

Jean Patou 1932

Lucien Lelong 1934

1930

1931

1932

1933

1934

1934

1930

1930

1932

1931

1930

1934

1932

1931

1932

1930

1931

1932

1933

1933

1933

1934

1934

1934

1930

1932

1934

1933

1931

1930

1933

1933

1931

1934

Chanel 1935

Chanel 1939

Creed 1937

Paquin 1939

1935

1937

1938

1939

1939

1936

1937

1939

1939

1935

1935

1939

1936

1937

1938

1939

1935

1936

1935

1936

1936

Day Wear 1937–1939

1937

1937

1939

1937

1939

1935

1936

1937

1938

1939

1937

1935

1939

1935

1936

1936

1935

1935

1936

1936

1937

1938

1938

1937

1938

1938

1938

1939

1939

1939

1939

1939

1939

1939

Couture Wear 1930–1934

[1] Norman Hartnell 1930. Bias-cut green crepe evening dress, semi-fitted sleeveless bodice with low wide V-shaped neckline incorporating an asymmetric diagonal panel from one shoulder to low hipline, graduated tucks from under the bust to the waist corresponding with the asymmetric panel and tucks of the narrow knee-length overskirt; flared bias-cut underskirt, cut in one with the dress, forms a small train; draped asymmetric hip-belt with tied ends on one hip. Hair with side parting, waves and curls to jawline. Coloured glass brooch pinned above one side of bust. [2] Jacques Heim 1931. Pale pink satin bias-cut sleeveless evening dress, low draped cowl neckline, semi-fitted bodice tightly fitted around the waist and hips by means of complicated panel seams, floor-length bias-cut skirt flares from low hipline. Short hair with centre parting, flattened to the head and with a single roll of curls on jawline. Double row of pearls. Satin shoes with pointed toes. [3] Jean Patou 1932. Bias-cut white satin evening dress, low back neckline, wide twisted shoulder straps forming a cape-effect over the shoulders, fitted bodice from bust to low hipline by means of complicated panel seaming, floor-length bias-cut skirt flares from hipline, back train. Short permed and waved hair. Long coloured glass earrings. [4] Lucien Lelong 1934. Bias-cut silk and patterned silk-chiffon evening dress, semi-fitted sleeveless bodice with low scooped neckline, wide tucked hip yoke and bias-cut frill dipping at back to form short train over full bias-cut skirt. Short permed hair with side parting. Glass bead necklace, wide bangles. Black satin shoes.

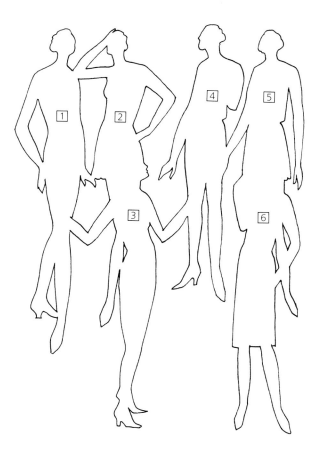

Underwear 1930–1934

[1] 1930. Hip-length elasticated pink cotton one-piece corselette, adjustable shoulder straps, seamed cups, double thickness fabric on the shaped front and side hip panels, back hook and bar fastening, adjustable suspenders. Flesh-coloured silk stockings. Brown velvet mules with low heels and pointed toes. [2] 1931. Waist-length fitted cotton brassiere covered with bands of machine-made lace, narrow satin shoulder straps, back hook and bar fastening. Patterned pink satin knickers, wide flared legs with scalloped edges, elasticated waist. [3] 1932. Hip-length elasticated peach-coloured cotton-satin one-piece corselette, fitted cups and low back trimmed with machine-made lace, intricately seamed bodice, back and side hook and bar fastening, adjustable shoulder straps and suspenders. Flesh-coloured silk stockings. Brown velvet house shoes, low heels, pointed toes. [4] 1933. Short pale pink silk camisole top, pintucked detail at bust level, shaped neckline trimmed with machine-made lace, narrow ribbon shoulder straps. Machine-embroidered cotton hip-girdle, elasticated front and side panels, back fastening, adjustable suspenders. Pale silk stockings. [5] 1934. Short pale blue cotton slip, narrow ribbon shoulder straps, bloused bodice with scalloped and embroidered neckline and hem, elasticated waistline. [6] 1934. Long patterned turquoise crepe-de-chine fitted slip, ribbon straps, fitted bustline trimmed with machine-made lace, matching hemline, princess-line panel seams from under bust to hem of flared skirt, side fastening. Flesh-coloured silk stockings. Turquoise satin house slippers trimmed with silk pompons, pointed toes.

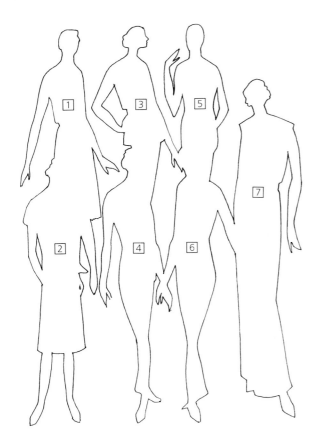

Leisure Wear 1930–1934

1 1930. White linen tennis dress. Sleeveless semi-fitted bodice, decorative tucked panel seams, V-shaped neckline, self-fabric covered belt, deep hip yoke, knife-pleated skirt. White beret. White canvas shoes with wide bar straps, pointed toes and flat heels. 2 1931. Tennis outfit. Waist-length white knitted cotton top, short puff sleeves, front opening with square buttons matching the turned-back revers. White linen skirt, narrow hip yoke, inset flap pockets, centre-front inverted box pleat. White canvas shoes, bar straps, pointed toes and flat heels. 3 1930. Knitted blue cotton beach top and shorts. Halter neck bodice with wide binding of white cotton, piped on each side with red to match the buckled belt and the covered side seams of the short flared shorts. 4 1930. Knitted red cotton bathing costume. Asymmetric bodice draped from one shoulder, the hem of the hip-length skirt bound with red, white and blue knitted cotton braid. Red rubber beach shoes trimmed with a blue and white motif, pointed toes and flat heels. 5 1932. Green elasticated-cotton bathing costume, deep scooped back, pink elasticated-cotton straps and threaded belt, high-cut legs. Pink rubber bathing hat. 6 1934. Yellow stretch-rayon bathing costume. Fitted bodice, halter neckline with cut-away front, waistbelt in self-fabric threaded through a covered ring, high-cut legs. Yellow canvas beach shoes, asymmetric bar straps, pointed toes and flat heels. 7 1932. Cotton beach top and trousers. Red and white striped knitted cotton top, short cap sleeves and wide sailor collar. Fitted red cotton trousers, high waistband, wide red leather buckled belt, pressed creases flared from knee to ankle. Red beret. Red canvas beach shoes with buttoned bar straps, pointed toes and flat heels.

Day Wear 1930–1932

1 1930. Herringbone wool wrapover coat, wide revers; top-stitching on collar, cuffs buckled waistbelt and hip-level patch pockets. Brown felt hat, narrow brim turned down on one side, green petersham band trimming. Brown leather gloves. Green leather clutch purse. Silk stockings. Brown and cream leather shoes, rounded toecaps and high heels. 2 1931. Double-breasted mid-calf-length beige gabardine raincoat, wide revers, large collar, inset sleeves with button detail at wrists, waistbelt with self-fabric covered buckle, welt pockets on hipline. Beige gabardine hat, shallow crown, narrow brim, self-fabric band and bow trimming. Leather gloves. Silk stockings. Brown and cream leather lace-up brogues, square toes and low heels. 3 1931. Bias-cut patterned green silk formal afternoon dress, low V-shaped neckline, narrow inset sleeves, tucked cuffs with points over the hands, intricately seamed bloused bodice and mid-calf-length skirt. Green silk-organdie hat with small crown and wide stitched and wired brim, silk flower decoration matching the corsage worn on one shoulder of the dress. Silk stockings. Brown leather shoes, almond-shaped toes and high heels. 4 1932. Brown crepe-de-chine dress; wrapover bodice trimmed with cream and yellow spotted silk to match the inset diagonal yoke, the inset elbow-length half cuffs and the buckled waistbelt; mid-calf-length skirt. Permed hair, set into formal waves and curls, high side parting. Silk stockings. Brown leather shoes, blunt toes and high heels. 5 1932. Mid-calf-length crepe-de-chine formal afternoon dress and knee-length jacket. Dress with tie neckline and bloused bodice in patterned crepe-de-chine, matching the godets and insertions in the full plain silk skirt and repeated on the unfitted jacket in the bodice and the narrow inset sleeves. Lacquered fine straw hat, small shallow crown, wide wired brim edged with wide band of silk. Leather gauntlet gloves. Leather clutch purse. Silk stockings. Leather shoes with almond-shaped toes.

Day Wear 1933–1934

1 1933. Sleeveless cream linen dress, high round neckline edged with decorative saddle stitching to match the shaped tucked seams on the semi-fitted bodice and on the front of the flared mid-calf-length skirt. Edge-to-edge collarless blue and white striped linen bolero jacket with short sleeves. Cream straw hat with shallow crown and wide wired brim. Elbow-length cream cotton gloves. Silk stockings. Brown and cream leather lace-up shoes, almond-shaped toes and high heels. 2 1933. Purple wool suit, semi-fitted belted collarless jacket with stepped diagonal front button fastening, narrow inset sleeves, flared skirt. Fox-fur stole worn around shoulders. Small brimless felt hat, worn at an angle, self-felt trim. White leather gauntlet gloves. Silk stockings. Beige and cream leather shoes, rounded toes and high heels. 3 1934. Semi-fitted lilac linen dress, high round neckline and short sleeves, spotted silk buckled waistbelt to match the scarf with outsized bow detail, the narrow band on the lilac linen beret and the gauntlet gloves. Silk stockings. Beige leather shoes with almond-shaped toes. 4 1934. Silk afternoon dress, waistbelt with plastic clasp; the flared skirt, the lower part of the bloused bodice and the sleeves from elbow to wrist in plain ivory silk; the upper part of the bodice, the outsized bow and the inset upper sleeves in patterned grey silk. Matching tiny hat worn at an angle and trimmed with two tiny lacquered red feathers. Silk stockings. Brown leather shoes with rounded toes and high heels. 5 1934. Brown silk dress spotted with white, low square neckline, narrow inset sleeves with flared plain white silk cuffs matching the silk flowers trimming the front of the hip-length fitted and ruched bodice; flared skirt with central gathered panel. Small hat in matching brown and white spotted silk with plain white silk brim. Silk stockings. White leather shoes trimmed with light brown, half round tongues, almond-shaped toes and high heels.

Evening Wear 1930–1934

1 1930. Pale pink silk-satin bias-cut evening dress, gathered halter neckline incorporating low scooped front, curved seaming under bust, matching seaming on hipline, double circle skirt with uneven hemline. Short permed hair, set into waves and curls, side parting. Silk stockings. Pale pink satin shoes, almond-shaped toes and high heels. 2 1931. Pale blue silk-georgette evening dress, low scooped neckline to waist at back, semi-fitted sleeveless bloused bodice; fitted skirt yoke from waist to low hip-level, narrow bias-cut diagonal panels with a swathe of pale blue chiffon at the base, knotted at the back, ends left to trail; full-length circular-cut skirt. Long hair with centre parting, set into waves and arranged into bun at nape of the neck. Pearl necklace and earrings. 3 1932. Full-length pale pink crepe-de-chine evening dress; cowled and gathered neckline, the outer edge trimmed with beads; fitted bodice; skirt cut into narrow curved bias-cut panels from under bust to hemline. Short waved hair with side parting. 4 1933. Pale green silk-taffeta sleeveless evening dress, waist-length V-shaped back neckline, wide revers cut in one with wide shoulder straps, fitted ruched bodice, bias-cut panelled skirt, bustle-effect at base of back neckline. Short hair set into rows of formal waves. 5 1934. Green silk-velvet sleeveless evening dress, low V-shaped back neckline emphasized by double cape collar, fitted bodice, back fastening with row of tiny self-fabric covered buttons ending with outsized bow forming bustle-effect; narrow skirt with wide centre-back inverted box pleat, slight train. Short permed hair set into rows of formal waves.

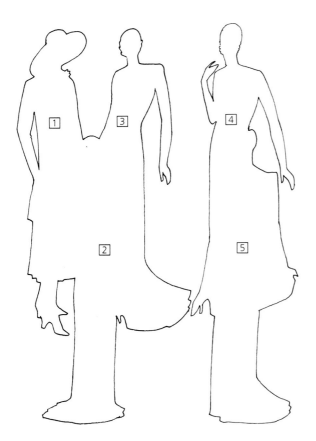

Bridal Wear 1930–1934

1 1930. Cream and white patterned silk wedding outfit; hip-length jacket with long tie neckline, tight inset sleeves, tucked detail above wrists matching panels on the unfitted edge-to-edge jacket; dress with low scooped neckline, semi-fitted bodice, narrow central panel to the belted waist, continuing through to hem of mid-calf-length knife-pleated skirt, silk flower corsage worn on one shoulder. Cream lacquered straw hat, wide brim edged with a wide binding of the dress fabric, matching band around high crown. Cream silk stockings. Cream leather shoes, almond-shaped toes and high heels. 2 1931. Ground-length silk-crepe wedding dress, central shaped panel of plain cream silk running from pearl-edged boat-shaped neckline through the fitted bodice to the hem of the flared skirt, patterned silk leg-of-mutton sleeves, points over the hands, self-fabric covered buttons from wrists to below elbows matching side panels of bodice and skirt. Headdress of pearls and silk flowers, cream silk-chiffon veil. 3 1933. White silk-satin wedding dress, fitted bodice, high shaped waist seam, padded shoulders, narrow inset sleeves, points over the hands, self-fabric covered buttons from wrists to below elbows, high round neckline edged with silver kid leather leaves and pearls, matching headdress, bias-cut skirt with long train. 4 1933. White corded-rayon wedding dress, fitted bodice and long flared skirt cut in one, opening from the high round neckline to the hem of the flared skirt, self-fabric covered buttons, padded shoulders, inset three-quarter-length sleeves with button trim. Pearl-embroidered wired silk-organdie headdress, fine silk-tulle veil. 5 1934. White crepe-de-chine wedding dress, fitted bodice, straight slashed neckline, padded shoulders, sleeves inset with cartridge pleats, points over the hands, self-fabric covered buttons from wrists to below elbows, bias-cut skirt and gathered train from a shaped hip seam. Skullcap embroidered and beaded with pearls.

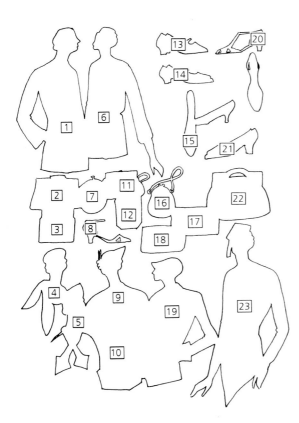

Accessories 1930–1934

1 1930. Hip-length edge-to-edge collarless knitted rayon cardigan and matching sweater, flared inset sleeves, embroidered decoration from wrists to below elbows, matching patch pockets. Amber beads and earrings.
2 1930. Yellow suede clutch bag, plastic trimming. 3 1931. Tapestry embroidered bag, silver frame, long handle. 4 1930. Knitted beret with large bow motif, matching knitted scarf. 5 1931. Small green felt hat, upturned asymmetric brim, brooch trim. Top-stitched green felt necktie.
6 1930. Hip-length yellow rayon blouse, gathered waistline, high round neckline, horizontal embroidered band across bodice and sleeves, repeated on hemline. Blue rayon scarf, wooden scarf ring. 7 1931. White silk clutch purse embroidered with flowers, plastic trim. 8 1934. Gold kid evening shoes, open sides, cut-away detail on fronts, ankle straps, high heels.
9 1933. Pink felt hat, asymmetric upturned brim trimmed with silk flowers. 10 1934. Orange felt trilby hat, high pointed crown, narrow brim, rouleau bow detail. 11 1932. Brown leather clutch bag, brooch trim, plastic frame. 12 1933. Red, white and blue striped canvas beach bag, long cord handle. 13 1930. Beige canvas shoes, orange leather heels, toecaps and trim. 14 1931. Crocodile leather shoes with buttoned bar straps, brown leather heels and trim. 15 1933. Blue and grey leather shoes, low bar straps trimmed with a bow, low heels. 16 1933. Pink satin evening bag with bead embroidery, ivory clasp and long handle. 17 1934. Leather and crocodile clutch purse. 18 1934. White plastic clutch purse striped with blue. 19 1933. Green felt hat with turned-down brim, white plastic bow trim. Striped velvet necktie and stickpin brooch. Grey leather gauntlet gloves. Blue and grey leather clutch bag. 20 1932. Silver kid evening shoes, open sides, cut-away fronts, low heels. 21 1934. Blue and white brogue shoes, almond-shaped toes, thick heels. 22 1934. Embroidered canvas beach bag, wooden handles. 23 1934. Small cream crocheted mortar-board with long tassel. Waist-length knitted cotton sweater, low round neckline trimmed with single knotted bow on one side, long inset sleeves.

Couture Wear 1935–1939

1 Chanel 1935. Three-piece wool-jersey suit, hip-length fitted striped jacket, V-shaped neckline and pointed collar, diagonal fastening with large covered buttons, narrow buttoned belt, long tight sleeves with plain wool turned-back cuffs to match flared skirt with inverted box pleats either side the front panel, short bolero jacket with narrow collar and revers, padded shoulders, elbow-length inset sleeves. Brimless skullcap in matching striped fabric, brooch trim. Red leather envelope purse. Flesh-coloured silk stockings. Black leather shoes with triangular buckle trim. 2 Creed 1937. Black wool day dress trimmed with red, white and blue striped piqué, high stand collar, fitted bodice with front button opening, padded shoulderline, narrow inset sleeves with triangular cuff detail, flared skirt. Black straw hat with stiff flat brim, shallow crown covered with striped piqué to match dress. Red leather gloves. Flesh-coloured silk stockings. Black leather shoes with high pointed tongues, pointed toes and high thick heels. 3 Chanel 1939. Black wool two-piece suit, fitted hip-length jacket, wide padded shoulders, narrow inset sleeves flaring out at split wristline, button trim, small collar, edge-to-edge fastening, buttons in sets of two, flared skirt. Silk blouse, ruffled at neck and wrists. Large beret set onto wide band, outsized star brooch trim. Flesh-coloured silk stockings. Black and white brogue shoes, snub toes and high thick heels. 4 Paquin 1939. Fitted grey wool coat; outsized collar, part-covered and trimmed with fur; narrow inset sleeves, fitted bodice and slim skirt, self-fabric covered buttons, matching buckled belt. Grey felt hat with narrow curled brim, small crown trimmed with black petersham band. Black leather gauntlet gloves. Flesh-coloured silk stockings. Black and grey leather brogue shoes, snub toes and high thick heels.

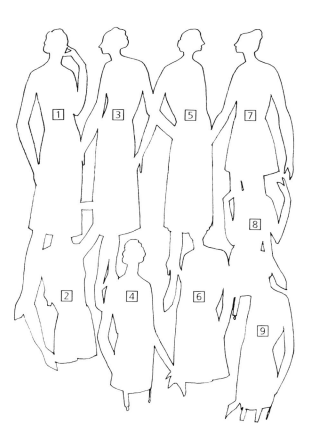

Underwear 1935–1939

1 1935. Knee-length peach-coloured silk-satin slip, seamed under bust; neck edge trimmed with border of machine-made lace and pintucks, matching the hem detail; narrow ribbon shoulder straps. 2 1936. Bias-cut cream silk camiknickers, ribbon straps, neckline and knicker legs edged with fine machine-made lace border, embroidered flower motif above one side of hemline. 3 1937. Cream crepe-de-chine slip, ribbon straps, decorated on bustline and on one side of hem with embroidered flower design. 4 1937 Waist-length cream silk camisole top, narrow ribbon shoulder straps, neck edge trimmed with fine machine-made border lace and rows of pintucks. High-waisted ribbed-cotton hip-girdle, double-fabric front control panel, side buckles and adjustable straps, back zip fastening, elasticated suspenders. 5 1938. Knee-length fitted blue silk slip, ribbon shoulder straps, bustline trimmed with appliqué lace and embroidery. 6 1939. Turquoise patterned silk camiknickers, narrow ribbon shoulder straps, fitted bodice, low neckline trimmed with lace and embroidery to match hem of wide flared knicker legs, side zip fastening. 7 1939. Pink silk brassiere, narrow ribbon shoulder straps, embroidered detail between bust cups, back hook and bar fastening. Pink silk camiknickers, elasticated waistline, side button fastening on embroidered shaped yoke, wide flared knicker legs edged with fine machine-made lace. 8 1939. Pink cotton-satin brassiere, ribbon shoulder straps, stitched shaped cups part-covered with machine-made lace, back hook and bar fastening. High-waisted elasticated cotton-satin hip-girdle, stiffened waistbelt with back hook and bar fastening, lightly boned front panel, machine-stitched side panels, side zip fastening, adjustable suspenders. 9 1939. Cotton-satin brassiere, adjustable shoulder straps, fitted and stitched cups, back hook and bar fastening. High-waisted hip-girdle, lightly boned and shaped front panel, elasticated side panels, side zip fastening, adjustable suspenders.

Leisure Wear 1935–1939

1 1935. Three-piece green knitted cotton suit. Sleeveless top with high round neckline, sleeveless edge-to-edge bolero jacket, small flap pockets at bust level trimmed with rouleau bows, fitted shorts with narrow turn-ups, wide red leather belt threaded through round green plastic buckle. Green canvas shoes, buckled bar straps and peep-toes trimmed with red, low thick heels. 2 1935. Red and white spotted elasticated rayon fitted bathing costume, shaped neckline ruched between bust, narrow halter straps. 3 1936. Elasticated rayon fitted bathing costume patterned with large green leaves, front button opening extending to each side the hipline, halter straps fastening at back of neck. 4 1937. Tennis outfit. Semi-fitted striped cotton blouse, narrow shirt collar, tucks on each side of front opening, decorative buttons to match the cuffs of the short inset sleeves, padded shoulders, narrow yoke, flared skirt in matching fabric, double inverted box pleats at front and sides, leather buckled belt. Rolled-down cotton ankle socks, lace-up canvas shoes with flat heels. 5 1938. Playsuit in pink cotton checked with white, semi-fitted blouse, small stand collar, narrow yoke, padded shoulders, inset bishop-style sleeves, front buttoned strap opening, short flared culottes, buttoned waistband. Wide headband. Pink and white striped canvas shoes, cord lacing over the instep and ankles, peep-toes and flat heels. 6 1939. Orange rayon two-piece bathing costume, short fitted bodice ruched between bust, shaped neckline edged with self-fabric frills, narrow shoulder straps, top attached to fitted shorts by centre-front point of bodice, bow trimming. 7 1939. Knitted cotton tennis dress, sleeveless bodice, high round neckline with small ribbed collar, decorative laced detail on upper bodice matching the tiny patch pockets on the hipline, buckled waistbelt, flared knee-length skirt. Canvas shoes with buttoned bar straps, round toes and flat heels.

Day Wear 1935–1936

1 1935. Pink and cream checked wool day dress, button-through semi-fitted bodice with two patch pockets matching those on each side of the inverted box pleat in the mid-calf-length straight skirt, padded shoulders, inset sleeves with narrow buttoned wrist cuffs, plain cream cotton collar, bow tie and buckled waistbelt. Cream lacquered straw hat, shallow crown with threaded feather trim, narrow brim dipping over to one side. Silk stockings. Cream leather shoes with almond-shaped toes and fringed tongues. 2 1935. Afternoon top and skirt in pale blue rayon patterned with white flowers, hip-length bloused bodice; top-stitched buttoned waistbelt matching the trimming on the tied neck detail, the cuffs on the short puff sleeves and the tops of both hip-level patch pockets; mid-calf-length flared skirt with centre-front inverted box pleat and knife-pleated side panels. Cream lacquered straw hat, narrow brim and shallow crown, wide white petersham band and bow. Long cream cotton gloves with top-stitched turned-down cuffs. Silk stockings. Cream leather shoes with rounded toes and high heels. 3 1936. Brown rayon day dress with all-over pattern, bloused bodice with ruching on each side of the central seam, padded shoulders, long gathered inset sleeves, points over the hands, button fastening to below elbow, wide suede belt knotted at front, mid-calf-length flared skirt falling from shaped yoke seam. Short permed hair. Silk stockings. Brown suede shoes, high tongues trimmed with tiny buckles, rounded toes, high heels. 4 1936. Camel-coloured wool double-breasted coat, large top-stitched collar and revers matching seams on the long raglan sleeves, the buttoned wrist straps, the buckled belt and the hip-level patch pockets. Cream felt hat, shallow crown and narrow brim, curled feather trim. Silk stockings. Brown suede shoes with rounded toes, bow trim and high heels. 5 1936. Tailored suit in lightweight cream wool pin-striped with pale grey, fitted jacket, wide collar and revers, two-button fastening, two welt pockets, padded shoulders, inset sleeves, straight skirt with wide box pleat. Navy blue shirt and cream spotted silk tie. White lacquered straw trilby hat trimmed with wide navy blue petersham band. Pale brown leather gauntlet gloves and clutch purse. Silk stockings. Blue and white leather shoes, rounded toes and high heels.

Day Wear 1937–1939

1 1937. Yellow rayon day dress patterned with random green spots; high round neckline with narrow plain white collar matching the wrist cuffs on the gathered inset sleeves, the covered buttons and the wide buckled waistbelt; bloused button-through bodice; raised panel seams run from the padded shoulders to the hem of flared skirt. Short permed hair. Silk stockings. Grey leather shoes with rounded toes and high heels. 2 1937. Two-piece suit in light and dark red rayon-velvet printed in white. Waist-length fitted button-through jacket, waistcoat-pointed hem, small collar, padded shoulders, gathered inset sleeves, points over the hands, covered buttons from wrists to below elbows, straight skirt with narrow box-pleated hemline. Short permed hair. Silk stockings. Grey suede shoes, rounded toes and high heels. 3 1937. Two-piece suit in green linen flecked with blue, semi-fitted collarless jacket, pointed scalloped button opening from neckline to belted waist matching cuff detail on the inset sleeves, padded shoulders, tiny triangular breast patch pockets, spotted silk handkerchief in one pocket matching small hat and gloves, flared skirt. Silk stockings. Blue and white leather shoes with rounded toes. 4 1939. Spotted rayon day dress, semi-fitted button-through bodice; high round neckline bound to match bow-tie, cuffs on the inset sleeves and the buckled waistbelt; panel seams from padded shoulders through to the hem of the knee-length box-pleated skirt. Hair arranged into curls on top of head. Silk stockings. Brown and white leather shoes, rounded toes and high heels. 5 1939. Pink rayon-crepe day dress; semi-fitted bloused bodice, V-shaped neckline edged with cream and lilac bands to match the cuffs of the elbow-length inset sleeves and the inset waistbelt; padded shoulders, narrow yoke, knee-length flared skirt with narrow shaped front panels. Hair worn in soft roll over forehead and swept up over ears. Silk stockings. Brown and cream leather shoes with rounded toes and high heels.

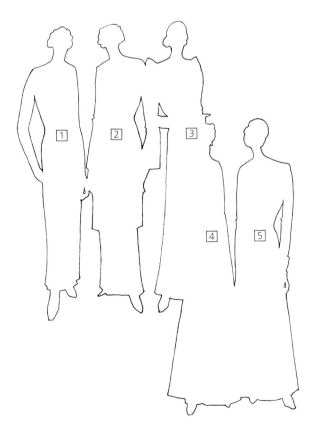

Evening Wear 1935–1939

1 1935. Gold-coloured silk-satin evening dress, halter neck with V-shaped front, seamed under the bust and bound with self-fabric through to the back of the neck, fitted bias-cut bodice and ankle-length skirt. Short permed hair. Gold satin shoes. 2 1936. Knee-length blue satin jacket, high round neckline, small collar with beaded and sequined edge to match the edge-to-edge front fastening and the hems of the inset flared sleeves, large beaded and sequined motifs on front of fitted bodice and on sleeves. Wide cream silk-satin pyjama trousers. Short permed hair, side parting. Cream satin pumps with flat heels. 3 1937. Dark red velvet evening dress, plain velvet fitted bodice with high shaped waistline, straight slashed neckline, padded shoulders, full-length multi-coloured printed velvet leg-of-mutton sleeves, tiny self-fabric covered buttons from wrists to below elbows, full-length flared skirt in matching fabric. Short permed hair set into waves and curls, side parting. Gold kid evening sandals. 4 1938. Blue silk-taffeta evening dress, wide self-fabric shoulder straps, matching band and bow trimming on top edge of semi-fitted bodice and on waistline, panelled ankle-length skirt covered with black silk-tulle to match bodice. Hair worn in high bun and decorated with silk flower. Glass bead bracelet. Satin evening pumps.
5 1939. Black corded-silk evening suit, hip-length fitted jacket with edge-to-edge fastening, large patch pockets, padded shoulders, tight inset sleeves, large cream silk bow at throat of high round collarless neckline, long flared skirt. Small fur beret worn on one side of head. Hair worn in large bun at back of head. Long cream kid gloves. Silver kid evening sandals.

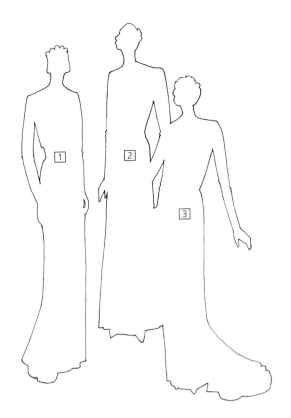

Bridal Wear 1935–1939

1 1935. Finely striped white crepe-de-chine wedding dress, semi-fitted bodice, high round neckline with plain white satin peter pan collar matching the wide draped cummerbund, centre-front opening, self-fabric covered buttons in sets of three, padded shoulders, gathered inset sleeves, points over the hands, bias-cut front panel running from neckline through to hem of flared skirt, long train. Headdress of wired pearls in the shape of a formal tiara, full-length embroidered silk-tulle veil. Hair cut in page-boy style with side parting. 2 1937. Cream crepe wedding dress, high round neckline with small stand collar, narrow yoke, padded shoulders, gathered inset sleeves, points over the hands, hip-length fitted bodice, shaped seam under bust, fastening from neck to hipline with tiny self-fabric covered buttons, ruching each side the opening, bias-cut skirt, central gathered panel. Tiara of wired pearls, long silk-tulle veil. White kid shoes, small bow decoration, almond-shaped toes. 3 1939. Finely corded white silk-crepe wedding dress, fitted panelled bodice and flared skirt cut without a waist seam and in one with the long back train, high neckline with small grown-on collar at front, padded shoulders, fitted inset sleeves, points over the hands, tiny self-fabric covered buttons from wrists to below elbows. Headdress of wax orange blossom, long embroidered tulle veil. Hair dressed in curls over ears and forehead and with side parting. White kid shoes with almond-shaped toes. Large bouquet of yellow tea roses, lily of the valley and various ferns and leaves.

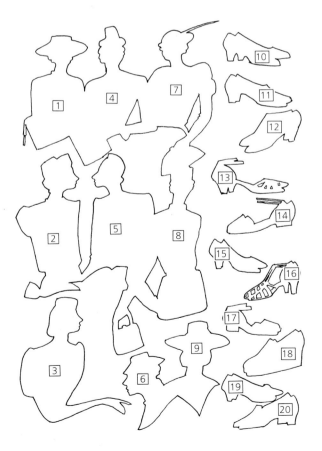

Accessories 1935–1939

1 1935. Cream lacquered straw hat, small crown trimmed with blue petersham band, narrow turned-down brim. Pearl earrings and necklace. Cream leather gauntlet gloves. Outsized cream leather clutch bag, decorative stitching, zip fastening. 2 1937. Top-stitched felt hat, upturned brim, tall crown with flat top. Glass bead necklace. Leather gauntlet gloves, matching belt with round plastic buckle. 3 1939. Small pillbox hat covered with spotted silk, black net snood. 4 1936. Felt hat with tall narrow crown and padded brim. Grey cotton gauntlet gloves. Grey suede clutch bag. 5 1938. Small felt hat trimmed with self-fabric pleated bow. Short cream leather gloves, matching bag with padded handle and plastic clasp faster. 6 1939. Small blue laquered straw hat, tiny crown trimmed with red and white ribbon matching the back strap. 7 1936. Grey felt hat, narrow brim, shallow crown, trimmed with white petersham band and long red feather. White fox-fur stole. White leather gauntlet gloves. White leather clutch bag and matching belt. 8 1938. Brimless fur hat and matching muff. 9 1939. Red lacquered straw hat, narrow flat-topped crown, wide straight brim with turned-down edge. 10 1935. Black patent and brown leather shoes with almond-shaped toes and high heels. 11 1935. Brown leather shoes, almond-shaped toes, cut-out laced detail. 12 1936. Blue and white lace-up brogue shoes, high thick heels. 13 1936. Red evening shoes, open sides, strap fronts, ankle-strap fastenings. 14 1937. Green canvas shoes, open sides and toes, flat leather heels. 15 1938. Blue suede shoes, almond-shaped toes, high thick heels, shallow platform soles. 16 1938. Silver kid evening shoes, open sides, strap fronts, T-strap fastenings, high heels. 17 1938. Orange leather shoes, open sides and toes, ankle straps, thick platform soles. 18 1939. Green suede shoes, high tongues, wide strap fastening with pink ribbons, matching pink leather-covered cork wedge heels. 19 1939. Black patent leather shoes with small grey leather tongues, almond-shaped toes and high heels. 20 1939. Brown leather shoes, stub toes, high tongues and low thick heels.

Norman Hartnell 1942

Strassner 1942

Cristobal Balenciaga 1940

Digby Morton 1944

Norman Hartnell 1944

1940

1940

1941

1941

1942

1942

1943

1944

1940

1940

1944

1943

1941

1944

1940

1940

1941

1941

1941

1942

1943

1943

1944

1944

1944

1944

Evening Wear 1940–1944

1940

1940

1941

1944

1940

1943

1944

1940

1942

1941

1941

1944

1940

1940

1941

1942

1940

1942

1940

1942

1943

1942

1942

1944

1943

1944

1944

1943

1943

1943

1944

Jacques Fath 1945

Giuseppe Mattli 1949

Cristobal Balenciaga 1947

Christian Dior 1947

Molyneux 1948

Underwear 1945–1949

1945

1946

1948

1949

1946

1948

1947

1947

1948

1945

1946

1948

1948

1948

1947

1949

1945

1945

1947

1948

1947

1947

1948

1948

1948

1949

1949

1949

1949

1945

1946

1948

1949

1948

1949

1945

1946

1949

1949

1945

1948

1946

1949

1948

1945

1946

1948

1949

1948

1945

1946

1947

1948

1949

1947

1949

1947

1947

1949

1949

1949

1949

Couture Wear 1940–1944

[1] Cristobal Balenciaga 1940. Black wool jersey dress, button-through fitted bodice, long inset fitted sleeves, padded shoulders, ruched yoke in violet wool jersey matching hip basque of the knee-length gathered skirt. Pale grey fox-fur hat trimmed with black petersham bow at back, large muff in matching fur. Black suede shoes, ankle straps, almond-shaped toes and thick high heels. [2] Strassner 1942. Dark blue ribbed-wool coat, fitted bodice, edge-to-edge hook and bar fastening, wide collar and revers, padded shoulders, fitted inset sleeves with false wrist cuffs, red tassel decoration on patch pockets and on panel seams running from shoulders to knee-length flared hemline. Blue felt hat, large upturned brim, worn on back of head. Long hair, deep fringe and large side curls. Short blue leather gloves. Flesh-coloured nylon stockings. Blue leather sling-back shoes with high heels and platform soles. [3] Norman Hartnell 1942. Knee-length tan wool dress, semi-fitted bodice, padded shoulders; narrow yoke, tiny collar, decorative tabs, covered buttons, fitted inset sleeves and tailored belt all in contrasting brown wool. Large brown felt breton-style hat worn on back of head. Long hair dressed into deep fringe with waves and curls at sides and back. Flesh-coloured nylon stockings. Brown leather court shoes with high thick heels. [4] Norman Hartnell 1944. Green wool edge-to-edge collarless coat, wide turned-back top-stitched revers, padded shoulders, narrow inset sleeves, knee-length flared skirt in matching fabric, beaver fur dicky front with high round collarless neckline and waistcoat-pointed hem, matching cushion muff and trimming on small green wool hat. Brown leather shoes, almond-shaped toes, curled tongue decoration and thick high heels. [5] Digby Morton 1944. Light blue and brown herringbone wool suit, fitted hip-length tailored jacket, wide revers, padded shoulders, fitted inset sleeves, hip-level flap pockets, straight knee-length skirt. Light brown felt pillbox hat with self-fabric looped bows on each side. Short brown leather gloves. Flesh-coloured nylon stockings. Brown suede sling-back shoes with high wedge heels, platform soles and peep-toes.

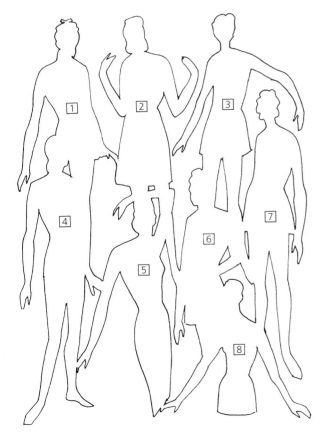

Underwear 1940–1944

[1] 1940. Camiknickers in pale blue crepe-de-chine patterned with sprays of flowers, high seam with gathers under bust, fine rouleau shoulder straps tied into bows, frilled neck edge and hemline. Hair dressed into curls, tied with velvet ribbon, left loose and rolled at back. [2] 1940. Short patterned silk slip, narrow rouleau shoulder straps, high waistline emphasized by rows of fine pintucks. Hair drawn back over ears with loose curls at back and a rolled fringe over forehead. [3] 1941. Fine cream cotton cross-over brassiere with pintucked detail and narrow shoulder straps, matching wide-legged knickers, pintucked waistband and pointed yoke, side-button fastening. Hair dressed into curls on top of head. [4] 1941. Flesh-coloured elasticated cotton satin hip-length corselette, stitched and wired uplift brassiere covered with flesh-coloured lace, narrow adjustable shoulder straps and suspenders, side fastening. Hair dressed back over ears and left loose at back. Nylon stockings. [5] 1942. Tailored cotton brassiere trimmed with lace, narrow adjustable shoulder straps, back fastening. Long-line Latex girdle, deep waistband, front figure control panel and adjustable suspenders. Page-boy hairstyle with rolled fringe. Nylon stockings. [6] 1942. Cream silk camiknickers; lace trimming on neckline, side seams and hems; rouleau shoulder straps, bloused bodice with elasticated waist. Curled hair, centre parting. [7] 1943. Stitched and wired uplift brassiere, fine lace trimming, narrow adjustable shoulder straps, back fastening. Pink silk knickers, deep waistband, wide leg, trimmed at each side seam with appliqué flowers, shaped front panel. Curled hair with side parting. Nylon stockings. [8] 1944. Waist-length black cotton-satin wired uplift brassiere covered with black lace, narrow shoulder straps, elasticated side panels, back fastening. Hair dressed in waves and curls high on head.

Leisure Wear 1940–1944

1 1940. Cycling outfit. Hip-length tailored striped wool jacket, single-button fastening at waist, shawl collar, padded shoulders, inset fitted sleeves, knee-length culottes in matching fabric. Red silk blouse with open neck. Short permed hair with side parting. Long knitted brown wool socks. Brown leather lace-up shoes with flat heels. 2 1940. Beach wear. Red knitted cotton sweater, high round neckline, short sleeves. Flower-printed white cotton knee-length skirt, gathered from wide waistband. Hat with wide brim covered in matching printed cotton. Page-boy hairstyle with rolled fringe. Canvas shoes with flat heels and ribbon tie fastenings. 3 1944. Cycling outfit. Hip-length brown herringbone wool jerkin, fitted sleeveless bodice buttons from the high round collarless neckline to waist, large flap-and-patch pockets at bust level, straight-cut trousers with turn-ups in matching fabric. Yellow wool cable-knit jumper. Red silk scarf tied into turban around head, concealing hair. Large clip-on earrings. Lace-up leather shoes with flat heels. 4 1941. Tennis outfit. Spotted white cotton collarless button-through top, short cuffed sleeves, wide waistband joins the top to the wide pleated shorts. Waved and curled hair, side parting. 5 1943. Tennis outfit. Striped white cotton blouse buttoning at front from small pointed collar to waist, padded shoulders, short inset sleeves with shaped cuffs, narrow yoke, short box-pleated skirt in matching fabric, wide waistband and buckled self-fabric belt, side zip fastening. Short permed hair, side parting. 6 1944. Tennis outfit. Checked white cotton blouse buttoning from peter pan collar to waist, padded shoulders, short inset sleeves with shaped cuffs, yoke seam with inset flap pockets, fitted shorts in matching fabric, wide waistband, turn-ups, pressed central creases, side hip pockets, side zip fastening. Long hair dressed away from face and into large curls at back.

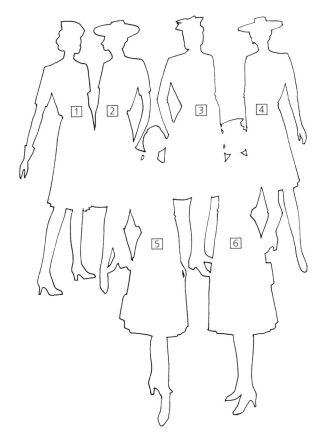

Day Wear 1940–1942

1 1940. Day dress, blue and cream striped rayon crepe, over-patterned in white, semi-fitted bodice, high yoke, padded shoulders, short sleeves, high round neckline edged with self-fabric band and bow tie, matching trim on narrow waistbelt, knee-length skirt, knife pleats stitched down to hip level. Small natural straw breton hat. Hair dressed in large curls and waves. Small clip-on earrings. Short cream cotton gauntlet gloves. Nylon stockings. Blue and white leather court shoes with high heels. 2 1940. Green linen day dress, semi-fitted bodice, padded shoulders, short sleeves, small collar, decorative top-stitched seams from shoulder to hip incorporating a narrow yoke and large hip-level patch pockets, knee-length flared skirt with centre-front seam buttoned from waist to hip. Brown lacquered straw hat, tiny flat-topped crown, wired brim. Clip-on earrings. Short cotton gloves. Leather clutch bag. Brown and white leather court shoes. 3 1941. Knee-length fitted checked wool coat, double-breasted fastening, wide collar and revers, padded shoulders, fitted inset sleeves, flared skirt, bias-cut side panels. Brimless felt hat with self-fabric trim. Curled and waved shoulder-length hair. Small clip-on earrings. Short leather gloves. Nylon stockings. Leather shoes with peep-toes and low thick heels. 4 1941. Edge-to-edge lightweight wool coat; front edges, hems of the fitted inset sleeves and the double rouleau tie-belt in contrasting colour; padded shoulders, smocked half yoke, knee-length flared skirt. Small lacquered straw hat, wired brim, upturned around outer edge, tiny flat-topped crown. Blue leather shoes trimmed with large bow at front. 5 1941. Beige wool coat; top-stitched detail on the buckled waistbelt, on the imitation breast pockets, on the large collar and on the cuffs of the inset fur-fabric sleeves. Hair obscured under red fabric turban except for waved fringe at front. Clip-on earrings. Leather gloves, bag and matching shoes. 6 1942. Green wool wrapover coat, wide collar and revers, inset sleeves, padded shoulders, self-fabric tied waistbelt, hip-level round patch pockets with piped openings, knee-length flared skirt. Red felt beret with black headband. Leather gloves and large clutch bag. Brown and cream lace-up leather shoes with high heels.

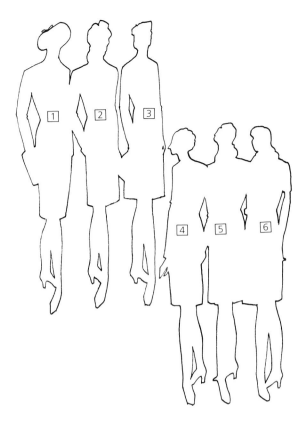

Day Wear 1943–1944

1 1943. Green wool suit, hip-length fitted jacket, buttons from high round neckline with small shawl collar to waist seam, padded shoulders, fitted inset sleeves, top-stitched half yoke, large flap pockets, knee-length wrapover skirt. Felt hat with wide turned-back brim, rouleau bow trimming. Clip-on earrings. Fur muff. Leather shoes, fringed tongue trim, round toes, high thick heels. 2 1943. Grey wool suit, hip-length fitted jacket, small wing collar, two-button fastening, top-stitched edges and decorative seams incorporating bust-level patch pockets with small piped openings, padded shoulders, fitted inset sleeves, narrow knee-length wrapover skirt. Tiny red felt hat, flat-topped crown, curled brim. Hair in large waves and curls. Clip-on earrings. Black leather shoes with white pipings, high thick heels. 3 1944. Red wool suit, hip-length fitted jacket, three-button fastening from narrow rounded collar and revers to natural waist position, padded shoulders, inset sleeves, bust-level piped pockets, knee-length box-pleated skirt. Brown felt hat, narrow brim, small flat-topped crown, petersham ribbon bow trim. Short brown leather gloves, matching outsized bag. Brown suede leather shoes, high tongues, square toes, medium-high thick heels. 4 1944. Hip-length checked wool jacket, large single-button fastening under wide collar, self-fabric buckled waistbelt, padded shoulders, half yoke, inset sleeves, outsized hip-level patch pockets. Straight knee-length light brown wool skirt. Short permed hair. Cream suede leather shoes, bow trimming, high thick heels. 5 1944. Patterned rayon crepe dress, neckline open to waist, yellow crepe mock blouse buttoning from high collarless neckline to waist, matching cuffs on the three-quarter-length inset sleeves, padded shoulders, curved inset panel from under bust to hip-level, bow trim on centre-front waist, gathered knee-length skirt. Waved and curled hair, side parting. Blue leather peep-toe shoes, white pipings, high thick heels. 6 1944. Cream linen wrapover dress, narrow spotted silk shawl collar, matching waistbelt and bow trim, padded shoulders, yoke seam, short inset sleeves, knee-length straight skirt. Shoulder-length hair, deep fringe. Leather shoes, cut-out decoration, round toes, thick high heels.

Evening Wear 1940–1944

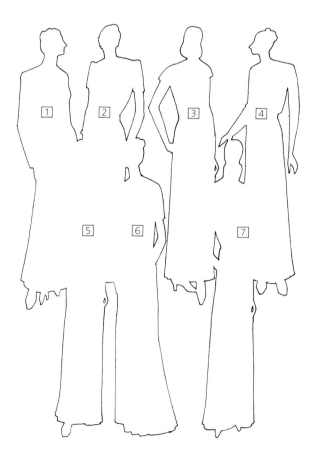

1 1940. Red wool crepe evening suit, hip-length fitted jacket, self-fabric covered buttons from narrow shawl collar to waist, curved side panel seams with gathered hip-level patch pockets, padded shoulders, fitted inset sleeves, long flared skirt. Long hair worn in curls on top of head. Silver kid shoes. 2 1940. Blue, grey and white striped taffeta top, fitted bodice, padded shoulders, short gathered inset sleeves, gathered hip basque open at front, blue crepe narrow stand collar and matching floor-length skirt with pleated central panel, wide gold-kid waistbelt. Long hair worn in bun at back. Gold clip-on earrings. 3 1941. Ankle-length blue rayon dress, beaded long-line fitted bodice, sweetheart neckline, padded shoulders and cap sleeves, straight skirt with gathered front panel. Hair worn in net snood. Silver kid sandals with high heels. 4 1944. Green crepe dinner dress, semi-fitted bodice, flared square neckline infilled with self-fabric frill, padded shoulders, fitted inset sleeves, narrow self-fabric buckled waistbelt, ankle-length skirt with gathered front panel from two hip-level curved seams. Hair worn in curls on top of head. Silver peep-toe shoes. 5 1940. Green crepe dinner dress, fitted bodice, padded shoulders, fitted inset sleeves trimmed at wrists with two bands of gold and silver sequins to match trim on high round neckline, shaped front panel seam from under bust to hip-level floor-length gathered skirt. Long curled hair. 6 1943. Gold lamé dress, fitted bodice slashed at the back from the collarless neckline to the deep swathed waistband, padded shoulders, short inset sleeves, floor-length skirt with gathered back panel. Hair dressed into curls on top of head. 7 1944. Gold satin top, deep V-shaped neckline, padded shoulders, inset short puff sleeves; deep stitched shaped waistband from under the bust decorated with row of self-fabric covered buttons, floor-length black satin wrapover skirt bound with black velvet. Long hair worn in roll at back of neck. Gold kid sandals.

Bridal Wear 1940–1944

1 1940. Pale blue rayon-crepe wedding dress, fitted hip-length bodice, shaped seam under bust, high round neckline, shaped yoke frilled with self-fabric, padded shoulders, short gathered puff sleeves, knee-length skirt gathered from shaped hip seam. Small hat with asymmetric brim in matching fabric, trimmed with posy. Short white gloves. White leather shoes, seamed wrapover effect, high heels. 2 1941. Floor-length wedding dress, fitted hip-length underbodice with fine flesh-coloured chiffon; collarless and sleeveless yoke, topped with machine-made lace, re-embroidered and scattered with seed pearls, matching the inset leg-of-mutton-style sleeves; straight neckline bound with silk-satin to match waistbelt and piped seams between each tier of the full tulle skirt. Headdress of satin roses and wired pearls, long silk-tulle veil. Short white kid gloves and matching shoes. 3 1941. Silk-chiffon wedding gown, floor-length full gathered skirt, fitted horizontally ruched bodice from high hip-level to over bust, vertically ruched yoke, padded shoulders, inset ruched sleeves, frilled wristline, high round padded neckline trimmed with collar of wax and silk flowers to match the tiny headdress with shoulder-length veil. 4 1944. White taffeta wedding gown striped with silver, fitted bodice, inset sleeves, embroidered and beaded off-the-shoulder collar infilled with silk organdie, full gathered skirt from V-shaped waist seam. Headdress of wax flowers with long silk veil. White satin shoes. 5 1942. Pink silk-crepe wrapover wedding dress, diagonal seams, self-fabric waistbelt tied in large bow on one side, padded shoulders, fitted inset three-quarter-length cuffed sleeves, knee-length flared skirt. Fine cream straw hat with wide wired brim, posy pinned into hair. Pearl earrings and matching necklace. Pink silk gloves. Cream leather sling-back shoes with ankle straps, peep-toes and high heels.

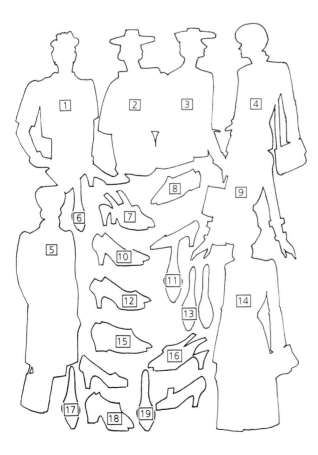

Accessories 1940–1944

1 1940. Waist-length edge-to-edge collarless fur jacket, padded shoulders, elbow-length sleeves. Blue straw hat with open crown, spotted veil. Long brown leather gloves. Brown leather folded envelope bag. 2 1940. Elbow-length fur cape, stand collar, satin bow-tie fastening. Cream straw hat, flat brim turned up around edge, narrow crown, petersham trimming. Long black suede gloves, matching bag with double handles. 3 1941. Hip-length double-breasted striped wool jacket. Straw hat, brim turned up on each side, small crown, petersham trimming. Leather gloves with scalloped cuffs. Leather bag with double handles. 4 1942. Hip-length wool jacket. Large red felt beret. Leather shoulder bag, short gloves. 5 1943. Three-quarter-length fur coat, waist-length shawl collar, single fur-button fastening, padded shoulders, inset leg-of-mutton-style sleeves. Straw hat, upturned brim, braided edges. Short brown leather gloves, matching metal-framed bag. 6 1940. Blue leather shoes, red platform soles, heels and studded trim. 7 1940. Blue and white leather sling-back shoes with peep-toes, punched decoration and satin bow trimming. 8 1942. Suede shoes with low wedge heels. 9 1943. Hip-length belted wool jacket, three-quarter-length cuffed sleeves. Deep fur scarf worn around shoulders. Small brown straw hat, green petersham band. Short gloves with turned-down cuffs. 10 1942. Brown and white leather court shoes. 11 1942. White leather peep-toe shoes with rouleau bow trimming. 12 1942. Dark green and yellow brogued court shoes. 13 1944. Black suede shoes with peep-toes and cut-out decoration. 14 1944. Knee-length black Persian lamb coat, small shawl collar, padded shoulders, inset flared sleeves, wide black patent-leather belt. Brimless velvet hat. Short gloves. Small clutch bag. 15 1943. Pink suede lace-up shoes, high wedge heels. 16 1944. Brown leather sling-back shoes, platform soles and high heels. 17 1943. Green leather shoes, brown square toecaps, high heels and bow trimming. 18 1943. Brown leather lace-up brogue shoes. 19 1944. Brown leather shoes, contrasting brown suede uppers and high heels, brown leather bow trimming.

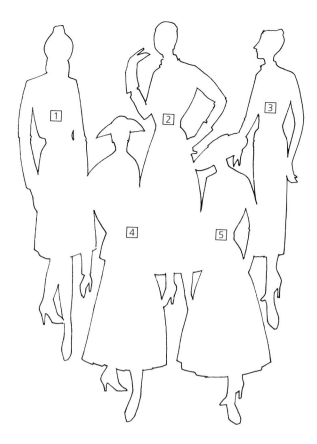

Couture Wear 1945–1949

1 Jacques Fath 1945. Grey wool suit, hip-length edge-to-edge jacket, padded shoulders, inset cuffed shirt-type sleeves, buttoned waistbelt, button-down flap-and-patch pockets, knee-length flared skirt. Blue and white striped silk shirt blouse. Blue felt hat with tall narrow crown and turned-back brim. Flesh-coloured nylon stockings. Black leather court shoes, rounded toes and high thick heels. 2 Cristobal Balenciaga 1947. Lilac wool dress, fitted bodice buttoned from the stand collar to the self-fabric buckled belt at the small waist, padless slightly rounded shoulders, three-quarter-length inset sleeves, mid-calf-length skirt with knife-pleated side panels. Brimless purple felt hat with attached silk-chiffon scarf passing over crown and under chin. Purple bead necklace and clip-on earrings. Long purple suede gauntlet gloves. Flesh-coloured nylon stockings. Purple suede court shoes, high thick heels. 3 Giuseppe Mattli 1949. Dark blue wool day dress, fitted bodice, wing collar, long dolman-style sleeves, swathed hip sash, narrow mid-calf-length skirt. Hair dressed away from face into curls at back. Clip-on earrings. Flesh coloured nylon stockings. Black leather court shoes, rounded toes and high thick heels. 4 Christian Dior 1947. 'New Look' suit, hip-length fitted silk jacket buttoned from narrow revers to tightly fitted waist, rounded unpadded shoulders, narrow inset sleeves with two-button detail on wrists, front panel seams from sloping shoulders to hemline, mid-calf-length knife-pleated black silk skirt. Natural straw hat with shallow crown and wide turned-down brim. Black leather gloves. Flesh-coloured nylon stockings. Black suede court shoes, rounded toes and high thick heels. 5 Molyneux 1948. Dark brown silk day dress, high round neckline edged with cream Russia braid to match the side hip pocket edges and the cuffs of the semi-inset fitted sleeves, mid-calf-length full skirt. Fabric-covered hat, wide wired flat brim and shallow crown. Nylon stockings. Brown suede court shoes with high heels.

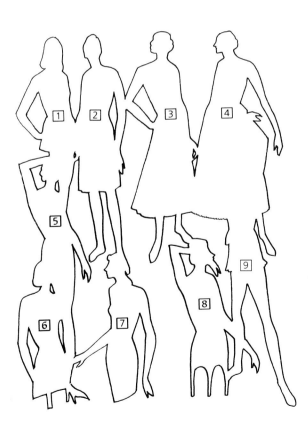

Underwear 1945–1949

1 1945. Pale pink silk camiknickers, shaped yoke seam with gathers under bust, pointed waist seam, narrow shoulder straps, neckline bound with self-fabric and trimmed with rouleau bow matching the hems of the wide knicker legs. Long page-boy hairstyle. 2 1946. Knee-length patterned silk fitted petticoat, shaped front panel, gathers under bust, neck and hemline trimmed with border of lace, narrow ribbon shoulder straps. Hair worn in rolls on the top of head. 3 1948. White spotted cream cotton brassiere, narrow shoulder straps, back fastening, mid-calf-length waistslip in matching fabric, full gathered skirt from deep hip yoke. Permed and waved hair with side parting. 4 1949. Waist-length striped cotton brassiere and combined camisole, fine lace trimming, narrow shoulder straps, back fastening, mid-calf-length waistslip in matching fabric, wide gathered frill around hem, trimmed with lace. Permed hair. 5 1946. Black cotton satin brassiere, wired cups with lace insertions, adjustable shoulder straps, back fastening, black stretch cotton pantie-girdle, deep waistband, double front panel, adjustable suspenders. Nylon stockings. Short permed hair. 6 1947. Pink elasticated cotton-satin brassiere with stitched and wired cups, narrow shoulder straps, back fastening, hip-girdle in matching fabric, stitched front panel, small centre-front elastic gusset, side zip fastening. Short page-boy hairstyle. 7 1947. Apricot waist-length knitted wool camisole top with deep waist rib, satin ribbon shoulder straps, fitted panties in matching fabric with deep waist rib. Long hair with rolled fringe. 8 1948. Strapless black elasticated-satin-and-lace boned and wired uplift brassiere, waist-nipper and adjustable suspender belt, side zip fastening. Hair worn on top of head in formal curls and rolls. 9 1948. Turquoise patterned silk brassiere with wired and darted cups, narrow shoulder straps, self-fabric frilled neck edge, back hook and bar fastening, fitted panties in matching fabric, frilled hems, side zip fastening. Flesh-coloured nylon stockings. Long waved and curled hair with centre parting.

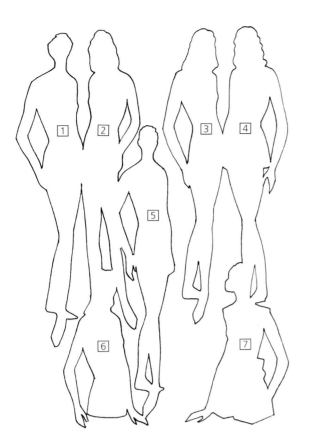

Leisure Wear 1945–1949

1 1945. Yellow and red shirred elasticated-cotton bathing costume, low neckline bound with self-fabric, narrow rouleau shoulder straps, short straight skirt cut in one with brief knickers. Red cotton scarf tied into turban around head. Red plastic clip-on earrings. Canvas sandals with peep-toes, ribbon trimming and fastening, thick rope soles. 2 1946. Blue fitted elasticated-cotton swimsuit with white spots, gathers between the fitted cups, rouleau halter-neck straps, decorative gathers above high-cut legs. Long hair, waved and curled. Leather strap sandals with flat heels. 3 1948. Pink rayon bikini, small bra top with gathered unfitted cups, back fastening, halter straps fastening at back of neck, frill of self-fabric trimming around neckline matching the hem of the short ruched skirt. Long curled and waved hair with side parting. Red canvas sandals with peep-toes and ankle straps; low cork wedge heels. 4 1948. Blue striped rayon beach dress trimmed around neckline with cuff of blue spotted rayon to match the tied knot, the wide halter straps and the waistbelt; fitted bodice, short box-pleated skirt. Shoulder-length curled and waved hair. White canvas sling-back sandals with low heels. 5 1948. Striped rayon bikini, draped cross-over bra top, narrow halter straps threaded through metal rings, back fastenings, fitted hip-length skirt in matching fabric. Hair worn in large plait across top of head. White canvas mules, peep-toes and flat heels. 6 1947. Pink, blue and white patterned bikini, small gathered bra top, narrow rouleau halter straps fastening at back of neck, fitted hip-length skirt, draped over-skirt knotted at front. Long straight hair dressed into large rolls. 7 1949. Pink and white striped linen beach set, sleeveless and collarless wrapover top, single-buttoned patch pocket, wide flared shorts with pressed central creases and single-buttoned patch pocket on the opposite side to the top, wide red silk sash tied into large bow on one side of waist. Short permed hair with centre parting.

Day Wear 1945–1948

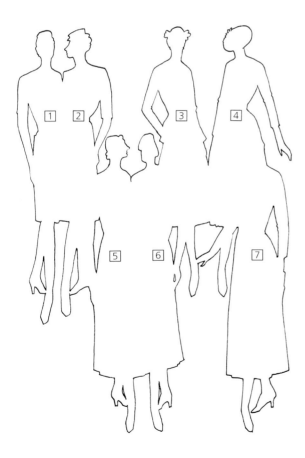

1 1945. Pink linen suit, fitted hip-length jacket, square buttons from neck to waist; white-spotted cream rayon peter pan collar matching the hem bindings of the short inset sleeves, the waistbelt and decorative bow, the lower turned-back facings and the patch pockets; knee-length skirt. Hair worn in curls on top of head. Pink suede peep-toe shoes with high heels. 2 1945. Cream linen suit, hip-length belted jacket, tailored collar and revers, buttons from neck to hipline, outsized patch pocket with piped middle opening, padded shoulders, elbow-length inset sleeves, knee-length box-pleated skirt. Tiny yellow lacquered straw hat, brown petersham band. Brown leather shoes with stitched detail. 3 1947. Red velvet fitted jacket buttoning from narrow stand collar to waistline, hip-length peplum with shorter split overpeplum, rounded shoulders, slim inset sleeves, mid-calf-length gathered black silk skirt. Small brimless straw hat trimmed with silk flowers. Short brown leather gloves. Large leather bag. Brown leather shoes with square toes and ankle straps. 4 1948. Grey flannel collarless dress, fitted bodice with rows of buttons each side the centre-front seam from neckline to the wide buckled waistbelt, rounded shoulders, three-quarter-length dolman-style sleeves, two large breast pockets, mid-calf-length sunray-pleated skirt. Felt hat with wide brim, silk flower trimming. Black leather court shoes. 5 1947. Mid-calf-length blue rayon dress spotted with red, collarless fitted bodice, inset cuffed sleeves, half-round patch pockets, button decoration, full skirt with centre-front box pleat. White felt skullcap. Short white cotton gloves with scalloped edges. White leather shoes, ruched and buttoned trim. 6 1947. Red and white striped cotton button-through mid-calf-length day dress, short inset sleeves with plain white cotton cuffs to match the collar and the pointed flaps on the large hip-level patch pockets. Red beret. Short white cotton gloves with narrow cuffs. Red leather court shoes. 7 1948. Green wool mid-calf-length button-through dress, three-quarter-length dolman-style sleeves, two surface darts from collarless neckline into the side panel seams which end in pressed knife pleats above the hemline, self-fabric waistbelt and covered buckle. Page-boy hairstyle. Short leather gloves and matching shoes with high heels.

Day Wear 1948–1949

1 1948. Blue wool day dress, fitted bodice, asymmetric button fastening matching the buttoned-down pockets in the mid-calf-length full skirt, small peter pan collar, fitted inset sleeves, self-fabric buckled waistbelt. Small brimless felt hat trimmed with looped ribbons on one side. Leather gauntlet gloves. Leather box-shaped bag. Leather court shoes. 2 1948. Brown wool day dress, fitted bodice, panel from under bust to waist trimmed on each edge with velvet ribbon and finished with small bows, grown-on collar, long dolman-style sleeves, gathered mid-calf-length skirt. Short permed hair with full fringe. 3 1949. Striped cotton dress with fitted collarless bodice, buttons to the waist, decorative buttons on the seams of the side panels of the mid-calf-length skirt, three-quarter-length dolman-style cuffed sleeves in plain cotton matching the buckled waistbelt. Short permed hair. Leather court shoes with low heels. 4 1949. Floral print cotton dress with fitted bodice; low V-shaped neckline edged with plain black cotton to match the buckled waistbelt, the flared cuffs on the short dolman-style sleeves and the hip-level band in the mid-calf-length skirt. Short permed hair. Black plastic clip-on earrings and matching necklace. Black leather sling-back shoes trimmed with white. 5 1949. Brown rayon dress, dolman-style sleeves, collarless fitted and ruched bodice, asymmetric side panel from under bust to hipline of wrapover swathed overskirt, narrow mid-calf-length underskirt. Short permed hair with side parting. White earrings and matching bead necklace. Brown leather court shoes, high thick heels. 6 1949. Plum-coloured wool-crepe dress, collarless fitted bodice, narrow inset sleeves, buttoned-down yoke from split centre-front seam to underarm, matching hip basque, self-fabric buckled waistbelt, narrow mid-calf-length skirt. Permed hair with centre parting. Black leather court shoes with high thick heels.

Evening Wear 1945–1949

1 1945. Floor-length green crepe dress, fitted bodice with narrow rouleau shoulder straps and flared skirt, hip-length black silk-chiffon over-bodice with short cap sleeves, high round neckline trimmed with shiny black sequins to match the waistbelt. Hair dressed into high curled fringe. Black satin-covered sandals. 2 1946. Beige crepe dinner suit, hip-length fitted jacket decorated with bands of horizontal tucks at bust and hip-level, tiny buttons from low square neckline to hem of box-pleated peplum, padded shoulders, short cap sleeves, straight ankle-length skirt. Hair dressed into large french pleat at back of head. Clip-on amber earrings and matching necklace. Grey suede peep-toe shoes. 3 1948. Mid-calf-length purple striped taffeta cocktail dress, fitted bodice, tiny self-fabric covered buttons from small stand collar to waistline, matching buttons on wristline of the fitted inset sleeves, bias-cut wrapover overskirt with irregular hemline, self-fabric full underskirt. Hair with centre parting worn with thick plait over top of head. Lilac satin-covered sandals, sling-backs and high heels. 4 1949. Pink rayon taffeta underdress with fitted bodice with flesh-coloured chiffon collarless and sleeveless yoke and a circular-cut skirt, covered by a brown machine-made lace overdress with a fitted bodice; buttons from bow-tied neckline to buckled self-fabric waistbelt, rounded shoulderline, short cap sleeves, mid-calf-length skirt cut in flared panels. Short permed and waved hair. Brown satin-covered shoes, tiny bow trimming and high heels. 5 1948. Floor-length pink silk-taffeta evening gown, asymmetric draped fitted bodice with large silk flower on one side, skirt with asymmetric graded gathered frill from side waist to side hip, deep hem frill. Permed and waved hair dressed away from face. White clip-on earrings and matching necklace. Long pink silk gloves. Pink silk-covered shoes. 6 1949. Floor-length pink silk-taffeta ballgown patterned with white flowers, fitted button-through bodice cuffed with pointed folds of self-fabric, wide shoulder straps, full overskirt cut in wide flared panels, open at one side to form two waterfall frills, self-fabric underskirt. Short waved hair, side parting. Large clip-on earrings and matching necklace. Long dark pink silk gloves.

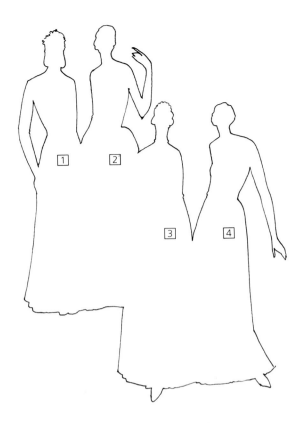

Bridal Wear 1945–1949

1 1945. Ivory satin wedding dress, hip-length fitted bodice cut in panels, sweetheart neckline with narrow grown-on collar, padded shoulders, fitted inset sleeves; rounded points over the hands decorated with appliqué stylized flowers and leaves, echoed above bust and around hipline; floor-length skirt cut in wide flared panels with an inset godet in each seam. Headdress of silk and wax flowers with long silk veil attached. Hair worn in net snood. 2 1946. White satin wedding dress, all-over pattern of bows, fitted bodice, low sweetheart neckline, padded shoulders, narrow inset sleeves, turned-down cuffs, self-fabric covered button trimming at wrists, floor-length skirt gathered from pointed waistline, looped up on each side to form mock panniers. Small white felt skullcap decorated with wax flowers, attached silk veil. Pearl necklace. 3 1949. White silk chiffon wedding dress, boned wrap-over draped bodice, embroidered and beaded infill to high round neckline, three-quarter-length ruched inset sleeves, floor-length skirt gathered from waistline and mounted over circular-cut silk-taffeta underskirt. Headdress of silk flowers and pearls, attached silk veil. Pearl earrings and choker necklace. 4 1949. White silk wedding dress, beaded boned bodice, white silk-chiffon yoke with beaded slashed neckline and long inset sleeves beaded from wrists to elbows, mid-calf-length panelled overskirt with pointed hemline, accordion-pleated underskirt. White silk skullcap with attached waist-length veil.

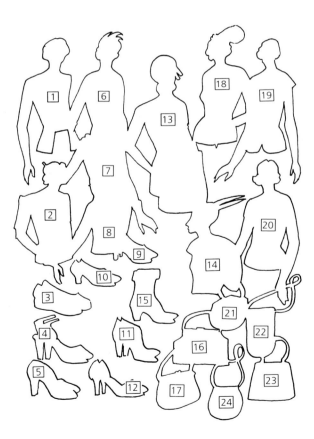

Accessories 1945–1949

1 1945. Knitted tan wool twinset, collarless waist-length sweater, collarless hip-length cardigan buttoning from bust to hem, padded shoulders, long cuffed inset sleeves. 2 1945. Hip-length knitted white cotton collarless cardigan, embroidered flower motifs, short puff sleeves. Knitted multi-coloured skullcap with spike, matching gloves. 3 1945. Red, white and blue leather shoes, high wedge heels and platform soles. 4 1949. Gold kid sling-back sandals, ankle straps and peep-toes. 5 1949. Black suede court shoes with scalloped sides. 6 1948. Brimless hat covered in fabric to match the dress, feather trimming. Bead earrings and necklace. 7 1946. Spotted pink silk brimless hat, large bow decoration. Corsage of silk flowers worn on one shoulder. Long white kid gloves with folded cuffs. 8 1946. Brimless green wool skullcap with flat top, matching waist-length jacket. 9 1947. Blue leather sling-back shoes, buttoned wrapover detail. 10 1946. Brown leather shoes, low tan suede heels, suede bow and trimming, striped platform soles. 11 1949. Blue leather ankle boots, punchwork decoration. 12 1949. Grey suede evening shoes, peep-toes, high heels and cut-away sides. 13 1948. Hip-length green velvet jacket, trimmed with braid frogging. Large leopard-fur muff. Black felt brimless outsized beret, bow trimming. 14 1949. Grey cotton blouse, wing collar and cap sleeves. Brimless felt hat trimmed with two long feathers. Yellow leather gloves with notched detail. 15 1948. Mid-calf-length boots, fur cuffs, side zip fastening. 16 1947. Blue leather bag, metal frame and clasp fastening. 17 1947. Brown leather bag, green leather inserts, metal frame and clasp. 18 1949. Hip-length fitted jacket, shawl collar, cuffed three-quarter-length inset sleeves. Brimless straw hat with feather trimming. 19 1948. Collarless knitted blue silk evening top; neckline, split peplum and cap sleeves decorated with embroidery. 20 1948. Collarless knitted white silk sweater, short wrapover sleeves, embroidered and beaded neckline. 21 1947. Brown leather bag, square top and rounded sides. 22 1949. Black leather shoulder bag, stud fastening. 23 1949. Light brown leather bag, padded handle, metal frame, clasp fastening. 24 1949. Unstructured yellow leather bag, pointed flap, large silver clasp, long handle.

Charles Creed 1951

Christian Dior 1953

Hardy Amies 1950

Lanvin 1953

Christian Dior 1954

1950

1952

1953

1953

1950

1951

1954

1954

1954

1950

1950

1951

1952

1952

1953

1954

1950

1950

1951

1951

1951

1952

1952

1953

1953

1954

1954

1954

Evening Wear 1950–1954

1950

1952

1953

1951

1954

1950

1953

1951

1954

Accessories 1950–1954

1951

1952

1950

1950

1950

1953

1952

1953

1953

1953

1952

1953

1953

1953

1953

1953

1954

1950

1954

1951

1953

1953

1954

1953

1954

1953

1953

1954

Hardy Amies 1956

Sybil Connolly 1955

Simonetta 1958

Alberto Fabiani
1959

Underwear 1955–1959

1955

1955

1956

1958

1959

1959

1955

1957

1958

1957

1958

1959

1959

1959

Day Wear 1955–1957

1955

1956

1956

1955

1956

1957

1958

1958

1959

1957

1958

1959

1955

1958

1958

1956

1959

1955

1957

1958

1958

1959

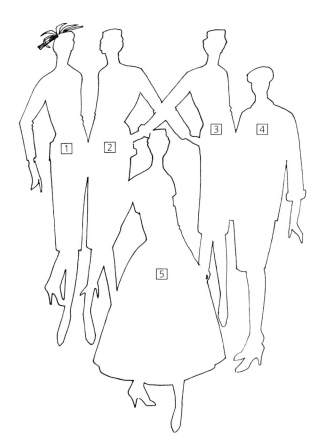

Couture Wear 1950–1954

1 Hardy Amies 1950. Green wool suit, hip-length fitted double-breasted jacket, wide lapels, long inset sleeves with single-button detail on wrists, sloping hip-level welt pockets, straight skirt in matching fabric. Brimless green felt hat trimmed with feathers. Black suede gloves with split turned-down cuffs, matching shoes with high heels. 2 Charles Creed 1951. Green velvet suit, hip-length fitted jacket, stand collar; front edges, hem and the cuffs of the inset sleeves trimmed with fur, matching the small velvet-covered brimless hat; bodice trimmed with fine braid, straight skirt in matching fabric. Black leather gloves and shoes. 3 Christian Dior 1953. Red wool afternoon dress, long cuffed dolman-style sleeves, short bodice, shirt collar with buttoned strap opening, fitted princess-line high-waisted skirt. Small pillbox hat covered with black silk. Black leather shoes, bow trimming. 4 Lanvin 1953. Wool tweed suit, long unfitted jacket, large lapels, edge-to-edge fastening and the hems of the wide three-quarter-length inset sleeves trimmed with fur, buttons decorate either side the front opening, hip-level flap pockets, straight skirt in matching fabric. Small brimless fur hat. Long grey leather gloves and shoes. 5 Christian Dior 1954. Black wool dress, off-the-shoulder neckline, short cap sleeves, upper bodice gathered from high waist seam, lower bodice fitted from under bust to high hip-level, gathered panelled mid-calf-length skirt worn over stiffened petticoats. Small pillbox hat. Long black suede gloves, matching shoes with cut-away sides and high heels.

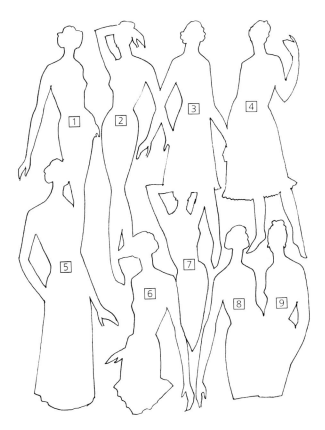

Underwear 1950–1954

1 1950. One-piece elasticated pink cotton-satin corselette, lightly boned cups covered with lace, adjustable shoulder straps, double thickness satin front panel, side fastening, adjustable suspenders. Flesh-coloured seamed nylon stockings. 2 1952. One-piece elasticated peach-coloured cotton-satin corselette, lightly boned cups covered with lace, adjustable shoulder straps, front hook and bar fastening to under bust, zip fastening to hip-level, V-shaped front control panel, adjustable suspenders. Flesh-coloured seamed nylon stockings. 3 1953. Knee-length pale peach-coloured rayon-satin petticoat, narrow ribbon shoulder straps, the fitted bodice and the flared hemline edged with scalloped ribbon and machine embroidery. Flesh-coloured nylon stockings. 4 1953. Knee-length pale green rayon petticoat, narrow ribbon shoulder straps, neck edge of fitted bodice trimmed with accordion-pleated self-fabric to match wider band around the hem of the flared panel skirt. Flesh-coloured nylon stockings. 5 1950. Knee-length pale blue cotton petticoat printed with forget-me-nots, narrow plain blue cotton rouleau shoulder straps, neck and hemlines bound with matching fabric and edged with narrow broderie anglaise. 6 1951. Waist-length blue and white spotted silk slip, matching short knickers with deep hem frills. 7 1954. One-piece elasticated black cotton-satin strapless corselette, stitched front panel, hook and bar fastening, stitched and wired cups, adjustable suspenders. 8 1954. Peach-coloured satin brassiere, stitched and wired wide-spaced cups, adjustable halter straps, front hook and bar fastening. Long-line girdle in matching fabric, side-front stitched control, front opening, adjustable suspenders. 9 1954. One-piece long-line corselette in white stretch cotton satin, wired cups covered with lace, stitched front panel control, front opening, adjustable suspenders.

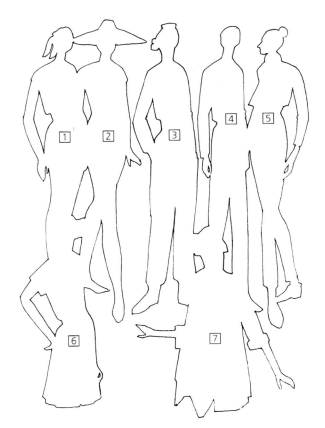

Leisure Wear 1950–1954

1 1950. Blue and white striped knitted cotton beach top, asymmetric V-shaped neckline and short cap sleeves. Fitted blue linen shorts, deep waistband with button fastenings, pressed central creases, narrow turn-ups. Short permed hair tied back with red cotton scarf knotted on one side.
2 1950. Blue linen sleeveless beach top, outsized sailor collar trimmed with inset bands of white linen, matching hemline detail. Fitted red linen shorts. Large straw hat, narrow crown and wide turned-down brim. Flat-heeled sandals with red leather straps. 3 1951. Ski wear. Water-proofed green cotton wind jacket, zip fastening from under the wide shirt collar to the hem, yoke seam running into the top of the long sleeves, large hip-level patch pockets with buttoned-down flaps, diagonal pockets with zip fasteners above the inset waistband. Dark yellow proofed-wool trousers gathered at ankles. Knitted brown wool hat with small crown and tassel trimming. Yellow wool mittens. Leather ski boots. 4 1952. Button-through waist-length suede cardigan, high knitted collar, matching inset batwing sleeves and hip yoke. Wool trousers, pressed central creases, turn-ups. Brown leather boots with thick soles. 5 1952. Red sweater, three-quarter-length raglan sleeves, fringed wool scarf threaded through loop just above bust. Fitted patterned-wool trousers, deep waistband, V-shaped yoke, diagonal welt pockets. Knitted wool hat trimmed with large pompon to match the sweater and socks. Fur-lined lace-up boots. 6 1953. Collarless white cotton tennis top, asymmetric buttoned opening, wide cap sleeves split on edge of shoulder seam, short pleated skirt in matching fabric. 7 1954. Sundress and coat. Yellow and brown striped cotton sundress, fitted bodice, narrow halter straps run from the back of the neck and widen to the waist, short split gathered skirt worn over brief knickers. Black cotton thigh-length edge-to-edge coat, wide three-quarter-length sleeves cuffed with sundress fabric to match the shawl collar and the lining. Red lacquered straw hat, pointed crown and turned-down brim.

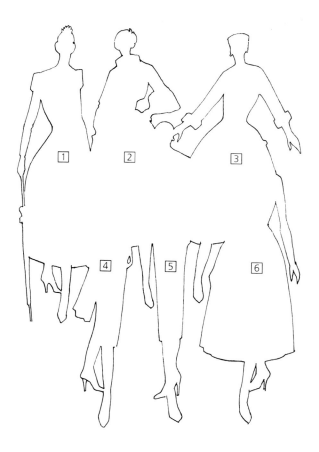

Day Wear 1950–1952

1 1950. Pale grey ribbed-silk day dress, fitted bodice and mid-calf-length princess-line skirt, low V-shaped neckline, self-fabric stole effect around shoulders, buttons above each side the bust, elbow-length inset sleeves, hip-level sloping welt pockets. Small brimless felt hat trimmed with a pompon of feathers. Long kid gloves. Umbrella with long handle. Black leather shoes, cut-away sides and high slender heels. 2 1950. Green checked wool coat, wide buttoned stand collar matching the cuffs on the full gathered inset sleeves and the hip-level welt pockets, bloused bodice with concealed opening and sloped shoulderline, buckled waistbelt, full gathered skirt. Brimless stiffened felt beret. Black leather gloves and shoes with buckle trim. 3 1951. Finely flecked wool-tweed coat, fitted bodice, two-button fastening, wide shawl collar with top-stitched edges matching the wide turned-back cuffs on the three-quarter-length sleeves, dropped shoulderline, hip-level pockets set into panel seams, mid-calf-length flared skirt. Brimless draped brown silk hat. Long brown leather gloves and shoes. 4 1951. Red and brown striped wool day dress, semi-fitted bodice, wide lapels, elbow-length raglan sleeves, front-button fastening, narrow skirt, long fringed scarf threaded through one side of wide buckled belt. Brown leather shoes, raised leaf trim and high heels. 5 1951. Purple wool-tweed tailored suit, hip-length fitted jacket; velvet peter pan collar, matching yoke, buckled waistbelt, hip-level pockets and buttons; three-quarter-length inset sleeves; straight skirt. Brimless purple felt beret. Long leather gloves. Black leather shoes with high slender heels. 6 1952. Grey silk princess-line afternoon dress, fitted bodice and mid-calf-length skirt, short grey velvet jacket, scooped neckline, shawl collar with ends which form tie fastening, three-quarter-length inset sleeves. Grey straw hat, narrow rolled brim, silk flower trim. Pearl earrings and choker necklace. Long pink silk gloves. Black leather shoes, peep-toes and high heels.

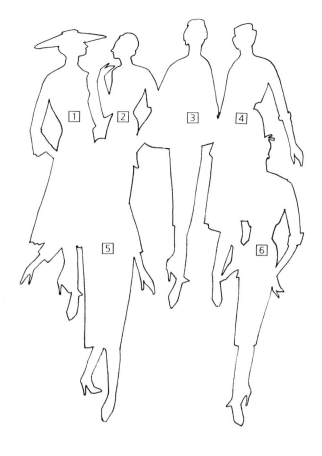

Day Wear 1952–1954

1 1952. Blue wool suit, hip-length top with cuffed hemline, large wing collar, three-quarter-length dolman-style sleeves split from hem to elbow, false turned-down cream patterned cuffs, matching bow-tied scarf, accordion-pleated skirt. Lacquered blue straw hat, tiny crown, wide wired brim. Long cream leather gloves. Blue leather shoes, bow trim and high slender heels. 2 1953. Tailored brown silk-tweed suit, hip-length fitted jacket, button fastening from U-shaped yoke seam, shawl collar, three-quarter length inset sleeves, hip-level pockets concealed in side panel seams, straight skirt. Beige hat with narrow rolled brim. Long beige leather gloves. 3 1953. Green wool tweed suit, checked with yellow and white, hip-length flared jacket, buttons from under large collar, long inset sleeves, button trim at wrists, flap pockets on hipline, straight skirt. Felt hat with turned-down brim and silk-swathed crown. Long yellow leather gloves. Brown leather shoes, almond-shaped toes and high slender heels. 4 1954. Cream linen day dress, semi-fitted bodice, V-shaped neckline forming wrapover loose flaps that fall to waistline, white cotton piqué buttoned-down flaps set into vertical seams above bust, three-quarter-length raglan sleeves cuffed in self-fabric with an under-cuff of white cotton piqué, narrow waistbelt, flared skirt, wide central box pleat. Small lacquered red straw hat, narrow brim and small flat-topped crown. Long white kid gloves. Red leather shoes, peep-toes and high slender heels. 5 1954. Unfitted red wool tweed coat, single-button fastening under large collar and revers, sloping flap pockets above bust, three-quarter-length inset sleeves, narrow hemline, split on the side seams, top-stitched detail on all edges and seams. Lacquered red straw pillbox hat. Long black suede gloves and shoes with cut-away sides and high slender heels. 6 1954. Lilac silk-tweed afternoon dress, bloused bodice above wide inset waistband, zip fastening from under large white silk collar, neckline infilled with self-fabric dolman-style sleeves, turn-back white silk cuffs, belt decorated with knot of self-fabric and long ends. Small grey velvet hat trimmed with purple velvet wired bow. Long white gloves. Grey leather sling-back shoes, peep-toes, cut-out decoration and high slender heels.

Evening Wear 1950–1954

1 1950. Pale pink silk-satin blouse, fitted bodice, short cap sleeves, off-the-shoulder neckline edged with deep jet-embroidered collar, dark pink floor-length velvet skirt gathered from waist, wide buckled black patent-leather belt. Short hair, waved and curled, side parting and large kiss curl. Jet drop earrings. Elbow-length black silk gloves. Black satin shoes with peep-toes. 2 1952. Mid-calf-length green silk-taffeta evening dress; fitted and boned strapless bodice embroidered with leaf shapes of bright green sequins, echoed from waist to hipline on the full gathered skirt; skirt worn over stiffened petticoats, narrow self-fabric waistbelt. Bead earrings and matching bracelet. Green satin shoes, pointed toes. 3 1953. Floor-length pink silk-chiffon evening dress, fitted boned bodice, intricate drapery, asymmetric draped shoulder detail and side front panel continued into layered skirt. Short hair set into large waves and curls, without a parting. Long drop earrings. Elbow-length satin gloves, shoes dyed to match. 4 1951. Multi-coloured glazed printed-cotton evening dress, halter neckline, wrapover fitted bodice, self-fabric buckled waistbelt, full floor-length wrapover skirt, waterfall of soft pleats to one side. Short-cropped straight hair combed forward. Large clip-on earrings. Elbow-length green satin gloves, shoes dyed to match. 5 1954. Floor-length blue silk-chiffon evening dress, fitted and boned bodice draped with chiffon, off-the-shoulder draped cap sleeves, scalloped waistline, full gathered layered skirt. Short hair set into large waves and curls, without a parting. Large drop earrings. Elbow-length pink silk gloves. Blue satin shoes with pointed toes.

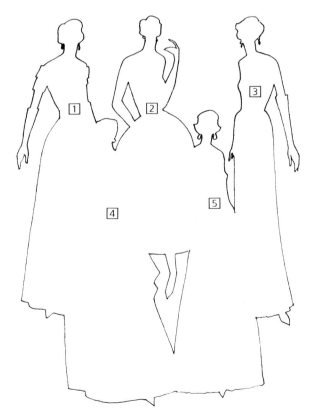

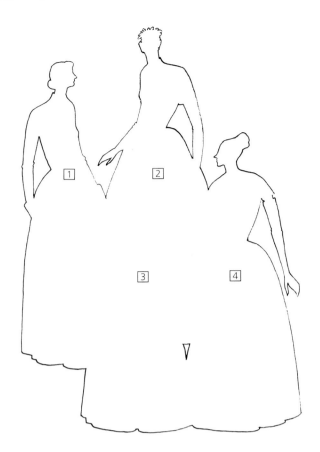

Bridal Wear 1950–1954

1 1950. White silk-brocade jacket, fitted bodice with pointed hip basque, self-fabric buckled waistbelt, covered buttons from under the grown-on collar to the hem, long fitted inset sleeves, plain white silk-taffeta skirt, central inverted unpressed box pleat, gathered side panels. Small brimless white silk-brocade hat embroidered with pearls, silk-tulle veil. White kid gauntlet gloves. 2 1953. Strapless princess-line wedding dress, fitted boned bodice, ruched detail on bustline, floor-length panelled skirt, short bolero-style jacket, grown-on collar and pointed edges piped with self-fabric, long dolman sleeves with points over the hands. Headdress of silk and wax flowers, long silk-tulle veil. 3 1951. Re-embroidered silk-brocade hip-length fitted bodice, self-fabric covered buttons from under the outsized shawl collar to the central point of the hip basque, fitted elbow-length inset sleeves, full gathered skirt from hipline, centre-front inverted box pleat. Heart-shaped headdress edged with pearls, long silk-tulle veil. Long silk gloves. 4 1954. White silk wedding dress, wide off-the-shoulder neckline framed with a tucked bertha-style collar, short tucked inset sleeves, fitted bodice and floor-length flared skirt cut without a waist seam, graduated diagonal tucks from above bustline to wide hem. Hair dressed away from face and through a bead-embroidered silk band into curls on top of head, long silk-chiffon veil. Long silk gloves meeting the hems of the short sleeves.

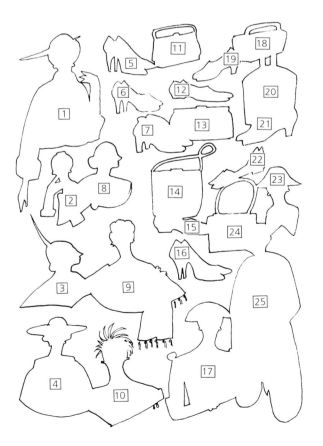

Accessories 1950–1954

1 1950. Waist-length edge-to-edge fur jacket. Brimless green felt beret, threaded feather trim. Long suede gloves. 2 1950. Pink wool draped turban. Pink leather gloves with white cuffs. Corsage of pink silk flowers. 3 1951. Small brimless green felt hat with long red feather trim. 4 1953. White straw hat with red velvet-covered crown and rose trim. 5 1950. Pink suede shoes, pointed toes and high heels. 6 1952. Blue leather shoes, cut-out detail around upper edge, pointed toes and high heels. 7 1953. Brown suede ankle boots, fur trim, pointed toes and high heels. 8 1952. Wired braid and bead hair ornament. Green bead earrings and necklace, large glass bead brooch pinned to organdie collar. 9 1953. Small evening hat of cut-out leather leaf shapes. Large clip-on earrings, matching brooches pinned to fringed stole. 10 1953. Feather evening hat, brooch clip matching clip on off-the-shoulder neckline. 11 1951. Brown leather bag, metal frame, thick handle. 12 1953. Flat-heeled leather shoes, buckle-and-strap fastening. 13 1953. Orange leather clutch bag, metal frame, clasp fastening. 14 1953. Unstructured green leather bag, clasp fastening, long handle. 15 1953. Flat-heeled red leather step-in-step shoes, blue heels and trimming. 16 1953. Yellow leather peep-toe shoes, cut-out sides, high heels. 17 1954. Large brimless straw hat. Elbow-length green fabric gloves. 18 1952. Blue leather vanity bag, strap fastening, thick handle. 19 1950. Brown leather shoes, punchwork decoration, high stacked heels. 20 1953. Red leather bucket-shaped bag, thick handle, gingham lining. 21 1953. Beige and blue two-tone shoes, thick heels. 22 1954. Flat-heeled beige canvas shoes, cut-out decoration, open sides and peep-toes. 23 1954. Straw hat, brim and shallow crown made in one piece. 24 1954. Brown leather bag, flap, strap fastening, thick rouleau handle. 25 1954. Brimless pink felt hat trimmed with self-fabric bow. Long grey fur stole. Grey leather gloves with gathered cuffs.

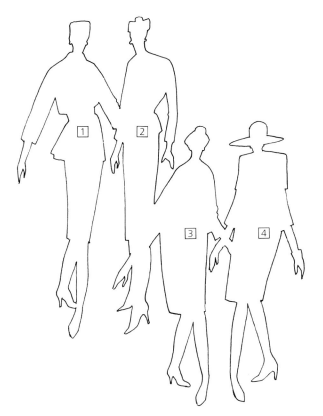

Couture Wear 1955–1959

1 Sybil Connolly 1955. Black wool tweed suit, long hip-length jacket tightly belted on waist with wide black patent-leather buckled belt, concealed opening, three-quarter-length dolman-style sleeves, wide round neckline edged with a black satin tied collar, narrow skirt in matching wool fabric. Brimless white fur hat. Long white kid gloves. Black leather shoes, almond-shaped toes, thin bar strap, high stiletto heels. 2 Hardy Amies 1956. Red wool tweed suit, hip-length tailored jacket, narrow collar and revers, front button fastening plus two overlapping tabs from the side panel seams, dolman-style sleeves, narrow skirt in matching wool tweed. Brimless black straw hat decorated with large black organdie bow and black feathers. Black leather gloves and shoes with pointed toes and high stiletto heels. 3 Simonetta 1958. Knee-length grey tweed bell-shaped coat, threaded tie-belt under the bust leaving the back loose, large single button under wide sailor collar, three-quarter-length dolman-style sleeves. Yellow felt hat with upturned brim, decorated with large feather pompon. Long yellow leather gloves. Black leather shoes, cut-away sides, pointed toes, high stiletto heels. 4 Alberto Fabiani 1959. Knee-length bell-shaped beige mohair coat, wrapover front with concealed fastening, wide elbow-length sleeves, outsized collar, button fastening and fringed hem. Brown lacquered straw hat, wide wired brim and high crown draped with brown silk. Short brown leather gloves. Brown leather shoes with bow decoration, pointed toes and high stiletto heels.

Underwear 1955–1959

1 1955. Pink nylon brassiere, adjustable shoulder straps and side/back securing straps, back fastening. Pink nylon satin waist-girdle, adjustable suspenders, side zip fastening. Flesh-coloured seamed nylon stockings. Short permed hair with long fringe. 2 1956. White nylon-satin long-line strapless brassiere, elasticated side panels, wired cups with lace trimming, back opening. White nylon mid-calf-length waist petticoat, fitted hip basque, gathered tiered skirt. Flesh-coloured seamed nylon stockings. Flat-heeled satin pumps, rouleau bow trimming. Long hair, centre parting and curled flicked-up ends. 3 1959. Blue nylon satin and lace brassiere, lightly boned cups, adjustable shoulder straps, back fastening. Blue nylon patterned pantie-girdle, lightly boned front panel, high waistband, side zip fastening. Flesh-coloured nylon stockings. Short straight hair combed forward. 4 1955. Pink cotton-satin brassiere, stitched and boned cups, adjustable shoulder straps, back fastening. Pink printed-cotton long-line girdle, elasticated side panels, side zip fastening, adjustable elastic suspenders. Flesh-coloured nylon stockings. Short hair set into large curls. 5 1958. Pale green nylon petticoat, fitted bodice decorated on bustline with appliqué embroidery, repeated on the hem of the knee-length scalloped flared panelled skirt, narrow ribbon straps, side zip fastening. Flesh-coloured nylon stockings. Pale green satin pumps decorated with rouleau bows. Short permed and waved hair. 6 1959. Blue nylon satin and lace strapless corselette, light boning, elasticated back panel, low scooped back neckline, long adjustable suspenders. Flesh-coloured nylon stockings. Long straight hair worn in a french pleat at back.

Leisure Wear 1955–1959

1 1955. Blue ribbed-cotton bathing costume; hip-length, fitted and boned, strapless bodice; short box-pleated skirt from inset bead-decorated hip-belt. Brimless yellow raffia sun hat with high pointed crown. Mule-style blue leather strap sandals. 2 1957. Floral printed-cotton bathing costume, wide V-shaped neckline, draped fitted bodice cut in one with the short wrapover skirt and side tiebelt, short knickers in matching fabric. Brimless green raffia sun hat with crown of raffia stalks. 3 1958. Red and white striped knitted-cotton bathing costume, wide V-shaped neckline, long fitted bodice. 4 1959. Sleeveless tennis dress, unfitted bodice and skirt cut without waist seam, worn unbelted, wide collar, short slit opening, rouleau ribbon tie fastening, hip-level flap pockets. Short white cotton socks. White canvas lace-up tennis shoes. 5 1959. Tennis dress, sleeveless hip-length unfitted bodice, buttons from straight slashed neckline to inset buttoned hip-belt, short flared skirt with wide-set facing knife pleats. Short white cotton socks. White canvas lace-up tennis shoes. 6 1959. Sleeveless princess-line white cotton tennis dress, low V-shaped back neckline, flat collar with scalloped edge to match the hemline of the short flared skirt, back zip fastening. White canvas lace-up tennis shoes. White cotton hairband. 7 1957. Elasticated white ribbed-cotton bathing costume, rouleau halter straps and inserted panels at bust-level in contrasting colour. White cotton headscarf, patterned with outsized red spots. 8 1958. Elasticated-cotton bathing costume patterned with random design of turquoise and white spots, low scooped neckline, gathers over bust, deep scooped armholes.

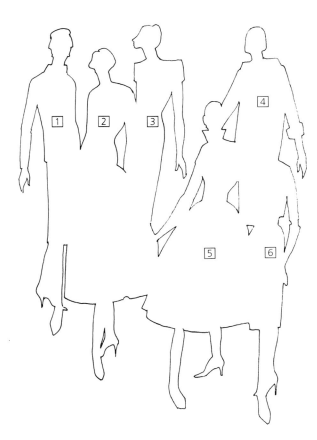

Day Wear 1955–1957

1 1955. Green corded cotton-velvet suit, hip-length unfitted jacket, self-fabric covered buttons from under narrow stand collar to hem, long inset sleeves, bias-cut front side panels incorporating welt pockets, straight skirt. Black straw hat, soft crown and turned-down brim. Black leather gloves and shoes with pointed toes and high stiletto heels. 2 1955. Floral printed glazed-cotton day dress, fitted hip-length bodice, double-breasted fastening, square collarless neckline, long inset sleeves, full skirt worn over stiffened petticoats, pleats either side flat central panel. Permed hair set into large curls. Leather shoes with pointed toes and high stiletto heels. 3 1956. Red wool afternoon dress, wide off-the-shoulder neckline, small cap sleeves, complex wrapover-effect bodice above the bust, fitted bodice and straight skirt cut without a waist seam, large welt pockets set on hipline. Hair worn in french pleat at back. Long white gloves. 4 1956. Unfitted wool-tweed coat, double-breasted fastening, wide-set top-stitched collar, dropped shoulderline, long inset sleeves with wide split cuffs, top-stitched edges and seams. Brimless yellow suede hat set onto shiny black leather band. Long yellow suede gloves. 5 1956. Green striped glazed-cotton day dress, fitted bodice, wing collar, short inset sleeves, wide self-fabric buckled belt, full skirt with central inverted box pleat worn over full stiffened petticoats. Large black plastic clip-on earrings. Elbow-length black cotton gloves. Grey suede shoes with black patent-leather pointed toecaps and high stiletto heels. 6 1957. Dark blue wool suit, short bolero-style jacket, double-breasted fastening, wide collar and revers and buckled waistbelt of the dress edged with red braid, elbow-length inset sleeves, sleeveless dress with low neckline and straight skirt. Brimless red felt hat trimmed with large blue silk rose. Elbow-length gloves. Blue leather shoes with pointed toes and high stiletto heels.

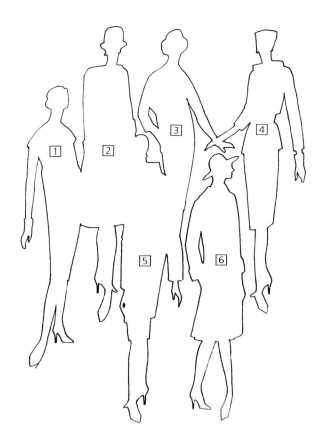

Day Wear 1957–1959

1 1957. Printed-cotton day dress, wide self-fabric buckled belt under bust, short cap sleeves, single-button trim, mock fly fastening from the high round neckline to the hem of the straight skirt. Permed hair set into large curls. Short blue cotton gloves. Blue leather shoes with pointed toes, decorative T-strap fastening, high stiletto heels. 2 1958. Red wool-tweed coat checked with grey and white, buttoned belt under bust, single-button fastening under the wide-set collar, three-quarter-length cuffed inset sleeves, full knee-length skirt. Black lacquered straw hat, narrow brim and high crown bound with red ribbon. Red leather gloves. Black leather shoes, pointed toes and high stiletto heels. 3 1958. Unfitted knitted yellow wool day dress, elbow-length batwing sleeves, buttons from under the peter pan collar to the point of the V-shaped yoke seam, buttoned-down flap pockets on bustline. Permed hair set into large curls. 4 1959. Brown wool suit, hip-length jacket, buttons from under the wide-set standing-band tie collar, buckled waistbelt, three-quarter-length inset sleeves, straight skirt in matching fabric. Brown straw pillbox hat. Long brown leather gloves, matching shoes with decorative asymmetric strap fastenings, pointed toes and high stiletto heels. 5 1958. Unfitted multi-coloured wool-tweed three-quarter-length coat, outsized turned-down stand collar with single button to match the front fastening, three-quarter-length raglan sleeves, pockets set into side panel seams, matching knee-length straight skirt. Felt pillbox hat, braid motif on front. Short lilac leather gloves, matching shoes with pointed toes and high stiletto heels. 6 1959. Blue wool suit, straight hip-length double-breasted jacket, large fur collar, matching cuffs on the three-quarter-length inset sleeves, waist-level flap pockets, box-pleated skirt, sleeveless and collarless blouse in matching fabric. Blue felt hat with high crown and wide straight brim. Long blue leather gloves. Brown leather shoes with pointed toes and high stiletto heels.

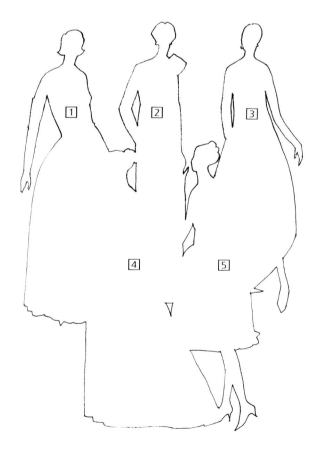

Evening Wear 1955–1959

1 1955. Boned strapless bodice in blue lace, with an inserted asymmetric curved panel of bound ruched blue silk chiffon, continued into the full skirt in two widening sweeps, skirt finished with a deep frill of layered blue silk chiffon. Straight hair, side parting, flicked-up ends. Long blue silk gloves. 2 1958. Bust-length black velvet bodice, elbow-length inset sleeves, asymmetric deep V-shaped neckline with looped cream silk-taffeta scarf threaded through one side, falling from under the bust in two mid-calf-length fringed panels, straight floor-length cream silk-taffeta skirt. Short hair set into large curls. Elbow-length gold satin gloves. 3 1958. Red taffeta trapeze-line dress, strapless bodice covered by two large loops of taffeta from under the bust and above the central unpressed box pleat; flared skirt with uneven hemline, knee-length at front and trailing to floor at back. Hair dressed away from face and into french pleat at back. Long black silk gloves. Red satin shoes, bow decoration, pointed toes and low stiletto heels. 4 1956. Pink silk-taffeta evening dress, boned strapless underbodice, long flat bow under bust, frilled unfitted overbodice, wide flared panel of unpressed pleats from under bustline to hem of the wide flared skirt, slight back train. Hair dressed away from the face and into curls at back of head. Long drop earrings. Elbow-length cream satin gloves. 5 1959. Black silk-taffeta cocktail dress, sleeveless fitted bodice, low deep V-shaped neckline to waist-level at back ending with large self-fabric bow, knee-length bell-shaped skirt plus an open self-fabric overskirt with deep frilled edge. Hair dressed away from face and into french pleat at back. Long black silk gloves. Black satin shoes, flat silk rose decoration, pointed toes and low stiletto heels.

Bridal Wear 1955–1959

1 1955. White brocade fitted bodice; wing collar, front seam and the cuffs of the fitted inset sleeves edged with a pattern of embroidery and bugle beads, repeated around scalloped hem of the short gathered overskirt; finely pleated silk-organdie tiered underskirt. Tiny beaded pillbox hat, waist-length silk-tulle veil. 2 1957. Patterned silk-chiffon wedding dress, low scooped neckline, long inset fitted sleeves and gathered skirt, mounted over pale blue silk-taffeta dress with boned strapless bodice and full gathered skirt. Headdress of velvet ribbon bows at each side of head, long silk-chiffon veil. 3 1958. Cream silk-grosgrain princess-line wedding dress, fitted boned strapless bodice edged with lace, flared panelled skirt worn over stiffened petticoats, bust-length bolero-style lace jacket with scalloped edges, long fitted sleeves. Beaded headdress, two-tier silk-tulle veil. 4 1958. White silk-seersucker wedding dress, fitted bodice to hip-level, off-the-shoulder neckline with wide asymmetric wrapover collar, elbow-length inset sleeves, swathed hip-belt, central unpressed box pleat, side panels of unpressed knife pleats. Small beaded headdress, floor-length silk-tulle veil. White satin shoes with pointed toes. 5 1959. Pale pink lace wedding dress, wide scooped neckline with scalloped edge, long fitted bodice decorated with two rouleau bows on hipline, knee-length bell-shaped gathered skirt with scalloped hem, pink silk-taffeta strapless boned underbodice with gathered stiffened bell-shaped skirts. Tiny beaded pillbox hat, short pink silk-organdie veil. Pink satin shoes with pointed toes and high stiletto heels.

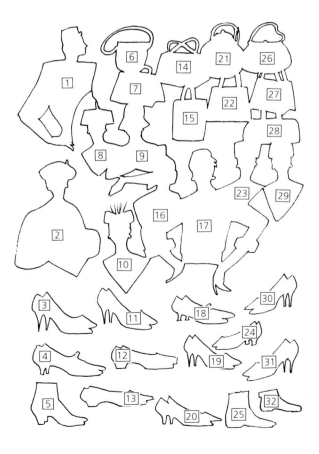

Accessories 1955–1959

1 1955. Brimless felt hat, bow trim. Bust-length wrapover fur stole, short sleeves. 2 1957. Brimless swathed silk hat, silk rose trim. Fur wrap, short sleeves, inset pockets. Long leather gloves. Bead bracelet. 3 1955. Beige leather shoes, cut-away sides, decorative straps, high stiletto heels. 4 1956. Cream and brown two-tone shoes, bar straps, pointed toes, medium-high stiletto heels. 5 1956. Ankle boots, elasticated sides, pointed toes, thick heels. 6 1955. Shoulder bag, long handle, strap-and-buckle fastening. 7 1955. Leather bag; metal frame, clasp and handle. 8 1956. Brimless hat, wide crown, self-fabric bow trim. 9 1956. Felt hat, turned-down brim, tall crown, wide band. Fur shoulder stole, fur button fastening. Long suede gloves. 10 1957. Cocktail hat, taffeta bow trimmed with feathers. 11 1955. Leather shoes, cut-away sides, pointed toes, high stiletto heels. 12 1957. Lace-up leather shoes, low heels. 13 1957. Leather shoes, pointed toes, side bow trim, flat heels. 14 1956. Leather bag, double handle. 15 1957. Unstructured leather bag, metal clasp fastening, thick handle. 16 1957. Evening hat, twisted roll tied at back, pointed crown, bead embroidery. 17 1958. Brimless draped fabric hat. Waist-length persian lamb jacket, three-quarter-length cuffed sleeves, leather-trimmed shawl collar, matching waistband and large decorative buttons. 18 1956. Leather shoes, bar straps, pointed toes, low louis-style stiletto heels. 19 1957. Leather shoes, pointed toes, high stiletto heels. 20 1958. Leather shoes, peep-toes, punchwork decoration, high stiletto heels. 21 1957. Ponyskin bag, double handle, metal frame, amber clasp fastening. 22 1958. Leather bag, metal frame and clasp, single rouleau handle. 23 1959. Brimless felt flat-topped hat, petersham band and bow trim. 24 1958. Leather shoes, petersham bows, pointed toes, louis-style heels. 25 1959. Ankle boots, elasticated sides, flat heels. 26 1958. Unstructured leather bag, metal clasp, rouleau handle. 27 1959. Leather bag, metal frame, envelope flap, clasp fastening. 28 1959. Leather bag, metal frame, clasp fastening, double handles. 29 1959. Brimless felt hat, silk rose trim. 30 1959. T-strap leather shoes, pointed toes, high stiletto heels. 31 1959. Leather shoes, cut-out decoration, pointed toes, high stiletto heels. 32 1959. Ankle boots, knitted cuffs, pointed toes, flat heels.

Michel Goma 1960

Mary Quant 1963

André Courrèges 1964

Michael 1964

Underwear 1960–1964

1960

1961

1963

1962

1963

1964

1964

1960

1962

1963

1960

1961

1964

1964

Day Wear 1960–1962

1960

1960

1961

1961

1961

1962

1962

1962

1963

1963

1964

1964

Evening Wear 1960–1964

1960

1962

1961

1963

1964

1963

1960

1961

1964

Accessories 1960–1964

1960

1960

1960

1960

1960

1960

1960

1960

1961

1961

1962

1962

1962

1962

1962

1963

1963

1964

1964

1964

1964

1964

1964

Grès 1966

Foale & Tuffin 1965

Guy Laroche 1968

Geoffrey Beene 1969

1965

1965

1966

1967

1967

1968

1969

1965

1965

1966

1968

1966

1967

1969

Day Wear 1965–1967

1966

1966

1966

1965

1965

1965

1967

1968

1968

1969

1969

1969

1969

Evening Wear 1965–1969

1965

1966

1968

1969

1969

1965

1966

1968

1969

1969

1968

1968

1969

1969

1969

1969

1965

1966

1968

1969

Accessories 1965–1969

1965
1965
1966
1967
1966
1966
1966
1968
1967
1969
1965
1966
1965
1965
1965
1966
1967
1968
1969
1966
1968
1969
1968
1968
1969
1968
1968
1969

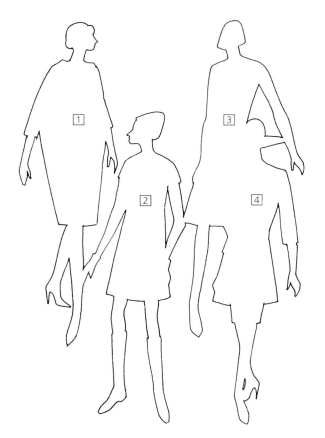

Couture Wear 1960–1964

[1] Michel Goma 1960. Scarlet wool velour coat, semi-fitted at front, fastening with three outsized covered buttons and flaring from the shoulder-line at the back into a narrow hem, flap pockets set into low-set front waist seam, three-quarter-length dolman sleeves, large stand-away collar. Fur hat with turned-back brim. Long leather gloves. Leather shoes with pointed toes and high stiletto heels. [2] André Courrèges 1964. Short semi-fitted cream fine wool dress with slashed neckline top-stitched to match centre-front channel seam and hem of short sleeves. Vertical welt pockets placed above hip-level. Domed brimless fur hat. Short leather gloves. Mid-calf-length leather boots with rounded toes and flat heels. [3] Mary Quant 1963. Sleeveless cream cotton shift dress, high round neckline trimmed with plain plum-coloured cotton bow with long ends, matching the inset band above the low waist seam, knee-length flared skirt with inverted box pleats. Plum-coloured ribbed cotton tights. Black leather pumps with pointed toes and flat heels. [4] Michael 1964. Long lilac silk-tweed Norfolk-style jacket, fastening with three outsized buttons; wide hip-length belt threaded through straps running from shoulder to hem, narrow knee-length skirt in matching fabric. Pale lilac glazed straw hat with high crown and wide brim, trimmed and lined with darker lilac straw. Long suede leather gloves. Leather shoes with fine rouleau decoration, pointed toes and high stiletto heels.

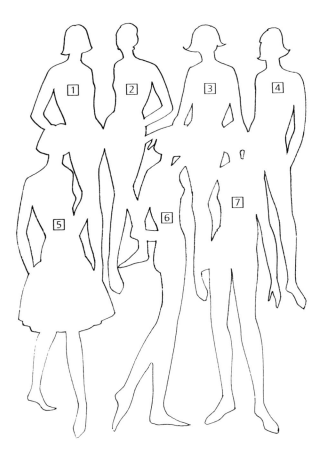

Underwear 1960–1964

[1] 1960. Elasticated peach satin bra trimmed with lace, lightweight pre-formed cups with wired seams, wide-set shoulder straps, back fastening. Hip-girdle in fine elasticated peach-coloured satin, lace edging at waist and hem, appliqué ribbon and lace flowers on centre front and hipline, six ribbon suspenders. [2] 1961. One-piece lightly boned strapless corselette in black elasticated nylon with black nylon lace insertions over flesh-coloured elasticated nylon, back fastening, six ribbon suspenders. [3] 1963. Pale blue corselette in Lycra power net with stretch Lycra satin side panels, lightly wired pre-formed cups with Lycra lace trim, adjustable stretch straps, back opening, side zip fastening, six suspenders. [4] 1964. Pale green Lycra bra with lightly wired pre-formed cups covered with French lace and trimmed with fine lace edging, adjustable ribbon straps, back fastening. Matching pantie-suspender, front and half side panels covered with lace, trimmed with lace edging and narrow satin ribbon, ribbon suspenders. [5] 1962. Cream cotton bra with adjustable shoulder straps, pre-formed cups with scalloped edge trimmed with lace, elasticated front panel, back fastening. Cream nylon waist slip, gathered skirt from hip yoke, waistband and skirt trimmed with nylon lace. [6] 1963. Pull-on corselette in peach-coloured Lycra power net with firm satin front panel and double Lycra side hip panels, nylon voile cups with foam insert, low wide-back stretch straps, six suspenders. [7] 1964. White Lycra bra and suspender set. Bra with wide-set adjustable shoulder straps built up from the top of the cups, padded with foam and lightly wired, lace trimming, back fastening. Suspender belt with V-shaped front panel in firm satin.

Leisure Wear 1960–1964

1 1960. Green linen trouser suit, unstructured shirt-style jacket with single-breasted fastening, long sleeves gathered into cuff at wrist, all edges and larger patch pockets with top-stitched decoration, narrow trousers with pressed crease. Large straw hat and casual bag with raffia decoration. Mule sandals. 2 1960. Black, grey and white cotton swimsuit, fitted and lightly boned bodice, pre-formed and boned cups, short flared skirt, narrow rouleau halter straps. Red cotton headscarf tied at back of neck. 3 1962. Red, white and blue bri-nylon bikini, fitted top with low scooped neckline and wide shoulder straps, ending just below the bust, panties fit on the hipline and have narrow sides. 4 1963. Sleeveless tennis dress; fitted bodice to low hip, short gathered skirt, back-button fastening, scalloped edges. 5 1961. Blue and white knitted cotton top with short sleeves and wide slashed neckline. White bell-bottom trousers, cut low on hip, wide red leather belt with large buckle. Leather mule sandals with squat heels, metal stud decoration. 6 1964. Brief cotton bikini in leopard-spot print, pre-formed bra top lightly boned with foam inserts, narrow rouleau halter straps, panties lowcut on hip with brief sides. Matching headscarf. 7 1964. Light grey cotton sleeveless tabard top with square neckline, open sides held with buttoned belt on hipline, braided edges, matching narrow ankle-length trousers. Large red canvas bag with bamboo handle. Red leather sandals.

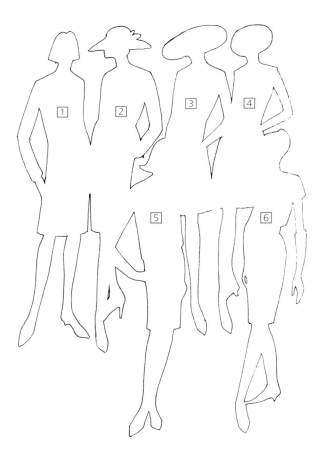

Day Wear 1960–1962

1 1950. Sleeveless knee-length dress in black and grey striped wool, low round neckline, straight unfitted bodice to low hip-belt, buttoned-down patch pockets, straight skirt. Black knitted wool sweater and matching stockings. Black suede shoes with low heels, pointed toes and buckle trim. 2 1960. Cream silk suit, semi-fitted collarless jacket, single-breasted fastening with outsized buttons, narrow rouleau belt on waistline, three-quarter-length sleeves, narrow knee-length skirt. Cream straw hat with large brim and shaped crown trimmed with large silk rose. Long pink suede gloves. Leather shoes with pointed toes, fine crossed strap decoration, high stiletto heels. 3 1961. Pale blue silk-tweed collarless and sleeveless top and flared skirt, narrow belt tied into stylized bow on centre front. Large pale blue straw hat with wide upturned brim. Beige leather gloves, matching leather shoes with wide cross straps and pointed toes. 4 1961. White Tricel collarless top with cap sleeves, flared skirt with red and blue ribbon braid trimming. Glazed red straw breton hat, short cotton gloves. Leather shoes with wide strap, blunt toes and low thick heels. 5 1961. Amber and oatmeal plain wool-tweed collarless dress with fringed elbow-length sleeves, bodice bloused on hipline, buttons from neck to hem with suede-covered buttons, matching belt. Small rust-coloured pillbox hat. Leather gloves. Leather shoes with wide instep straps and almond-shaped toes. 6 1962. Fine black wool dress with shallow boat-shaped neckline, short sleeves, bodice bloused gently into wide black calfskin belt, narrow knee-length skirt. Long black suede gloves. Black suede leather shoes with cut-off almond-shaped toes and low stiletto heels.

Day Wear 1962–1964

[1] 1962. Dark mustard-coloured wool semi-fitted coat, single-breasted fastening with two large self-fabric covered buttons, decorative seam into narrow sloping welt pocket, detachable fur collar and revers. Large felt pillbox hat with fine leather trim. Two-tone leather shoes with elongated square toes. [2] 1963. Crease-resistant linen and Terylene sleeveless dress in white and prune, threaded tie neckline, armhole and waist seam decorated with saddle stitching, flared knee-length skirt. Leather shoes with cross-over strap, elongated square toes and low stiletto heels. [3] 1963. Blue wool semi-fitted sleeveless dress with white piqué peter pan collar, centre-front opening with brass buttons, decorative channel seams from shoulder to hem of flared skirt. Leather shoes with squared-off toes and low thick heels. [4] 1964. Bright yellow rayon suit with collarless semi-fitted double-breasted jacket piped in navy blue rayon to match the scalloped hem of the flared skirt. Bonnet of blue organza petals tied under chin. Short blue leather gloves. Blue leather shoes with almond-shaped toes. [5] 1962. Turquoise wool semi-fitted coat with double-breasted fastening, four outsized buttons, shaped standing-band collar, bracelet-length sleeves, flared knee-length skirt. Brimless domed hat covered with ostrich feather strands. Long leather gloves. Dark grey leather shoes with inset band of cream, pointed toes and high stiletto heels. [6] 1964. Seven-eighths-length coat in camel-coloured wool, double-breasted fastening, collar standing away from neck, flap pockets, three-quarter-length sleeves, worn over white gabardine dress. White felt hat with narrow downturned brim. Short cotton gloves. Mid-calf white leather boots with flat heels and round toes.

Evening Wear 1960–1964

[1] 1960. Evening gown, gold lamé and bead embroidered organza top with wide low round neckline bound with silk and edged with gold beads to match hem of short sleeves. Separate overskirt of heavy cream silk faille gathered into a waistband which ties into large bow on one side. Elbow-length cream kid gloves. Gold kid shoes with pointed toes, decorated with tiny bow. [2] 1962. Dark cream duchesse-satin evening gown with draped asymmetric bodice embroidered and beaded with a design of leaves and flowers, narrow full-length skirt with back split. Elbow-length orange satin gloves. Gold kid shoes with pointed toes and ruched decoration. [3] 1964. Violet double-crepe dress with cowl bodice, cap sleeves, deep waistband decorated with large self-fabric knot flower and bow, ankle-length wrapover skirt. Elbow-length gloves in stretch satin. Satin-covered shoes with pointed toes, buckle trim and high stiletto heels. [4] 1961. Short evening or cocktail dress, pink silk taffeta covered with pale grey lace. Wide square neckline, sleeveless fitted bodice, knee-length skirt gathered from low hip seam decorated with two large pink silk-taffeta bows, scalloped hem. Pink silk-taffeta-covered clutch bag. Pink satin shoes with pointed toes and high stiletto heels. [5] 1963. Blue heavy silk-crepe sheath dress with fitted and boned strapless bodice, narrow decorative rouleau halter straps from single scallop of neckline, narrow skirt with back split and pleat. Elbow-length gloves of light blue stretch satin. Gold kid shoes decorated with blue rosette.

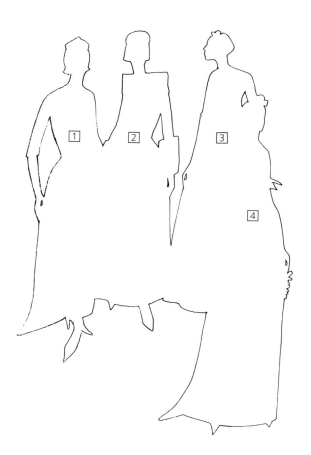

Bridal Wear 1960–1964

1 1960. Cream pure silk-satin wedding dress with high slashed neckline decorated at each end with fine rouleau bows which 'support' long self-fabric train, fitted bodice with elbow-length tight dolman sleeves, mid-calf-length bell-shaped skirt. Pillbox hat embroidered with beads and sequins with attached floor-length pure silk-tulle veil. Elbow-length cream kid gloves. Matching shoes with pointed toes, bow trim and high stiletto heels. 2 1961. Rich silk-brocade dress and jacket, short-cropped waist-length jacket with three-quarter-length sleeves trimmed with deep cuffs of white mink matching the deep high stand collar, bell-shaped skirt with wrapover side pleat. Pillbox hat with floor-length silk-tulle veil. Satin shoes trimmed with silver buckles, pointed toes. 3 1963. Cream silk-moiré gown with high waistline emphasized by narrow self-fabric belt and flat bow, shallow boat-shaped neckline, elbow-length dolman sleeves, full-length flared skirt with facing wide-apart unpressed pleats and short back train. Headdress of silk roses, lily-of-the-valley and ribbon. Short tiered silk-tulle veil. 4 1964. Satin ribbon-embroidered white nylon gown with low scooped neckline edged with wide satin binding to match hem of three-quarter-length sleeves and deep waistband of the fitted bodice, full-length bell-shaped skirt with matching train attached to each side of the back. Satin-covered pillbox hat trimmed with flat bow, silk rose and floor-length silk-tulle veil. Short gloves. Satin shoes with pointed toes.

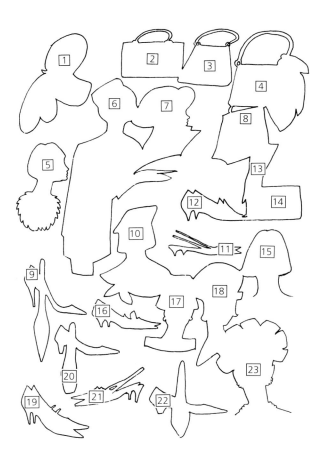

Accessories 1960–1964

1 1960. Felt cloche hat with silk ribbon insertions, tiny brim held back by jewelled brooch. Fox-fur scarf. Large pearl clip earrings. 2 1960. Leather-lined baby-crocodile bag with brass fastening and fittings. 3 1962. Matt leather unstructured bag, strap-and-buckle fastening. 4 1963. Unstructured plastic bag with brass fastening and fittings, brightly coloured nylon scarf with fringed edges. 5 1960. Short blond acrylic wig. Matching necklace and earrings of gold leaves and beads. 6 1960. Felt pillbox hat, large lozenge-shaped clip-on earrings, long and wide fringed wool scarf held on one shoulder with large silver and copper brooch, three-quarter-length leather gloves. 7 1961. Felt hat with fur-covered brim. 8 1964. Polished baby-calf bag, over rigid frame with snap fastening. 9 1960. Calf-skin shoes with high stiletto heels, low-cut vamp, side-draped detail and pearl clasps. 10 1962. Beret with stiffened bow trim, matching scarf with fringed edges. 11 1964. Suede and leather sling-back shoes with almond-shaped toes and low squat heels. 12 13 14 1964. Set of shoes, gloves and clutch purse in fine leather, all with flower motifs as main design feature. 15 1964. Jewelled hair decoration. 16 1960. Leather shoes with low squat heels, pointed toes covered with checked fabric. 17 1964. Upturned flowerpot hat with threaded self-fabric strip. 18 1962. Green velvet crown gathered onto wide band and trimmed with wide flat bow. 19 1962. Two-tone leather shoes with punchwork decoration, high louis heels, strap fastening and pointed toes. 20 1961. Black patent-leather shoes with low squat heels, squared-off toes and grosgrain ribbon trimming. 21 1963. Fine kid sling-back shoes with basketwork front and high stiletto heels. 22 1964. Suede leather shoes with almond-shaped toes, squat heels and buckle trim. 23 1964. Silk-organza loops sewn onto velvet headband, bead necklace and earrings.

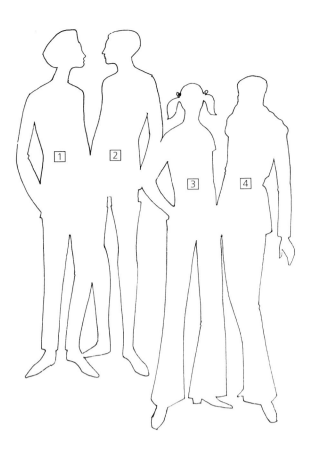

Couture Wear 1965–1969

1 Foale & Tuffin 1965. Camel-coloured wool trouser suit, long semi-fitted jacket, wrist-length set-in sleeves, three-button off-set front fastening, flap pockets, wide-set collar, top-stitched edges, narrow trousers with pressed creases. Brimless fur hat. Leather ankle boots with almond-shaped toes and low heels. 2 Grès 1966. Collarless and sleeveless cream wool tunic, decorative seaming around hipline and forming an inverted V-shape on centre of bodice. Worn over all-in-one fine wool knitted body suit. Thigh-length suede boots with almond-shaped toes and flat heels. Fur bonnet fastening under chin. 3 Guy Laroche 1968. Pale cream wool-jersey collarless jumpsuit with short sleeves, front opening with buttons, high yoke seam, flap-and-patch pockets with top-stitching to match other edges and seams, trousers flare out from knee with pressed creases. Cream leather shoes with blunt toes and thick squat heels. 4 Geoffrey Beene 1969. Oatmeal-coloured trouser suit, long jacket with raglan sleeves gathered into cuffs at wrists, outsized button-down patch pockets at hip-level, wide collar and revers, all edges top-stitched, fitted trousers flare out from knee, pressed creases. Knitted pull-on hat with matching polo-neck sweater. Leather two-tone shoes with blunt toes and low squat heels.

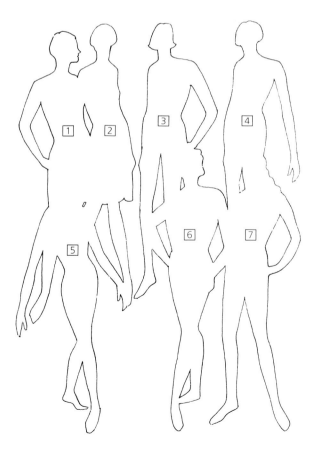

Underwear 1965–1969

1 1965. Dark brown and white fine Lycra bra with wide elasticated shoulder straps, back fastening. Long-leg pantie-girdle in dark brown heavy Lycra with white Lycra trimming. 2 1965. Pink nylon fitted slip with black nylon lace centre panel, shaped bra top, adjustable shoulder straps, fine lace trimming, side opening. 3 1966. Flesh-coloured fine Lycra all-in-one body stocking, stretch straps, high-cut legs, minimum seaming. 4 1967. Halter-neck bra in lilac stretch-nylon lace, lightly boned and stitched cups, elasticated bands at neck and under bust with plastic cup fastenings, cut low at back. Matching stretch-nylon briefs cut low on hip. 5 1967. Multi-coloured Lycra bra with deep scooped neckline, boned and stitched cups, adjustable straps, lace edging, front fastening. Matching low-slung Lycra briefs with high-cut legs. 6 1968. Mini-length mint green transparent nylon bra slip, flower embossed bra with light boning, adjustable straps, lace-edged hem.
7 1969. Black stretch-nylon lace all-in-one body stocking and tights, low scooped neckline, deep armholes, stretch straps, minimal seaming, stretch-to-fit, no openings.

Leisure Wear 1965–1969

1 1965. Orange slubbed-linen beach dress with wide slashed neckline, deep square armholes, large patch pockets with turned-back fringed flap matching hem of short flared skirt. Orange plastic mules. 2 1965. Yellow, green and blue flower-printed hip-length bri-nylon blouse, semi-fitted with narrow band collar tied into bow with long ends, flared sleeves. Fitted blue bri-nylon trousers flaring from knee. Canvas shoes with square toes and flat heels. 3 1966. Ribbed green plastic ski jacket with shiny green plastic appliqué design on front, buckled stand collar and cuffs, vertical welt pockets in side panel seam, zip fastening. Stretch-jersey ski pants. Leather mittens. Buckled ski boots. 4 1968. Red and white knitted cotton beach top cropped to just below bust and held by elasticated band, slashed neckline and cut-away armholes. Shorts in matching colour are gathered on elasticated waistband. Large lacquered straw hat. Glass beads. Leather mules with thick soles and low heels. 5 1966. Pink, white and blue geometric patterned Lycra swimsuit, deep plunge neckline caught at bustline with tiny plastic flower and ending in large keyhole, wide shoulder straps, minimal seaming, no openings. 6 1967. Bri-nylon swimsuit with deep plunge neckline to below waist held in place by three metal rings, wide shoulder straps, minimal seaming, no openings. 7 1969. Cotton mini-length beach dress with deep plunge halter neckline to below waist held under bust by narrow belt and stylized bow. Hair tied back with spotted scarf. Leather mule sandals with wide two-tone cross-over straps.

Day Wear 1965–1967

1 1965. Double-breasted brown tweed jacket, brown checked wool-tweed flared mini-length skirt matching jacket collar, jacket and skirt bound with dark yellow braid. Felt breton hat with wide upturned brim. Short yellow leather gloves. Brown leather shoes with squared-off toes, bar strap and low thick heels. 2 1965. Coffee and cream braid horizontally striped knitted dress with bound round neck, short sleeves, flared mini-length skirt with stripes running vertically. Leather hip-belt. Leather shoes with square toes and bow decoration. 3 1966. Mini-length dress of white crocheted cotton with round neck, elbow-length sleeves with flared scalloped cuff to match hem of skirt, narrow suede hip-belt. Dress worn over white cotton mini-length slip. Leather shoes with square toes and rouleau bow trim. 4 1966. Bright yellow plastic mini-length raincoat, tab and button fastening; sleeve tabs, epaulettes and large flap-and-patch pockets top-stitched to match all other edges. Sectioned plastic cap with outsized peak. Long yellow plastic boots with round toes and flat heels. 5 1965. Yellow wool double-breasted mini-length coat with top-stitched seams, high-yoke, wide-set collar and hip-level welt pockets. Coat worn over dress with polo-neck collar. Knee-high gaiters in fabric to match coat, worn over flat-heeled leather pumps. 6 1967. Dark lilac linen double-breasted coat with flared mini-length skirt, wide peter pan collar, narrow sleeves, flap pockets. Straw hat with upturned brim. Short leather gloves. Leather shoes with high tongue, decorative leather laces, square toes and low squat heels.

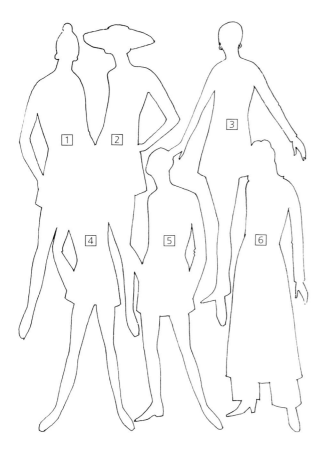

Day Wear 1968–1969

1 1968. Light green wool suit; belted hip-length jacket with top-stitched scalloped hem matching collar, three-quarter-length sleeves, seams and hem of flared mini-length skirt. Knee-length boots in cream leather with scalloped cuff, round toes and flat heels. 2 1968. Navy blue wool-crepe mini-length dress with halter neckline bound to match hip-belt in contrasting colour. Glazed and stiffened straw hat with deep crown and wide flat brim. Leather shoes with strap-and-chain decoration, square toes and low thick heels. 3 1969. Pale pink wool mini-length coat with decorative raised and top-stitched seams; collar and cuffs in cream wool. Cream felt brimless hat. Cream shiny leather knee-length boots with cut-out disc decoration at knee level, round toes and low thick heels flaring out at base. 4 1969. Grey flannel mini-length dress with shirt collar and sleeves, front fastening with brass buttons. Red leather and brass hip-belt. White knitted cotton knee socks. Red leather shoes with squared-off almond-shaped toes. 5 1969. Black and white rough-tweed mini-length dress with taped square neckline, armholes, high-yoke seam, panel seams and welt pockets. Worn over pale grey cotton shirt. Grey and white spotted silk tie. Black leather shoes, high vamp with chain decoration, almond-shaped toes, low square heels. 6 1969. Mid-calf-length shiny red plastic double-breasted coat with shirt collar, long tight sleeves, welt pockets set vertically into side panel seams, top-stitching detail on all edges. Worn over baggy trousers. Suede boots with round toes, high thick heels and narrow platform soles.

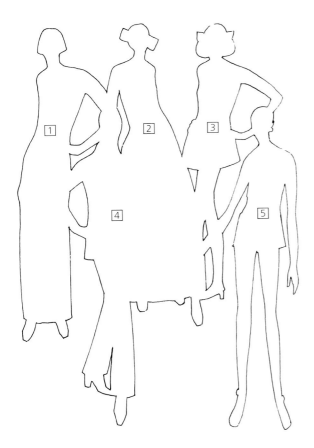

Evening Wear 1965–1969

1 1965. Semi-fitted beaded evening dress patterned with giant black spots on cerise background, high bib neckline held with wide shoulder straps, long straight skirt. Black satin shoes with square toes and thick heels. 2 1968. Pure silk evening gown printed with outsized leaves and flowers of red, black and white; fitted bodice with halter neckline ending in high stand collar, stiff wide belt decorated with flat bow, full-length flared skirt. Satin bow decoration worn at back of head. Red satin shoes with square toes. 3 1969. Black wool-crepe mini-length evening/cocktail dress with Y-strap neckline, low-cut fitted bodice, wide waistband. Hair held back with outsized stiff black satin bow. Satin shoes with straight-across vamp, square toes, ankle straps and high thick heels. 4 1966. Black velvet evening trouser suit, masculine-style jacket, waistcoat and trousers each trimmed and edged with satin braid. White silk blouse with ruffled collar and cuffs worn with satin bow tie at neck. Jewelled cufflinks. Black satin boots with long square toes and high thick heels. 5 1969. Shiny cream plastic sleeveless truncated top with round neckline; bodice dips to centre front and connects to flared mini-length skirt by large cream, black and red plastic disc. Shiny cream Lycra tights. Flat-heeled cream plastic sandals with ankle strap fastening under plastic disc.

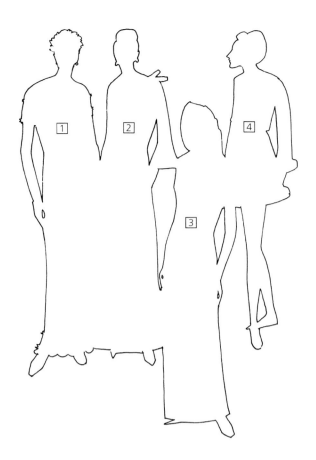

Bridal Wear 1965–1969

1 1965. Strapless silk sheath dress with scalloped hem decorated with organdie flowers, worn with truncated top of silk organdie covered with organdie flowers, low round neck with scalloped edge matching short sleeves and hem. Headdress covered with silk of the dress and decorated with organdie flowers, long silk-tulle veil attached. Short gloves. Satin shoes with round toes and thick heels. 2 1966. Textured silk-satin wedding dress with wide stand collar ending in an asymmetric bow from which a diagonal raised seam crosses the semi-fitted bodice and flared skirt to the hem, flared sleeves with side split. Small sectioned pillbox hat in matching silk with silk-tulle veil attached. Satin shoes with almond-shaped toes and thick heels. 3 1968. Wool-crepe semi-fitted wedding dress with high round neckline beaded and embroidered to match the design on the wrists of the long tight sleeves, separate hood of matching wool-crepe. Satin shoes with round toes and low thick heels. 4 1969. Ribbon-lace collarless top bound at waist and neck with silk-satin ribbon, the hem of the flared sleeves and skirt edges with bands of white mink to match the separate bonnet which ties under chin. Knee-high white plastic boots with almond-shaped toes and squat heels.

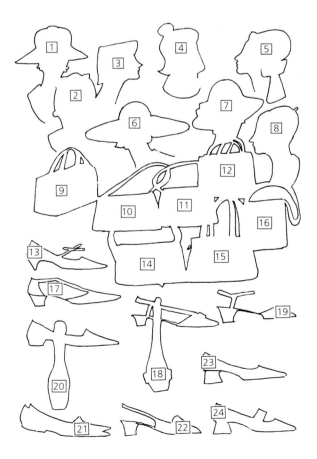

Accessories 1965–1969

1 1965. Hat with tall navy blue straw crown and wide down-turned cream brim. Pearl clip-on earrings. 2 1966. Felt pillbox hat trimmed with large flat petersham bow. 3 1965. Cream linen brimless pull-on hat decorated with machine top-stitching. 4 1966. Red wool beret with dark blue pompon. 5 1967. Blue chunky-weave straw bowler-type hat worn on back of head, trimmed with large blue and white spotted bow. 6 1968. Bright pink lacquered fine straw hat with high crown and wide wired brim turned up to one side. 7 1966. Grey felt hat with tall crown and wide brim, trimmed with wide herringbone petersham ribbon and flat disc brooch. 8 1969. Brimless patchwork hat of leather and suede, knitted welt. Leaf-shaped clip-on earrings, matching brooch. 9 1965. Biscuit-coloured suede handbag with two handles and matching top-stitched fastening. 10 1965. Fawn leather bag with single handle and looped strap fastening with clip, top-stitched detail. 11 1966. Blue linen bag with flap, press-stud fastening under rouleau bow. 12 1967. Light blue leather bag with flap, press-stud fastening. Two rouleau handles come from outsized eyelet holes. 13 1965. Rich orange-brown suede shoes with medium-high stiletto heels, strap and petersham ribbon decoration. 14 1969. Unstructured leather shoulder bag with long adjustable handle and strap-and-buckle fastening. 15 1968. Rust-coloured leather bag with adjustable handles, zip fastening plus strap-and-buckle trim. 16 1967. Unstructured green suede shoulder bag with deep flap and outsized black patent-leather dress-stud fastener. 17 1965. Leather shoe with toecap detail, ankle strap, open sides and thick heels. 18 1968. Lilac patent-leather sling-back shoe with large petersham bow decoration, high thick heels. 19 1969. Suede sling-back shoes with ankle straps and thick heels. 20 1966. Pink leather shoes with strap-and-buckle fastening, low thick heels. 21 1968. Shiny grey leather shoes with double strap-and-buckle decoration, flat heels. 22 1968. Leather sling-back shoes, buckle trim, thick heels. 23 1969. Black patent-leather shoes with black and white disc, square toes, thick heels. 24 1969. Canvas shoes covered with spotted silk, bar strap, high thick flared heels.

Yves Saint Laurent 1971

Ted Lapidus 1974

Calvin Klein 1970

Jean Patou 1972

1970

1970

1971

1971

1972

1972

1973

1974

1974

1970

1970

1971

1972

1973

1974

1970

1971

1971

1970

1971

1972

1972

1973

1974

1972

1973

1974

1974

Evening Wear 1970–1974

1970

1971

1973

1970

1972

1974

1970

1971

1972

1974

Accessories 1970–1974

1970
1970
1970
1970
1970
1970
1970
1970
1970
1970
1971
1971
1971
1971
1971
1971
1971
1972
1972
1972
1972
1972
1972
1972
1972
1972
1973
1973
1973
1973
1973
1973
1973
1974
1974
1974
1974
1974
1974
1974

John Bates 1975

Nina Ricci 1977

Pierre Cardin 1978

Sonia Rykiel 1975

Thierry Mugler 1979

Underwear 1975–1979

1975

1975

1976

1976

1977

1977

1978

1979

1979

1975

1976

1977

1979

1975

1976

1978

1979

1975

1975

1975

1976

1976

1976

1977

1977

1977

1978

1979

1979

Evening Wear 1975–1979

1975

1976

1977

1978

1979

1975

1976

1977

1979

1975

1975

1976

1978

1975

1976

1977

1977

1976

1978

1978

1977

1977

1978

1978

1979

1979

1979

1978

1979

1979

1979

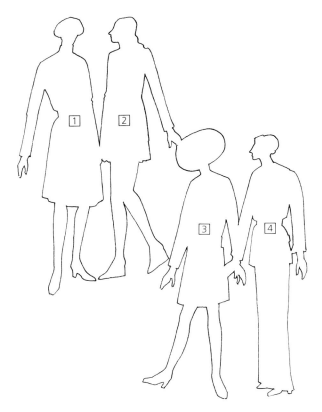

Couture Wear 1970–1974

[1] Calvin Klein 1970. Double-breasted camel-hair coat, brown leather buttons, wide collar and revers, long inset sleeves with buttoned wrist straps, self-fabric tie belt, outsized hip-level flap-and-patch pockets, knee-length flared skirt, decorative top-stitching on edges and seams. Orange knitted wool jumper with high polo-neck collar and long sleeves. Outsized peaked cap in the coat fabric. High tight-fitting brown leather boots, platform soles and low thick heels. [2] Yves Saint Laurent 1971. Hip-length double-breasted yellow satin jacket, self-fabric covered buttons, wide revers, padded shoulders, long narrow inset sleeves, outsized hip-level patch pockets, dark grey pleated-linen mini skirt. Long curled hair with side parting. Flesh-coloured tights. Blue leather peep-toe shoes, platform soles, high wedge heels, sling-backs and ankle straps. [3] Jean Patou 1972. Mini-length red wool coat, buttoned hip-belt, wide collar and long revers, hip-level patch pockets with self-fabric covered button trimming, long raglan sleeves, top-stitched seams and edges. Blue and white striped silk collarless blouse. Blue lacquered straw hat with wide upswept brim. Blue leather shoes, peep-toes, platform soles, high thick heels, sling-backs and wide strap over instep. [4] Ted Lapidus 1974. Brown wool trouser suit, hip-length edge-to-edge jacket, wide pointed collar, long raglan sleeves with wide buttoned wrist straps, large buttoned flap-and-patch pockets on the bustline matching the outsized pockets on the hipline, tie-belt, top-stitched seams and edges, wide flared trousers in matching fabric. Red knitted wool jumper with polo-neck collar and long sleeves, matching pull-on hat. Brown leather boots with platform soles and thick high heels.

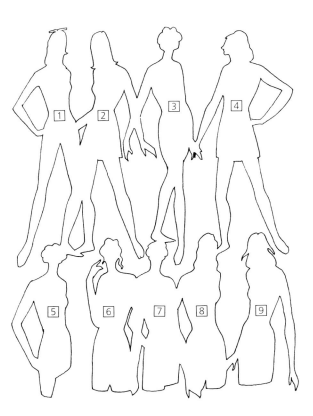

Underwear 1970–1974

[1] 1970. Lightweight peach-coloured Lycra bra, lace-covered cups wired and lightly padded, nylon lace edging, adjustable shoulder straps, back fastening; matching short-legged panties. Long hair tied back with ribbon, long fringe over eyebrows. [2] 1970. Lightweight orange cotton bra, wired cups, adjustable shoulder straps, back fastening; flared mini-length waist slip in matching fabric, cotton lace trimming. [3] 1971. One-piece pale orange Lycra body suit, shaped seaming over bust, high-cut legs, narrow shoulder straps, low back. Nylon wig dressed into large curls and deep fringe. [4] 1971. Mini-length white-spotted yellow cotton petticoat, built-in bra with wired and lightly padded cups, narrow shoulder straps, cotton lace trimming. Long curled hair with deep fringe. [5] 1972. Black cotton uplift bra with wired and lightly padded cups, trimmed with cotton lace; adjustable shoulder straps, edged with cotton lace; back fastening; black cotton panties with high-cut legs. Nylon wig dressed into large curls. [6] 1972. One-piece pale green cotton lace pantie-suit with built-in plain cotton bra, wired cups, adjustable shoulder straps, back fastening. Long curled hair dressed on top of head, long curled side bangs. [7] 1973. Waist-length pale orange Lycra bra, wired lightly-padded lace-covered cups and double Lycra centre and side panels, wide adjustable stretch shoulder straps; matching Lycra long-leg panties, double control panels, lace trimming. Short straight nylon wig, combed forward onto face. [8] 1974. Long-line pink stretch nylon body suit, built-in bra with wired cups, narrow stretch rouleau shoulder straps, high-cut legs. Long hair with deep fringe and curled side bangs. [9] 1974. Fine black cotton unstructured bra, narrow rouleau halter straps, back fastening; mini-panties with elasticated waistband. Long hair, centre parting and side bangs.

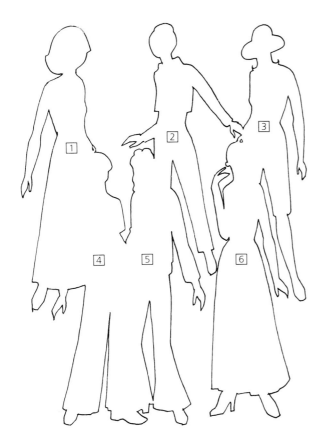

Leisure Wear 1970–1974

1 1970. Red and yellow striped cotton beach outfit; bra top, padded and wired cups, self-fabric bindings and halter straps, back fastening; ankle-length wrapover skirt, bound edges, bow tie fastening; large hat with upturned brim in matching fabric. Red leather sandals with cross straps and thick platform soles. 2 1970. Padded water-and-windproof cotton ski suit printed with all-over pattern of random-sized stylized flowers, short unfitted top with long raglan sleeves, wide knitted wool collar, fitted underbodice and trousers cut in one piece, V-shaped hip yoke. Close-fitting fur hat. Short knitted gloves. Leather ski boots. 3 1971. Country wear. Brown cable-knit fitted wool sweater, long tight sleeves, high polo-neck collar. Multi-coloured knitted-wool sleeveless sweater with low scooped neckline, worn with wide buckled leather belt. Knee-length brown cotton-corduroy breeches, wide buttoned bands at knee-level. Long beige wool knee socks. Dark red leather step-in walking shoes, flat heels and square toes. 4 1972. Multi-coloured spotted and striped cotton-lawn playsuit, short top finished with self-fabric frill under bust, slashed neckline and short inset sleeves, full trousers gathered from narrow hip yoke. Leather mule sandals with thick platform soles. 5 1973. Cream polyester-cotton shirt, long pointed collar, full inset sleeves with deep cuffs, velvet ribbon bow-tie. Waist-length sleeveless fitted multi-coloured sweater, low scooped neckline. Fitted orange striped wool trousers. Leather shoes with thick high heels and platform soles. 6 1974. Multi-coloured striped-and-flower-printed polyester-cotton ankle-length beach dress, low V-shaped halter neckline, wide inset band under bust, flared skirt with deep central inverted box pleat. Purple polyester-cotton turban. Purple leather shoes with ankle straps, black leather heels and platform soles.

Day Wear 1970–1972

1 1970. Grey flannel trouser suit, mini-length top, long flared raglan sleeves, grown-on collar and curved yoke cut in one piece; knee-length flared skirt attached to self-fabric tie-belt, split from waist to hem at front; narrow ankle-length trousers in matching fabric. Hair held back with silk scarf tied into large bow. Blue leather boots with thick high heels. 2 1971. Pink and cream herringbone wool suit, knee-length fitted double-breasted coat, wide collar and revers, long narrow inset sleeves, hip-level pockets set into the top-stitched side-panel seams, flared trousers in matching fabric. Pink wool beret. Cream leather boots. 3 1971. Yellow suede fitted waist-length jacket, stand collar, shaped yoke seam, narrow inset shirt sleeves, tight bodice with side-panel seams, zip fastening from under collar to hem of waistband, short fitted pants in matching suede. Short hair combed forward. Knitted wool tights. Long brown suede boots, flared cuffs over knees, low thick flared heels, rounded toes. 4 1970. Multi-coloured geometrically patterned wool dress and jacket, plain black wool cummerbund from under bust to high waistline, ankle-length gathered bell-shaped skirt, hem bound to match the stand collar and the edges and hems of bolero jacket. Brimless black fur hat. Fitted black leather boots, square toes and high thick heels. 5 1971. Yellow and orange checked wool trouser suit, fitted hip-length jacket, single-button fastening, wide collar and revers, long narrow inset sleeves, large bias-cut patch pockets, flared trousers in matching fabric. Herringbone wool cap. Cream silk shirt and striped wool tie. 6 1972. Ankle-length yellow-and-white spotted grey cotton day dress, slit neckline, shirt collar with long points, inset sleeves fitted to the elbow and flared and gathered into wide wrist cuffs, bias-cut skirt bound with plain yellow cotton to match the bow-tied waistbelt. Pale blue straw hat, tall crown and wide brim. Yellow leather sandals, wide straps, peep-toes and thick flared heels.

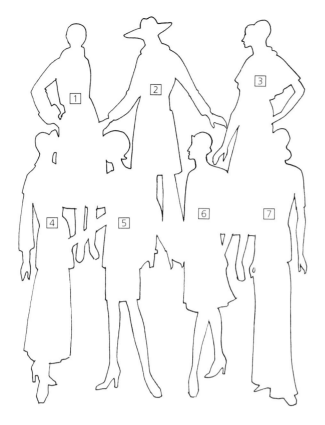

Day Wear 1972–1974

[1] 1972. Edge-to-edge knee-length sheepskin coat painted with stylized flowers, trimmed and lined with wool fleece, long inset sleeves, wide buckled waistbelt. Brimless wool hat. Long leather boots, rounded toes, thin platform soles. [2] 1973. Mini-length yellow wool coat, front zip fastening, pointed collar, low-slung belt, deep-pile imitation-sheepskin curved yoke and long inset cuffed sleeves. Polo-neck sweater. Flared trousers with turn-ups. Felt hat, crown trimmed with petersham band, wide brim. Leather boots, platform soles, high thick heels. [3] 1974. Midi-length fine white cotton-lawn day dress printed with flowers and leaves, cross-over bodice fastening on one side with self-fabric bow, short semi-inset flared sleeves, bias-cut skirt from low hip yoke seam. Yellow straw hat, turned-down brim, trimmed with silk daisies and artificial fruit. Green leather shoes, peep-toes, cut-out detail, platform soles, high thick heels. [4] 1972. Collarless hip-length knitted wool sweater in bold geometric pattern, short inset sleeves, tie-belt, hip-level patch pockets. Cream cotton blouse, long shirt sleeves, pointed collar. Ankle-length printed-cotton skirt, hat in matching fabric, wide turned-down brim. Brown leather boots, square toes, platform soles, high thick heels. [5] 1973. Hip-length fitted double-breasted tailored jacket in fine checked wool, wide collar and revers, long inset sleeves, hip-level flap-and-patch pockets. Mini-length skirt in bold checked wool. Felt hat with wide brim. Black and white leather shoes, square toes, platform soles, high thick heels. [6] 1974. Fitted hip-length brown and white striped knitted-cotton top, low V-shaped neckline, detail patch of alternative stripes, long tight inset sleeves; knee-length bias-cut skirt in knitted brown cotton striped with white. Straw hat, upturned brim edged with blue ribbon. Leather sling-back shoes, almond-shaped toes, high thick heels. [7] 1974. Orange linen trouser suit, hip-length fitted jacket, strap opening from under the long pointed collar to the wide buckled waistbelt, elbow-length sleeves, stitched cuffs matching the panels on the front bodice and the hip-level bound pockets, flared trousers. Orange wool beret. Orange leather shoes.

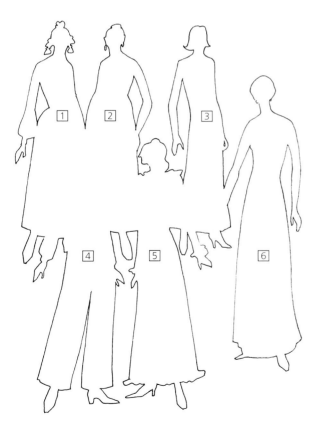

Evening Wear 1970–1974

[1] 1970. Ankle-length wool dinner dress printed with multi-coloured geometric patterns, fitted bodice, close-fitting stand collar; inset sleeves fitted to the elbow, ballooning out below and gathered into fitted cuffs; high waist position marked by self-fabric tie-belt with long ends; bell-shaped skirt, supported over stiff petticoats. Multi-coloured beaded cap, decorated with hanging bead tassels. Red suede boots with square toes. [2] 1971. Ankle-length vertically striped printed silk evening dress, fitted bodice with high waist position, low square neckline, long fitted inset sleeves, gathered skirt with band of horizontal stripes from knee-level to hem. Large glass bead earrings. Green satin boots with square toes. [3] 1973. Hip-length sleeveless knitted silver-Lurex evening sweater, low V-shaped neckline. Orange silk blouse, wide pointed collar, long narrow inset shirt sleeves. Ankle-length bias-cut orange panne-velvet skirt. Orange satin shoes, square toes, cut-away sides, ankle straps and medium-high thick heels. [4] 1970. Black ribbed-silk sleeveless bolero, rounded edges trimmed with wide metallic and beaded braid, echoed on the flared hems of the high-waisted self-fabric trousers. Collarless white silk blouse, inset shirt sleeves, bodice decorated with bead embroidery and feathers. Hair worn in side bunches, centre parting. Black satin shoes, almond-shaped toes, low thick heels, satin ribbon criss-cross trimming. [5] 1972. Ankle-length white silk-chiffon dinner dress, all-over embroidered design of wild flowers, fitted bodice, long tight inset sleeves; the hem of the flared skirt edged with layers of bias-cut frills, echoed on the wrists and neckline; white silk buckled belt. Gold kid shoes, almond-shaped toes, cut-away sides, platform soles, ankle straps and high thick heels. [6] 1974. Blue silk-crepe evening dress printed in white, fitted bodice ruched at bust-level, V-shaped halter straps, flared skirt with wide godet set into centre-front seam from knee-level to hem. Matching fabric turban trimmed with large jewelled brooch. Blue satin shoes.

Bridal Wear 1970–1974

[1] 1970. Cream silk princess-line wedding dress, slashed neckline, long fitted inset sleeves with scalloped beaded hems, panel seams embroidered with pearls and trimmed with wax leaves and flowers. Small beaded headdress, long silk-tulle veil edged with pearls. Cream silk shoes. [2] 1971. Trapeze-line beige silk wedding dress, inset fitted sleeves, small self-fabric buttons from wrists to elbows, short lace oversleeves with scalloped hems to match collarless floor-length tabard and pillbox hat. Beige silk shoes with almond-shaped toes. [3] 1974. White silk-ottoman wedding dress, fitted bodice with high waist position trimmed with lace flowers to match base of shallow grown-on collar, wide square yoke outlined with band of deep border lace, three-quarter-length fitted inset sleeves ending in wide wrist-length gathered frill, lace edging echoed on the floor-length hem of the dress and long detachable back train. Headdress of wax flowers and pearl beads, long silk-tulle veil. White silk shoes. [4] 1972. Cream silk-organdie wedding dress, fitted bodice, short puffed inset sleeves, fitted skirt flared from knee level, decorated with rows of fan-shaped pieces of pleated organdie, shoulder-wide double-layered organdie collar fastening with double ribbon bows with long trailing ends, wide cream satin waistband. Cream silk-organdie hat, wide wired double layered brim with scalloped edge, tall crown with self-fabric band. Cream satin shoes with pointed toes.

Accessories 1970–1974

[1] 1970. Green suede shoes, cut-out decoration, narrow bar straps, almond-shaped toes, brown leather platform soles, low thick heels. [2] 1970. Yellow suede shoes, wide buckled bar straps, brown leather platform soles, low thick heels. [3] 1970. Red leather shoes, high tongues, cross straps, brass trimming, square toes, low thick heels. [4] 1970. Pink suede shoes, diagonal ruched bar straps, square toes, thick platform soles. [5] 1970. Beige felt hat, wide brim, tall crown with band-and-buckle trim. [6] 1970. Yellow felt hat, turned-down brim, tall crown with wide white yellow-spotted band. [7] 1970. Green straw hat, stiffened brim with upturned edge, high crown with flat top. [8] 1970. Blue felt hat, wide crown, narrow upturned brim. Gold hoop earrings. [9] 1970. Mid-calf-length leather lace-up boots, thick heels, platform soles. [10] 1970. Green, red and white leather shoes, high wedge heels, platform soles. [11] 1971. Beige leather shoes, high tongues, square toes, stitched detail, low thick heels. [12] 1971. Green wool peaked cap. [13] 1971. Lilac pearlized leather sandals, ankle straps, rouleau strap fronts. [14] 1971. Green leather sandals, ankle straps, peep-toes, cut-out detail, thick platform soles, high heels. [15] 1971. Purple velvet pull-on hat, turned-back fitted brim. [16] 1972. Beige felt hat, turned-back brim. [17] 1972. Felt fedora hat, tall crown, wide curled brim. [18] 1972. Beige leather sling-back shoes, black patent-leather toecaps, platform soles, high thick heels. [19] 1972. Tri-colour leather mules, peep-toes, thick cork platform soles and high heels. [20] 1972. Pink suede sling-back shoes, peep-toes, high thick wooden heels and shaped platform soles. [21] 1973. Blue wool hat, bias-cut brim. [22] 1973. Sequin-covered pillbox hat. [23] 1973. Green felt hat, upturned brim. [24] 1972. Knee-length pink leather boots, thick platform soles, high heels. [25] 1972. Knee-length brown leather boots, stitched detail, low thick heels. [26] 1973. Red, white and blue leather lace-up shoes, low thick heels, platform soles. [27] 1974. Pale blue straw hat, unstiffened brim held on one side with artificial flower. [28] 1974. Red straw boater trimmed with blue and white ribbon. [29] 1974. Purple panne-velvet draped cap, silk flower trim. [30] 1973. Purple and green leather shoes, T-straps, cut-away sides, low thick heels, thin platform soles. [31] 1973. Yellow leather shoes, cut-away sides, ankle straps, pointed toes, high thick heels. [32] 1974. Blue leather shoes, red spotted decoration, pointed toes, high thick heels. [33] 1974. Red leather shoes, high vamp, elastic insertions, pointed toes, high thick heels. [34] 1974. White straw hat, close-fitting crown, unstiffened brim. [35] 1974. Red wool beret with stalk.

Couture Wear 1975–1979

1 John Bates 1975. Dark blue lightweight wool collarless overdress, split neckline, elbow-length kimono sleeves, bloused bodice, wide self-fabric waistbelt tied into large bow with trailing ends, top-stitched detail, cream silk underdress with bold dark blue chevron pattern, full sleeves gathered into deep cuffs, midi-length full skirt, matching scarf. Undecorated dark blue lacquered straw hat with high crown and wide brim. Dark blue leather shoes, cut-away sides, almond-shaped toes and high straight heels. 2 Nina Ricci 1977. Finely striped pale blue cotton collarless dress, bloused bodice, buttoned bias-cut strap from neckband to hipline, dropped shoulderline, inset shirt sleeves with deep cuffs, bust-level patch pockets matching outsized pockets on hipline of the full gathered skirt, tassled cord waistbelt. Brimless beret embroidered with wooden beads. Red canvas espadrilles with long ribbon straps. 3 Pierre Cardin 1978. Knee-length red wool coat, concealed fly fastening, high flared stand collar, strap fastening with leather buttons matching black leather belt, wide padded shoulders, flared inset sleeves. Wide black wool trousers, gathered at the ankles and tucked into short black leather boots with platform soles. Brimless black felt hat trimmed with large black felt bow on one side. 4 Sonia Rykiel 1975. White Indian cotton sleeveless dress, low scooped neckline and curved yoke cut in one piece, knee-length overdress, hip-level self-fabric sash, mid-calf-length underskirt in matching cotton. White cotton headscarf, twisted headband. White canvas boots, almond-shaped toes and thick heels. 5 Thierry Mugler 1979. Cream linen suit, fitted double breasted jacket, wide collar and revers, padded shoulders, wide epaulettes from waist-level, narrow inset sleeves, large patch pockets on hipline, top-stitched seams and edges, knee-length wrapover skirt. Cream silk scarf knotted in with the hair on one side of head. Cream and beige leather shoes with pointed toes and high straight heels.

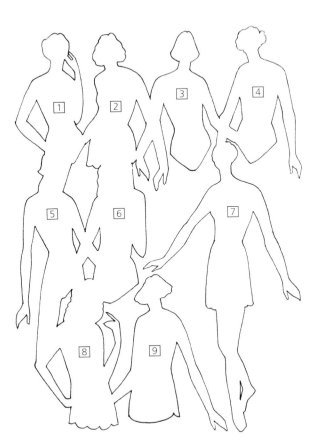

Underwear 1975–1979

1 1975. White cotton bra, broderie-anglaise-trimmed half-cups, light wiring, elasticated side panels and wide-placed shoulder straps, back opening; panties with narrow sides in matching fabric. Straight hair dressed into full roll around head and with long fringe. 2 1975. Pale green silk covered unstructured bra, cups trimmed and edged with lace, back fastening; knickers in matching fabric, wide hems and side panels trimmed with lace, elasticated waist. Permed hair with centre parting. 3 1976. White broderie-anglaise wired half-cup bra, elasticated wide-spaced shoulder straps, back fastening; matching panties. Chin-length straight hair with long fringe. 4 1976. Unstructured peach-coloured Lycra half-cup bra trimmed with nylon lace, halter straps, back fastening; matching panties. Permed hair worn high on head. 5 1977. Strapless moulded bra in sheer black nylon and Lycra; matching mini-panties. Long straight hair with centre parting. 6 1977. Flesh-coloured Lycra moulded bra, lightly wired under cups, narrow shoulder straps, front opening; moulded pantie-girdle in matching fabric. Long permed hair set into waves, centre parting and small fringe. 7 1979. Black lace-trimmed satin half-cup bra, light padding and wiring, front fastening; matching black silk mini-slip. Straight hair worn high on head, centre parting, long curled side tendrils. 8 1978. Pale blue silk camisole top, scalloped upper edge trimmed with fine lace, narrow rouleau shoulder straps; knickers in matching fabric, scalloped hems bordered with lace. Long crimped hair with centre parting. 9 1979. Lilac polyester-silk mini-slip, low scooped neckline, narrow rouleau shoulder straps, embroidery on bustline and on side hem. Short crimped hair with side parting.

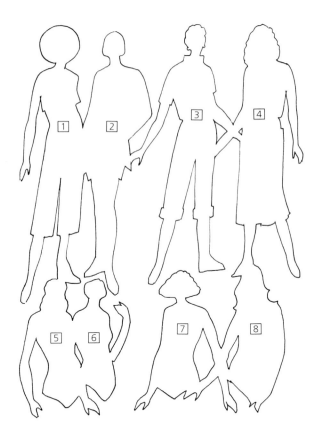

Leisure Wear 1975–1979

1 1975. Striped cotton playsuit; strapless bra top with short flared overtop to below bust-level, bare midriff; wide midi-length trousers, broad band of horizontal stripes above hem, narrow waistband. Yellow straw hat with wide wired brim. Mule-type strap sandals, high cork wedge heels. 2 1976. Purple striped cotton beach dress, hip-length unfitted sleeveless bodice, slashed neckline, bias-cut mini-length skirt with uneven hemline, self-fabric bias bindings to match the tie-belt. Purple canvas mules, peep-toes, platform soles and high wedge cork heels. 3 1977. All-in-one cotton playsuit, unfitted bloused bodice, button fastening from under the wide stand collar to the hipline, short inset sleeves, hip-level patch pockets, midi-length trousers with wide turn-ups. Blue cotton turban with twisted headband. Blue canvas espadrilles, peep-toes, thick rope-covered cork platform soles and high wedge heels, ribbon ties. 4 1979. Strapless cotton beach dress, bloused bodice gathered on waistline and above bust with threaded rouleau ribbon, midi-length skirt, buttoned strap opening from waistline to hem, large hip-level patch pockets. Red canvas shoes, peep-toes, ankle straps and high wedge heels. 5 1975. Dark blue cotton bikini; brief bra top, narrow halter straps, tiny wide-apart cups, back fastening; mini-briefs, rouleau ribbon-tied sides. 6 1976. Green Lycra one-piece swimsuit, rouleau halter straps fastening at back of neck, bib-front with cut-away sides, back and legs. 7 1978. Strapless dark blue moulded-Lycra one-piece swimsuit, sides cut-away on one side and fastening with rouleau ribbons. 8 1979. Striped Lycra swimsuit, halter neckline with polo-neck collar, back fastening; cut-away sides, back and legs bound with self-fabric narrow belt with decorative buckle.

Day Wear 1975–1976

1 1975. Printed rayon suit, fitted collarless jacket, short bias-cut inset sleeves, buttons from base of V-shaped neckline to waist, self-fabric covered buckled belt, hip-length peplum, knee-length flared skirt. Permed hair with side parting. Red plastic bracelets and earrings. Brown leather shoes, cut-away sides, ankle straps, almond-shaped toes and high thick heels. 2 1975. Cotton patchwork dress, fitted bodice, low V-shaped neckline, short inset sleeves, tie-belt, ankle-length flared skirt. Long permed hair with side parting. 3 1975. Patchwork dress, fitted bodice, scooped neckline, elbow-length inset sleeves with frilled cuffs, panne-velvet sleeveless bolero jacket, matching wide cummerbund and ankle-length underskirt, midi-length overskirt. Headscarf knotted at back of head. Hoop earrings. Canvas espadrilles, high wedge heels and ribbon fastenings. 4 1976. Wool suit, hip-length top with low scooped neckline worn under short bolero in contrasting colour, matching knee-length edge-to-edge unfitted coat with three-quarter-length inset sleeves, dropped shoulderline, low-placed patch pockets, straight-cut trousers gathered into cuffs on ankles, long scarf incorporating both fabrics, matching pull-on hat. Cream leather boots, almond-shaped toes and high thick heels. 5 1976. Knitted wool suit, long unfitted top, inset band above bust and below low U-shaped neckline, elbow-length inset sleeves, hip-level outsized patch pockets, midi-length straight skirt, long fringed scarf in matching fabric. Permed hair worn in bun on top of head. Long leather boots with pointed toes. 6 1976. Short striped-wool unfitted waistcoat, three-button fastening, two patch pockets. Collarless cream cotton shirt. Midi-length cotton-needlecord skirt, gathered from wide waistband, buckled leather belt, hip-level patch pockets. Felt trilby-style hat. Long permed hair. Long leather boots with square toes and flat heels.

Day Wear 1977–1979

1 1977. Green cotton suit; the hip-length top, slashed neckline, yoke, three-quarter-length flared sleeves and the hem of the knee-length flared skirt banded with pintucks and cream cotton lace; self-fabric tie-belt. Cream leather sling-back shoes, ankle straps, almond-shaped toes and high thick heels. 2 1977. Grey wool jersey dress, high polo-neck collar, wide elbow-length batwing sleeves gathered into fitted lower sleeves, unfitted bodice cut without waist seam and gathered into wide band above knees. Red velvet pull-on hat. Red leather court shoes with almond-shaped toes and high thick heels. 3 1977. Hip-length checked wool coat, front zip fastening from wide stand collar to above hem, unfitted bodice, low-slung leather tie-belt, padded dropped shoulderline, inset sleeves gathered into knitted wool cuffs. Green velvet-corduroy trousers tucked into tops of long brown leather boots with square toes and high thick heels. Brown felt hat with turned-down brim, high crown banded in pink. 4 1978. Cotton patchwork dress, button-through fitted bodice, narrow stand collar, square yoke, gathered inset sleeves with deep cuffs, waistbelt with round buckle, knee-length gathered skirt. Cream straw hat, tall crown with deep band, wide unstiffened brim. Long cream leather boots, pointed toes and high thick heels. 5 1979. Knee-length multi-coloured striped knitted-wool dress, fitted bodice, low square neckline, narrow straight skirt, wide red leather belt. Three-quarter-length multi-coloured striped knitted-wool coat, edge-to-edge, narrow high yoke in fabric to match the dress, padded shoulders, long inset sleeves. Red and green leather shoes, peep-toes, cut-away sides, ankle straps, high thick heels. 6 1979. Cream knitted-wool dress, fitted bodice, slashed neckline, graded buckled belt bound twice around waist. Cream leather shoes, cut-away sides, ankle straps, pointed toes and high thick heels.

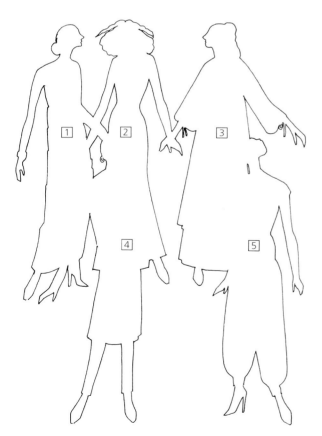

Evening Wear 1975–1979

1 1975. Red silk-jersey evening dress, strapless beaded and embroidered bodice with high waistline, bias-cut wrapover ankle-length skirt. Hair dressed into bun at nape of neck. Flower-shaped bead earrings, matching bracelet. Red satin shoes, peep-toes, cut-away sides, ankle straps, high slim straight heels. 2 1976. Red silk-jersey dress with all-over sequin embroidery and an asymmetric motif of beaded flowers from under the side bust to the opposite side hip, fitted bodice, low V-shaped neckline, narrow rouleau shoulder straps, ankle-length flared skirt with split from hem to thigh on one side. Permed hair with centre parting. Red satin sandals, peep-toes and ankle straps. 3 1977. Pink silk dinner dress, three-quarter-length inset sleeves gathered at wrists with threaded rouleau ribbon, gathered midi-length overskirt with high waist, short button-through bodice with low square neckline in a contrast pattern fabric to match the ankle-length underskirt. Permed hair drawn back away from face. Pink silk shoes with pointed toes. 4 1978. Blue silk jersey pants suit, sleeveless top with asymmetric bloused bodice, knee-length skirt slashed from hem to waist on one side, beaded motifs and scattered bugle beads repeated on hems of narrow ankle-length pants. Hair worn in asymmetric ponytail. Beaded loop earrings. Silver kid strap sandals. 5 1979. Turquoise silk-taffeta evening pyjamas, top-stitched fitted bodice from hipline to under bust, pleated self-fabric belt tied on one side, short bloused bodice, round neckline with split to bust-level, padded shoulders, top-stitched inset cap sleeves, trousers gathered into stitched ankle-length cuffs. Short permed hair with side parting. Turquoise satin strap sandals, long ankle straps and high narrow straight heels.

Bridal Wear 1975–1979

1 1975. Midi-length cream pleated silk-jersey dress, unfitted bodice, slashed neckline, padded shoulders, narrow cream satin yoke to match the low-slung bow-tied belt and the buttoned cuffs of the bishop-style inset sleeves. Brimless cream satin hat trimmed with pearls. Shoulder-length permed hair. Cream satin shoes with almond-shaped toes and high slender heels.
2 1976. Knee-length peach-coloured silk-crepe top, slashed neckline open on centre front to bustline, full bishop-style inset sleeves with deep cuffs, self-fabric tie-belt with tassled ends, skirt split to waist, full harem pants gathered into cuffs around ankles, satin bindings and trimmings. Peach-coloured felt hat with silk-crepe and satin-covered padded roll brim, waist-length silk-crepe veil. Leather mules with rounded toes and high wedge heels. 3 1977. White cotton blouse; low square neckline, banded with embroidered ribbon and edged with lace, matching the hems of the full inset sleeves gathered below the edges and flaring out over the hands; ankle-length panelled skirt gathered from lace-covered and trimmed hip yoke, trimming repeated at mid-calf-level and around hem. Coronet of fresh flowers. White satin shoes with almond-shaped toes. 4 1979. White silk suit, fitted jacket, short frilled peplum, square neckline infilled with pleated silk scarf, concealed opening, long fitted inset sleeves, self-fabric waist sash and bow with long bias-cut ends, midi-length gathered bell-shaped skirt. White silk pillbox hat trimmed with velvet rose at back, short circular net veil. White satin shoes, almond-shaped toes, trimmed with pearls.

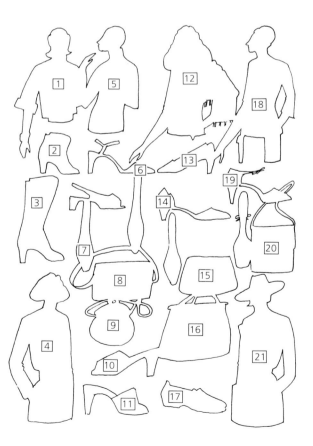

Accessories 1975–1979

1 1975. Waist-length quilted printed-cotton jacket, wide elbow-length inset sleeves with deep cuffs, front edge-to-edge fastening with ribbon bows, edges bound with striped cotton. Knitted wool polo-neck sweater. Pull-on knitted hat. 2 1975. Ankle-length leather boots, top-stitched detail, almond-shaped toes, high thick heels. 3 1976. Long leather boots, top-stitched detail, high heels. 4 1978. Sleeveless hip-length knitted wool sweater, low V-shaped neckline, wide buckled leather belt. Checked cotton shirt, long pointed collar, inset cuffed sleeves. 5 1975. Flower-printed fringed silk scarf worn over fitted ribbed knitted wool sweater. Pull-on multi-coloured knitted wool hat. 6 1976. Leather sling-back shoes, ankle-straps, cut-away sides, almond-shaped toes and high straight heels. 7 1978. Leather sling-back shoes with peep-toes, low thick heels. 8 1978. Unstructured leather bag, top and side zip fastenings, long shoulder strap. 9 1979. Unstructured leather bag with metal clasp, long rouleau handle. 10 1978. Mules with wooden platform soles and high heels, leather strap fronts. 11 1979. Leather mules, top-stitched front straps, high slender heels. 12 1976. Long wool scarf, decorative borders and fringed hems. Fitted knitted wool sweater. 13 1977. Suede shoes with almond-shaped toes and high heels. 14 1978. Multi-coloured leather shoes, cut-away sides and leaf-shaped fronts, medium-high heels. 15 1977. Unstructured leather clutch bag, threaded buckled strap, front fastening. 16 1979. Striped canvas beach bag. 17 1979. Flat lace-up leather shoes with thick crepe soles. 18 1978. Collarless wool-jersey blouse, bound neckline matching the hems of the flared three-quarter-length inset sleeves, patch pockets attached to hem on each side of hips. Sleeveless wool-jersey vest, low scooped neckline, bound edges. Pull-on hat in matching fabric, large flower motif on one side. 19 1977. Leather shoes, cut-away sides, rouleau decoration, high straight heels. 20 1977. Unstructured bag, flap with punchwork decoration and long handle. 21 1979. Double-breasted tailored jacket worn with narrow leather buckled belt. Cream cotton shirt, striped silk tie, spotted silk handkerchief. Large felt hat, tall crown with deep petersham band and wide brim.

Vivienne Westwood 1981

Luciano Soprani 1982

Kenzo 1980

Emanuel Ungaro 1983

Giorgio Armani
1984

JP

1980

1980

1981

1981

1981

1982

1982

1983

1983

1984

1980

1981

1982

1982

1984

1980

1980

1981

1981

1981

1982

1982

1982

1983

1983

1984

1984

Evening Wear 1980–1984

1980

1981

1982

1982

1984

1980

1981

1983

1984

Calvin Klein 1985

Karl Lagerfeld 1988

Oscar de la Renta 1985

Christian Lacroix 1987

Claude Montana 1990

Katharine Hamnett 1990

Underwear 1985–1990

1985

1986

1987

1987

1987

1988

1988

1988

1989

1989

1990

1990

1985

1986

1986

1987

1989

1990

1985

1985

1986

1986

1986

1987

1987

1988

1988

1989

1990

Evening Wear 1985–1990

1985

1986

1987

1988

1990

1990

1985

1986

1988

1990

1985
1985
1986
1986
1987
1987
1987
1988
1988
1989
1989
1989
1990
1990

Couture Wear 1980–1984

1 Kenzo 1980. Blue cotton-denim mini-length dress, unfitted bloused bodice, bias-cut collar forming a waterfall frill set into a wide waist-length strap opening, single-button fastening, long inset shirt-style cuffed sleeves, circular skirt with hip basque, top-stitched edges and seams, wide low-slung black leather belt. Brimless beret gathered onto narrow band. Black leather shoes with low heels and pointed toes. 2 Vivienne Westwood 1981. Printed cotton mini-length shirt, V-shaped neckline with long tie scarf collar, dropped shoulderline, full inset sleeves gathered at elbows and into cuffs at wrists, knee-high stockings in matching fabric, white sash knotted at front, matching underskirt. Short-cropped dyed blond hair. Gold kid sandals with long straps bound around the lower legs, low thick heels. 3 Luciano Soprani 1982. Pale brown linen blouson jacket, shoulder-wide shawl collar, padded shoulders, long inset sleeves gathered into narrow cuffs. White cotton blouse, bow-tie neckline. Mini-length red linen divided skirt. Beige nylon tights. Red leather peep-toe shoes. 4 Emanuel Ungaro 1983. Yellow flower-printed silk crepe-de-chine collarless blouse, buttoning from neck to waist, padded shoulders, short inset puff sleeves, red leather buckled waistbelt, matching headband. Flared mini-length skirt in contrasting pattern. Brown leather shoes, pointed toes and low heels. 5 Giorgio Armani 1984. Double-breasted hip-length grey checked wool tailored jacket, wide padded shoulders, long inset sleeves, wide collar and revers. Grey linen wrapover skirt finishing just above the knees. White straw hat, high crown banded with black ribbon matching the edge of the wide brim. Black leather shoes, pointed toes, cut-away sides, high slender heels.

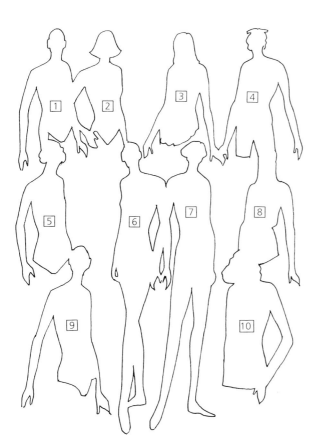

Underwear 1980–1984

1 1980. Pale yellow stretch-satin front opening bra, lace-trimmed wired and lightly padded cups, narrow adjustable shoulder straps, mini-panties in matching fabric. 2 1980. Orange stretch-satin front opening uplift bra, wired and lightly padded lace-trimmed cups, halter straps, mini-panties in matching fabric. 3 1981. Blue silk and lace combination camiknickers, ribbon shoulder straps. 4 1981. Sleeveless cream knitted-wool vest, deep scooped neckline, lace edging, long-legged knickers in matching fabric. 5 1981. Pale green silk camisole, lace motif and trimming, narrow rouleau shoulder straps, knickers in matching fabric. 6 1982. Pink stretch-satin body-shaper, lace-covered bra, lightly wired and padded cups, narrow adjustable shoulder straps, high-cut legs, lace trimming. 7 1982. Pink elasticated and stitched cotton body-shaper, pre-formed bra with lightly wired and padded cups trimmed with lace, elasticated shoulder straps, high-cut legs. 8 1983. Brown silk camisole and knicker combination, drawstring waist, wrapover bodice trimmed with lace, narrow rouleau shoulder straps. 9 1983. Pale grey nylon camisole top, straight neckline trimmed with lace and threaded ribbon, ribbon shoulder straps, scalloped shirt-tail hemline trimmed with border lace to match elastic-sided mini-briefs. 10 1984. Mini-length silk slip, neckline trimmed with lace to match the hem and split side seams.

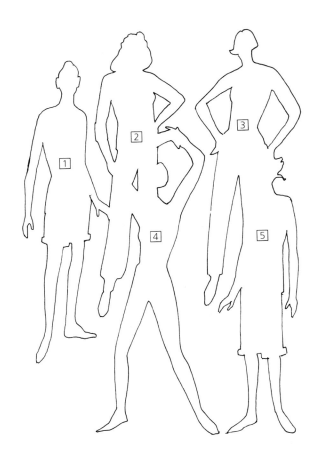

Leisure Wear 1980–1984

1 1980. Suede bra top, gathers under the self-fabric rouleau halter straps, ruched shaping on the centre front at bust-level. Cream linen bermuda-length shorts, deep waistband threaded with buckled brown leather belt, hip-level side pockets, fly fastening, central pressed creases, turn-ups. Cream suede pumps with pointed toes and flat heels. Hair dressed away from face and into small tight bun on top of head. 2 1981. Grey brushed-cotton exercise suit, hip-length top, low V-shaped neckline with pink brushed-cotton trimming matching inset band at waist-level, three-quarter-length sleeves, fitted pants gathered at waist and into cuffs around ankles. Pink cotton headband worn to hold back long permed hair. Pink canvas lace-up exercise shoes. 3 1982. Strapless elasticated white cotton tube printed with multi-coloured palm leaves, self-fabric rouleau tie-belt, matching ankle-length trousers, hip-level side pockets. Short hair with long fringe. Red stitched-leather strap sandals. 4 1982. Yellow striped Lycra all-in-one exercise suit, low U-shaped neckline; long tightly fitted sleeves, body and legs; straps under feet. Short hair dressed away from face. 5 1984. Unfitted hip-length red-white-and-blue striped cotton beach top, low neckline bound with red-white-and-blue spotted cotton, worn off one shoulder, blue-and-red striped cotton bermuda-length shorts with red-white-and-blue spotted turn-ups. Turban and headscarf made of a combination of fabrics. Blue canvas beach shoes with long laces.

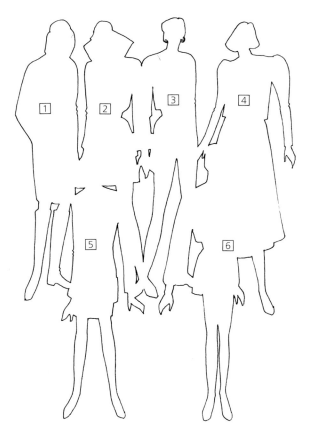

Day Wear 1980–1982

1 1980. Knee-length waterproof cotton coat, vertical lines of quilting, fastening from under the oustized collar to hip-level with loops and bone toggles, long inset sleeves gathered into cuffs, vertical hip-level pockets. Brimless knitted wool beret. Long suede boots with low thick heels. 2 1980. Short plastic wrapover raincoat, large collar and revers, padded shoulders, long cuffed inset sleeves, tie-belt on natural waistline, large hip-level flap-and-patch pockets. Leather shoes with peep-toes, cut-out decoration and ankle straps. 3 1981. Yellow wool mini-length dress, wide boat-shaped neckline, padded shoulders, elbow-length inset sleeves, wide self-fabric buckled waistbelt, hip-level patch pockets. Plastic hoop earrings. Red leather shoes with flat heels. 4 1981. Rust velvet dress and jacket printed with a multi-coloured paisley design, unfitted hip-length edge-to-edge jacket, padded shoulders, leg-of-mutton-style sleeves, dress with fitted bodice and midi-length gathered skirt. Brown leather shoes with openwork design. 5 1981. Blue wool tailored suit, fitted double-breasted hip-level jacket, wide shawl collar faced with satin to match the hip-level bound pockets and the covered buttons, padded shoulders, long inset sleeves. Gold hoop earrings. Blue leather peep-toe shoes. 6 1982. Multi-coloured knitted wool jumper, wide boat-shaped neckline, padded shoulders, long inset sleeves. Red wool mini-length skirt, gathered onto a wide waistband threaded with a blue leather buckled belt. Orange wool ribbed tights. Blue leather shoes with almond-shaped toes and flat heels.

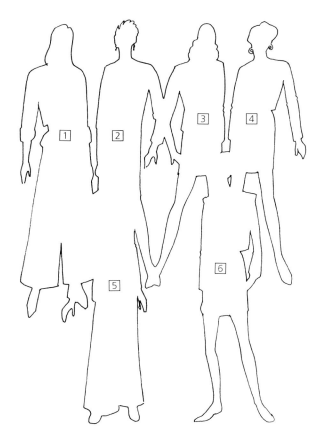

Day Wear 1982–1984

1 1982. Cream suede trouser suit, collarless top, padded shoulders, long raglan sleeves rolled to the elbows, front fastening with two studs under round neckline, fly fastening to the hem, buckled leather waistbelt, wide-legged trousers seamed above the ankles and gathered into a waistband, hip-level pockets. 2 1982. Collarless yellow crepe dress, unfitted bodice and knee-length skirt cut in one piece, padded shoulders; elbow-length pleated inset sleeves, gathered into top-stitched cuffs, matching the edges of the yoke, neckline and front opening; self-covered buttons. Bead earrings. 3 1983. Grey linen suit, short fitted tailored jacket, wide padded shoulders with stitched epaulettes, long inset sleeves gathered into cuffs, two-button double-breasted fastening, narrow collar and revers, mini-length tight skirt. Red plastic flower worn on edge of collar. Red leather shoes. 4 1983. Red cotton suit spotted with white, waist-length semi-fitted collarless jacket, two-button fastening under the wide white cotton buttoned-down revers, padded shoulders, long inset sleeves, mini-length tight skirt. White plastic hoop earrings. Red leather shoes. 5 1984. Beige linen trouser suit, hip-length unfitted collarless jacket, white linen central panel matching stitched cuffs on the inset sleeves, padded shoulders, wide-legged trousers. Beige felt hat, large crown and narrow straight brim. Large clip-on earrings. Beige leather shoes, pointed toes and decorative crossed straps. 6 1984. Brown cotton suit, hip-length blouson jacket, single-stud fastening under the narrow collar and revers, fly fastening to the waist, padded shoulders, epaulettes, shirt-style sleeves, large flap-and-patch pockets, deep hipband, ring and strap fastening, mini-length tight skirt. Large clip-on earrings. Brown leather shoes, pointed toes and flat heels.

Evening Wear 1980–1984

1 1980. Figure-fitting evening gown, embroidered all over with blue and green sequins, halter neckline, bare back with triangular cut-out to below waist, slightly flared skirt with deep centre-back split to mid-calf-level. Jaw-length hair swept back away from face. Blue satin shoes with pointed toes and high slender heels. 2 1981. Blue silk-taffeta evening gown, fitted bodice, halter neckline with attached elbow-length sleeves leaving shoulders bare, self-fabric frilled edges matching flower motif on the pleated pink silk cummerbund, floor-length gathered skirt. Jaw-length straight hair with side parting. Large clip-on earrings. 3 1982. Pink silk-taffeta ball gown, fitted bodice, decorated with large self-fabric bows, wide off-the-shoulder neckline, frilled edges matching the decoration on the elbow-length puff sleeves and repeated around the hem of the gathered floor-length skirt, gathered petticoats of nylon net. Long hair arranged in a french pleat at back of head. 4 1982. Blue silk-jersey top, draped asymmetric bodice, single inset leg-of-mutton sleeve, white silk-jersey trousers printed with outsized pattern of blue leaves and gathered onto wide waistband, knotted self-fabric rouleau belt, hip-level pockets. White kid shoes with peep-toes and high heels. 5 1984. Red silk-jersey dinner dress, fitted bodice ruched from above bust to low hip-level, matching open yoke with brooch trimming, padded shoulders, long tight inset sleeves, straight ankle-length skirt with side split from hem to above knee-level. Hair dressed away from face. Long drop earrings. Red satin strap sandals.

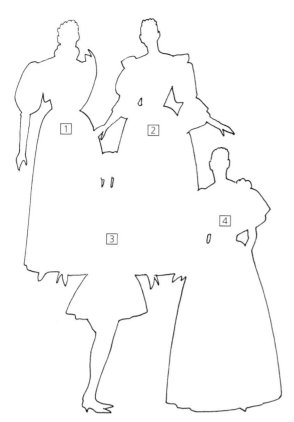

Bridal Wear 1980–1984

[1] 1980. Cream silk-taffeta bridal gown, fitted tucked bodice, circular-cut frilled collar; outsized leg-of-mutton sleeves, buttoned from wrist to elbow, cut into points over the hands; deep embroidered waistband with piped edges, matching waist-length sleeveless bolero jacket, ground-length gathered skirt worn over nylon net petticoars. Pearl bead headdress and long silk-tulle veil. Drop earrings. Satin shoes with pointed toes. [2] 1981. Cream striped white silk-taffeta wedding dress, fitted bodice, low scooped neckline edged with wide frilled collar covering the tops of the outsized elbow-length puff sleeves, two-tier frilled wrist-length cuffs trimmed with self-fabric bows, ground-length gathered skirt worn over stiff petticoats. Pearl tiara, long silk-tulle veil. [3] 1983. Mini-length pale pink silk-taffeta wedding dress, low V-shaped back neckline edged with wide self-fabric frill, ending on the waistline in large taffeta bow with long trailing ends, straight skirt with wide gathered frill. Headdress of pink silk taffeta roses and orange blossom. Satin shoes with pointed toes and low heels. [4] 1984. Cream satin bridal gown, sleeveless fitted bodice, wide neckline edged with deep frill reaching to bust-level at front and dipping to waist-level at back, large silk flower on one shoulder, wide self-fabric waistbelt, ground-length gathered skirt. Tiara of wax flowers, long silk-tulle veil.

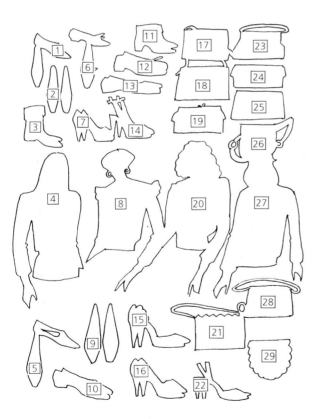

Accessories 1980–1984

[1] 1980. Suede shoes, braid and button trim, flat heels. [2] 1980. Leather shoes, high tongues, fringed leather trim. [3] 1980. Leather ankle boots, deep cuffs, flat heels. [4] 1980. Hip-length knitted wool sweater, straight neckline, padded shoulders, long inset sleeves, narrow leather waistbelt. [5] 1983. Leather shoes, cut-away sides, T-straps, flat heels. [6] 1980. Leather shoes, ribbon trim, flat heels. [7] 1981. Two-colour peep-toe shoes, high heels. [8] 1981. Polo-neck sweater, padded shoulders, frilled epaulettes, long inset sleeves. [9] 1983. Leather peep-toe shoes, laced leather insertions. [10] 1983. Canvas peep-toe shoes, striped trim, flat heels. [11] 1981. Leather ankle boots, suede trim, low thick heels. [12] 1981. Leather lace-up shoes, flat heels and thick soles. [13] 1981. Leather peep-toe shoes, bead trim, flat heels. [14] 1981. Canvas sling-back shoes, peep-toes, high heels. [15] 1984. Leather shoes, cut-away sides, pointed toes, scalloped detail, high heels. [16] 1984. Leather shoes, straight-cut fronts, pointed toes, high heels. [17] 1980. Leather bag, zip fastenings, long handle. [18] 1981. Canvas bag, double patch pockets, leather trim and long and short handles. [19] 1982. Mock snakeskin clutch bag. [20] 1982. Collarless knitted cotton tabard, buttoning on side of waistband. Tie neck blouse, long leg-of-mutton sleeves. [21] 1984. Leather bag, stitched fan detail, long handle. [22] 1984. Leather evening sandals, high heels. [23] 1980. Leather bag, zip fastening, front pocket with stud fastener, long handle. [24] 1981. Leather clutch bag with scalloped flap. [25] 1981. Leather envelope-shaped clutch bag. [26] 1982. Leather shoulder bag with long handle. [27] 1984. Hip-length jumper, V-shaped neckline, tie trim, padded shoulders, long sleeves. [28] 1983. Leather bag, scalloped detail, long handle. [29] 1984. Leather shell-shaped clutch bag, scalloped edge and stitched detail.

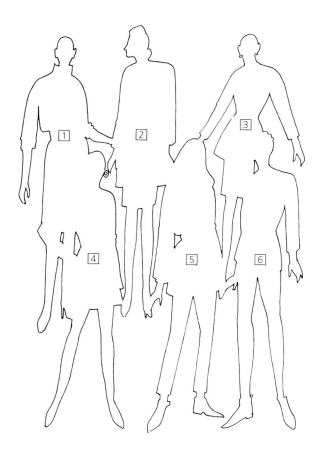

Couture Wear 1985–1990

1 Calvin Klein 1985. Knee-length fine wool gabardine coat, asymmetric fastening with two buttons under the high wide stand collar, strap-and-buckle fastening, padded shoulders, long raglan sleeves rolled to the elbows, wide buckled leather waistbelt, hip-level buttoned-down slanted flap pockets. 2 Oscar de la Renta 1985. Three-quarter-length pink wool coat, padded shoulders, long inset sleeves, black wool collar, covered buttons and slanted hip-level welt pockets, matching knee-length skirt. Black pillbox hat worn on front of head. Large clip-on earrings. Black suede gloves and matching shoes. 3 Karl Lagerfeld 1988. Blue silk tailored suit, fitted double-breasted jacket, narrow collar and revers, padded shoulders, long raglan sleeves, bodice banded in white silk from under bust to hem of the hip-length flared peplum, straight knee-length skirt. Grey tights. Dark blue leather shoes with pointed toes. 4 Christian Lacroix 1987. Hip-length tailored jacket in white silk crepe printed with brightly coloured flowers and appliquéd with raffia-stitched flowers, single-button fastening under wide collar and revers, padded shoulders, long tight inset sleeves. Mini-length fringed black raffia skirt. Hoop earrings. Black shoes with pointed toes. 5 Claude Montana 1990. Red wool mini-length wrapover coat, wide revers and an outsized collar forming a hood, padded shoulders, long inset sleeves gathered into narrow cuffs, tie-belt. Red wool drainpipe trousers. Purple wool polo-neck sweater. Short yellow cloth gloves. Red socks and purple leather ankle boots with pointed toes and flat heels. 6 Katharine Hamnett 1990. Yellow quilted-silk collarless jacket, padded shoulders, long inset sleeves gathered into knitted cuffs, front zip opening repeated on the waist-level pockets, short pants in matching quilted silk worn over black wool tights. Black wool balaclava. Black elastic-sided ankle boots with flat heels and pointed toes.

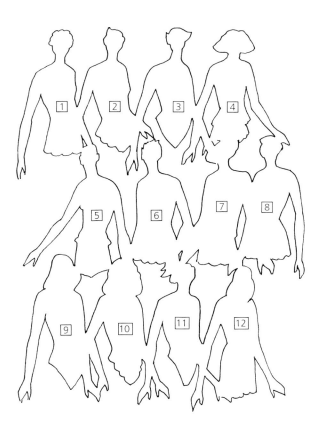

Underwear 1985–1990

1 1985. Mini-length cream cotton lace slip, scalloped neck and hemline, narrow ribbon shoulder straps. 2 1986. White silk crepe-de-chine camiknickers with all-over pattern of roses, neck and hemline trimmed with lace, ribbon shoulder straps. 3 1987. Black lace and Lycra body-shaper, deep plunge neckline with scalloped edges, infilled with fine Lycra, high-cut legs. 4 1987. Pale lilac bra and knicker set, front fastening bra trimmed with lace, adjustable shoulder straps, knicker legs decorated with flounces of lace on each side of hipline. 5 1987. Front fastening black cotton bra spotted with white, lace trimming, self-fabric rouleau shoulder straps, panties in matching fabric, lace suspender belt with elasticated and adjustable suspenders. 6 1988. Cream crepe-de-chine camisole top, V-shaped scalloped neckline, front-button opening, knickers in matching fabric, scalloped hemline. 7 1988. Hip-length cream crepe-de-chine camisole top, straight neckline and the hems of the matching knickers trimmed with lace. 8 1988. Front opening long-line strapless bra, lightly wired and boned bodice, moulded cups lightly padded and trimmed with lace, knickers in matching fabric. 9 1989. Strapless black Lycra body-shaper, spotted in white, light boning, high-cut legs. 10 1989. Strapless pink cotton bra, lightly boned, lace trimming, back fastening, matching cotton and lace panties. 11 1990. Nylon body-shaper printed with large stylized roses, ruched cups, halter straps, reinforced panel seams, high-cut legs. 12 1990. Strapless black Lycra body-shaper, fitted lightly boned bodice, black stretch-lace legs.

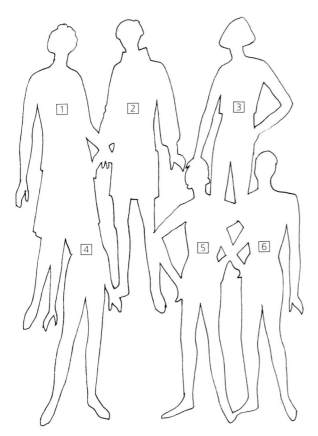

Leisure Wear 1985–1990

☐1 1985. White linen top and skirt printed with brown cartoon horses and uneven stripes, hip-length button-through sleeveless top, round neckline with plain white peter pan collar, gathered knee-length skirt. Permed hair dressed to one side. White cotton ankle socks worn with white canvas step-in shoes. ☐2 1986. Beige cotton anorak, zip fastener through high roll knitted wool collar, padded dropped shoulderline, knitted sleeves with deep cuffs, ribbed hemline, high waist position, top-stitched panel seams, large patch pockets. Short-cropped hair. Green cotton tights. Brown leather lace-up shoes with flat heels. ☐3 1986. Short yellow Lurex sleeveless beach top, low scooped neckline, matching asymmetrically draped sarong and mini-briefs. Short hair dressed away from face. ☐4 1987. Strapless white Lycra top striped with yellow and green diagonal wavy lines, matching pedal-pusher pants. Long straight hair. White canvas shoes with pointed toes and flat heels. ☐5 1989. Multi-coloured Lycra one-piece exercise suit, wide scooped neckline, short sleeves, bermuda-length shorts. Short hair lacquered into spikes. Large plastic clip-on earrings. ☐6 1990. Brown wool-jersey exercise suit, V-shaped neckline slashed to waist, bodice gathered from padded shoulders to waistline at front, long tight sleeves, high-cut legs. Short hair brushed away from face.

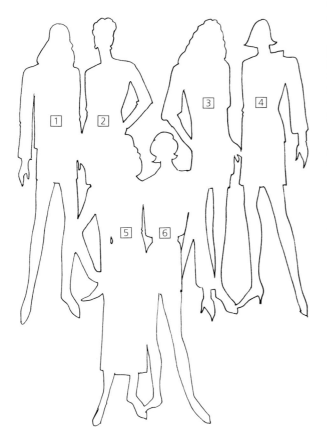

Day Wear 1985–1987

☐1 1985. Collarless hip-length edge-to-edge silk-tweed jacket, wide padded shoulders, long inset sleeves, large hip-level patch pockets. Beige silk collarless blouse worn over straight cream linen skirt. Brown leather shoes, pointed toes and flat heels. ☐2 1985. Green silk dress printed with all-over abstract pattern of darker green, wide boat-shaped neckline, padded shoulders, long inset sleeves ruched from wrists to elbows to match the bodice from under the bust to the hem of the short skirt. Black silk-organdie hat made up of leaf-shaped petals. ☐3 1986. Red knitted wool mini-length sweater dress, wide round neckline, padded shoulders, patterned yoke with fringed edges, elbow-length sleeves gathered into cuffs, low-set pockets, deep rib around hem. Red leather shoes with pointed toes and flat heels. ☐4 1986. Green patterned silk suit, fitted collarless jacket with wide buttoned wrapover panels of plain white silk, wide padded shoulders, long inset sleeves gathered into cuffs, short wrapover skirt. Black leather shoes with pointed toes and high slender heels. ☐5 1986. Bust-length double-breasted blue silk-tweed jacket, narrow collar and revers, wide padded shoulders, long inset sleeves, midi-length blue and white printed silk dress, fitted hip-length bodice and box-pleated skirt. Long permed hair held back with blue and white spotted scarf. Blue leather shoes with pointed toes and flat heels. ☐6 1987. Green cotton mini-length dress, wide revers, decorative zip fastening to hip-level, padded shoulders, long shirt sleeves, brown leather buckled waistbelt. Cream straw hat with an upturned brim. Brown leather shoes, pointed toes and flat heels.

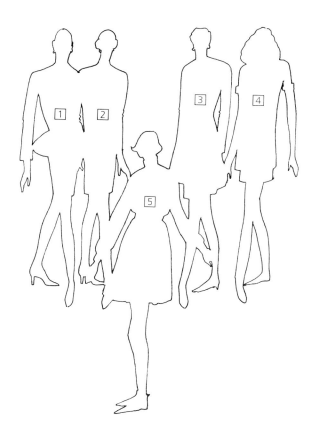

Day Wear 1987–1990

1 1987. Red wool tailored jacket printed with blue circles, padded shoulders, long inset sleeves, rounded collar and revers, fitted bodice, single-button fastening, deep flared peplum with flap pockets set into waist seam. Short plain red wool skirt. Red leather shoes with pointed toes and high slender heels. 2 1988. Collarless white cotton dress, padded shoulders, three-quarter-length inset sleeves, asymmetric button fastening from neckline to waist-level, single breast patch pocket, short straight wrapover skirt cut in one with bodice. White straw hat with narrow upturned brim. Leather shoes with pointed toes and high slender heels. 3 1988. Brown silk suit, collarless semi-fitted jacket with uneven hemline, padded shoulders, long inset sleeves, short straight skirt, top-stitched detail. Brown leather shoes, pointed toes and low heels. 4 1989. Three-quarter-length button-through striped cotton top, padded shoulders, short inset sleeves with narrow turned-back spotted cotton cuffs, matching the peter pan collar and the small decorative hankie in the breast pocket, short straight skirt. Blue leather shoes, pointed toes and flat heels. 5 1990. Short green wool hooded coat, padded shoulders, long inset sleeves gathered into elasticated cuffs, matching inset waistband, full gathered skirt. Green wool polo-neck sweater and matching tights. Brown leather elastic-sided ankle boots with pointed toes and flat heels.

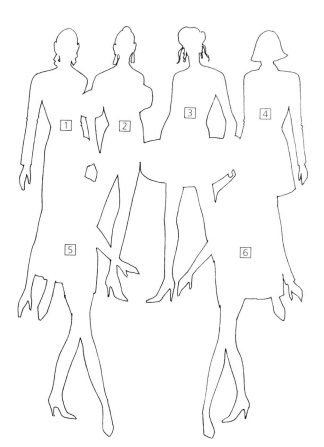

Evening Wear 1985–1990

1 1985. Lilac silk-jersey dinner dress, fitted draped bodice, low curved V-shaped neckline, padded shoulders, long inset sleeves, ankle-length straight skirt with gathered front panel. Hair dressed away from face. Long drop earrings. Satin shoes with almond-shaped toes. 2 1986. Silk-taffeta evening dress, embroidered and beaded fitted bodice, off-the-shoulder-neckline edged with braid, matching elbow-length puff sleeves, draped wrapover mini-length skirt in contrast colour. Hair dressed away from face and into small bun on top of head. Large drop earrings. Long black stretch-satin gloves. Black satin sling-back shoes with pointed toes and high slender heels. 3 1987. Strapless black taffeta evening dress, boned bodice ruched from the neckline to low hipline, black and yellow striped silk skirt arranged into informal ruches. Long hair dressed away from face with long side curls. Long drop earrings. Black satin shoes with cut-away sides, pointed toes and high slender heels. 4 1988. Long white silk fitted jacket, decorated with large geometric patterns embroidered in black sequins, narrow stand collar, wide padded shoulders, long inset sleeves, concealed fastening from waist to hem. Flared ankle-length black silk-jersey skirt. Black satin pumps. 5 1990. Gold all-over stretch sequin mini-length fitted tube dress with narrow wide-set shoulder straps. Jaw-length straight hair, dressed away from face and behind ears. Large gold hoop earrings, gold bead necklace. Gold kid sling-back shoes with pointed toes and high slender heels. 6 1990. Gold stretch-lamé mini-length dress, low asymmetric neckline infilled with black Lycra, long tight inset sleeves. Hair dressed away from face. Large drop earrings. Black satin sling-back shoes with pointed toes and high slender heels.

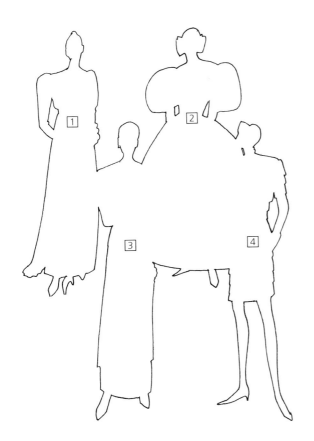

Bridal Wear 1985–1990

[1] 1985. Cream satin bridal gown, straight ankle-length skirt falling from high waist position, waist-length overbodice incorporating long back train, edges trimmed with wide border lace, high waist emphasized with self-fabric band trimmed with long flat bow, wide scooped neckline, long leg-of-mutton-style sleeves. Short bouffant silk-tulle veil gathered into headdress of silk flowers. Satin shoes trimmed with beads. [2] 1986. Ivory silk-taffeta bridal gown, fitted bodice with wide boat-shaped neckline, elbow-length puff sleeves, tight undersleeves to wrists, gathered overskirt dipping from knee-length at front and forming ground-length train at back, straight ankle-length underskirt. Hair dressed away from face and into french pleat at back, covered by large taffeta bow. White satin pumps. [3] 1988. Cream silk-jersey wedding dress, unfitted bloused bodice, boat-shaped neckline, narrow turned-down collar, matching cuffs on short dolman sleeves, sequin motif on padded shoulders, wrapover sequined hip basque, straight ankle-length underskirt, shorter overskirt gathered from under basque. Sequined turban. Long stretch satin gloves. Satin pumps. [4] 1990. Cream silk-crepe mini-length dress, graduated tiered tucks from the off-the-shoulder neckline to the hem, matching the elbow-length sleeves. Unstructured straw hat with wide turned-back brim. Large clip-on earrings, matching choker necklace. Cream satin pumps with low heels.

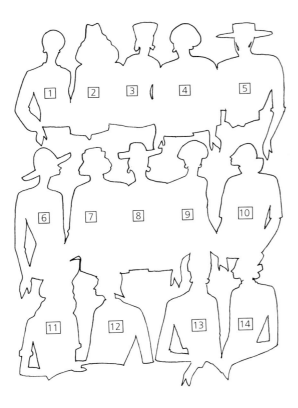

Accessories 1985–1990

[1] 1985. Stitched velvet beret on self-fabric band. Hip-length knitted cotton collarless sweater, padded shoulders, inset sleeves gathered into cuffs. Amber beads and earrings. [2] 1985. Small brimless hat with dented crown. Hip-length knitted cotton sweater, polo-neck collar set into V-shaped neckline, sleeves gathered into cuffs. [3] 1986. Lacquered straw hat with wide upturned brim. Belted wrapover jacket with wide collar. Large clip-on earrings. [4] 1986. Stiffened felt beret. Collarless double-breasted jacket. Large clip-on earrings. [5] 1987. Stiffened felt hat, flat-topped crown, straight brim and chin strap. Waist-length knitted cotton shirt, low round neckline, front button fastening, padded shoulders, three-quarter-length sleeves. [6] 1987. Straw hat, high rounded crown trimmed with deep ribbon band, wide upturned brim, collarless sweater with all-over pattern. [7] 1987. Straw hat with upturned brim. Knitted wool cardigan, long collar, fastening on the waistband, padded shoulders, batwing sleeves, inset cable-stitch bands running from shoulder to waist. [8] 1988. Straw hat with flat-topped crown, wide upturned brim. Knitted edge-to-edge cardigan and short top with V-shaped neckline. Large clip-on earrings. [9] 1988. Beret gathered onto wide band, brooch trim. Black cotton top, low neckline, front-button opening. [10] 1989. Knitted sweater with appliqué birds and leaves. Hair tied back with large bow in nape of neck. Large drop earrings. [11] 1989. Straw hat with upswept brim, braided edge. Waist-length jacket, buttoned-down white cotton revers matching cuffs on short sleeves. [12] 1989. Straw hat, deep crown, narrow turned-down brim. Waist-length knitted cotton top, wide polo-neck collar, silk rose trim. [13] 1990. Draped nylon-fur hat printed with leopard spots. Black knitted-cotton polo-neck sweater. Cotton gloves with nylon-fur cuffs. [14] 1990. Hair dressed into nylon-fur tube and black velvet bow. Short striped cotton top. Bead necklace and earrings.

Yves Saint Laurent 1994

Thierry Mugler 1991

Chanel 1992

Versace 1993

Rifat Ozbek 1997

1991

1992

1995

1993

1997

1993

1991

1997

1993

1995

1994

1994

Day Wear 1991–1994

1991

1994

1993

1991

1992

1994

1995

1997

1997

1996

1997

1995

1991

1993

1996

1992

1995

1997

1991

1992

1994

1996

1997

Dolce & Gabbana 2001

Gucci 2000

Dior 1998

Dolce & Gabbana
2006

Valentino 2005

Armani 1999

Underwear 1998–present day

1998

1999

2000

2000

2003

2005

2003

2006

2000

1999

2005

2005

1998

2000

2006

Day Wear 1998–2001

1998

2000

2001

1998

2000

2001

2003

2002

2004

2005

2005

2005

2006

1998

2002

2006

2003

1999

2001

2006

1998

2001

2006

2006

2000

2005

Accessories 1998–present day

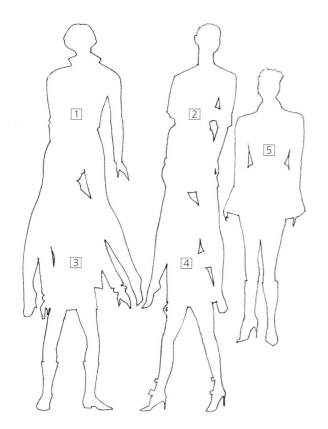

Couture Wear 1991–1997

1 Thierry Mugler 1991. Waist-length silver leather biker jacket, colour-sprayed on padded shoulders and upturned collar, asymmetric front zip fastening, matching slant pockets set into curved side-panel seams, decorative buckled straps above wrapover side seams. Square-neck checked cotton gingham catsuit, tight-fitting legs into ankle boots covered in matching fabric. 2 Yves Saint Laurent 1994. Round-neck black silk-velvet top, long inset sleeves with wide cuffs, worn pushed up to elbow. Contrast-colour silk-satin mini skirt with vertical black silk-velvet pockets set into side-panel seams, matching belt, covered buckle and hemline. Black suede open-toe sandals. 3 Chanel 1992. Hip-length striped wool-tweed edge-to-edge jacket with four button-trimmed patch pockets, shawl collar, edges and seams bound with plain wool braid. Round-neck knitted silk T-shirt. Denim mini skirt with fringed hemline, worn with gilt chain belt, matching jewelry. Coloured tights and calf-length leather biker boots. 4 Versace 1993. Hip-length fitted black wool jacket, fastening under high collar and revers with large gilt buttons, matching decoration on curved side-panel seams and clips on elbow-length slits on tight inset sleeves. Skin-tight ankle-length trousers in matching fabric. Small black suede shoulder bag suspended on gilt chains. Black suede shoes decorated with gilt buttons, buckles and bows, high heels and pointed toes. Large gilt earrings and chunky bracelets. 5 Rifat Ozbek 1997. Single-breasted silver satin fitted jacket with small collar and narrow revers, tight inset wrist-length sleeves, hip-level piped pockets in wide flared skirts. Wrapover mini skirt in matching fabric, side stud fastening on one side above hem. Knee-length silver kid boots with pointed toes and high shaped heels.

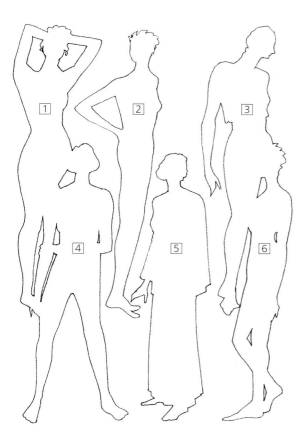

Underwear 1991–1997

1 1991. One-piece elasticated white cotton body, soft shaped cups with embroidered detail, adjustable shoulder straps, low-cut back, double-fabric front panel and high-cut legs. 2 1992. Blue stretch lace and cotton bra, soft shaped lace cups with looped cotton rouleau edging, back and halter straps in plain cotton, back fastening, briefs in matching fabrics and trim, high-cut legs. 3 1995. Unstructured pale green, pink and white knitted cotton cropped vest, low neckline and hem trimmed with wide lace, adjustable shoulder straps, no fastenings, briefs in matching fabric with fine lace trim on waist and on high-cut legs. 4 1993. One-piece fine stretch black lace body, underwired satin cups with lace-edged tops, adjustable buckled satin shoulder straps, high-cut legs with self-lace edges forming narrow frill. 5 1997. Fine white cotton pyjamas with all-over embroidered pattern in pale blue, loose-fitting hip-length jacket fastening with fine self-fabric rouleau loops and pearl buttons, low collarless neckline edged with white satin, matching hems of flared inset sleeves and wide flared full-length trousers. 6 1993. Red bias-cut stretch-fabric body, double-fabric cups with underwiring, wide shoulder straps, low-cut back, high-cut legs.

Leisure Wear 1991–1997

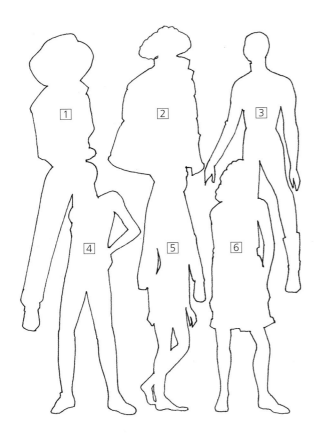

1 1991. All-in-one insulated silver fabric ski overall, large double-layer hood with padded outer edge in contrast colour, underbodice with zip fastening under high collar, overbodice with concealed zip fastening under two decorative buttons, wide inset waistband, full-length sleeves with elasticated cuffs, matching hems of fitted trousers, various zipped pockets, decorative seams with top-stitched detail. Insulated mittens. Short ski boots. 2 1997. Hip-length green nylon jacket with duck-down and feather interlining and blue fleece lining, joined with wide horizontal bands of top-stitching, high stand collar, long sleeves with elasticated cuffs, front zip fastening, side hip-level pockets. Round-neck white knitted cotton T-shirt. Blue and grey checked wool trousers, narrow legs, wide waistband, hip-level pockets. Slip-on casual shoes. 3 1993. Body-hugging one-piece silver stretch-nylon ski suit, two-colour hood, zip fastening from under chin to hip-level, two zipped pockets under contrast-colour yoke, full-length cuffed sleeves, seams and edges bound in contrast colour. Insulated short gloves. Long ski boots. 4 1995. Orange nylon cropped top, double-layer fabric on front bodice, wide band under bust, low neckline and cut-away armholes bound with contrast colour. Blue nylon tracksuit bottoms, narrow legs with stirrups, gathered and elasticated waist band, outer seams bound in contrast colour. Lace-up running shoes. 5 1994. One-piece stretch-fabric bathing costume with round neckline, cut-away armholes and inset stretch-lace panel at waist-level, high-cut legs. 6 1994. Knitted pink cotton cropped top with low V-shaped neck and long sleeves. Denim dungaree-style shorts, bib front with pockets and adjustable shoulder straps, loose-fitting inset waistband, wide legs with turn-ups. Lace-up suede shoes.

Day Wear 1991–1994

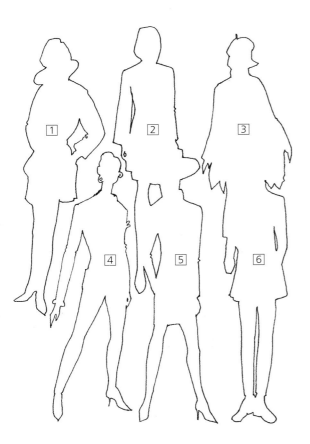

1 1991. Light brown soft leather edge-to-edge coat-dress with waterfall collar reaching to rounded hemline, buckled belt fastening, full-length sleeves with buttoned cuffs, top-stitched detail on seams and edges. Black wool round-neck top and matching mini skirt. Short ankle boots with high heels and pointed toes. 2 1994. Blue wool-crepe overdress, flared from under bust line with centre front slit, wide boat-shaped neckline and full-length flared sleeves. Cream silk underdress with wide shoulder straps and flared skirt. Blue tights. Leather shoes with bar straps and pointed toes. 3 1993. Three-piece knitted cashmere and wool mixture suit, hip-length top with polo neck, straight mid-calf-length skirt, three-quarter-length edge-to-edge loose-fitting jacket with long shawl-effect sleeves. Black wool beret. Black leather lace-up shoes with square toes. 4 1991. Two-piece peach-coloured lightweight wool suit, fitted hip-length double-breasted jacket with draped shawl collar, gilt buttons and long tight sleeves, skin-tight ankle-length trousers. Gilt earrings and bracelets. Leather shoes with high stiletto heels and pointed toes. 5 1992. Blue silk and wool mixture mini-length coat with narrow shawl collar set onto a low neckline, full-length fitted sleeves with button detail on hem, matching double-breasted front fastening, front wrapover edges cut into deep scallops. Fine pink straw hat with wide turned-back brim and deep crown. Leather shoes with high stiletto heels and buckle trim above pointed toes. 6 1994. Two-piece grey and black striped wool trouser suit, single-breasted jacket with high fastening under narrow collar and revers, long fitted sleeves and flared skirts, ankle-length drainpipe trousers. Pink and white striped cotton shirt with stand collar and long tails. Single-breasted blue and red striped velvet waistcoat. Black leather lace-up boots with low heels.

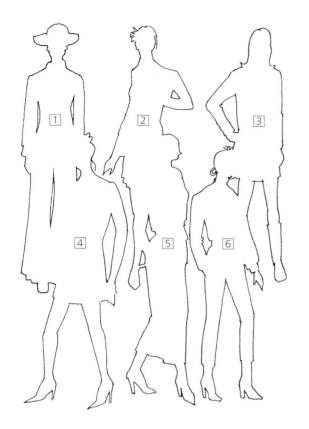

Day Wear 1995–1997

1 1995. Single-breasted collarless cream linen jacket with full-length fitted sleeves, button trim on hem, matching front fastening. Cream linen blouse with front button fastening to under wide collar and revers. Blue and cream patterned silk pyjama-style trousers, gathered from waist. Straw hat with wide up-swept brim and large crown. Sandals with small platform soles.
2 1997. Pale green silk and wool mixture single-breasted fitted jacket with small collar set onto low neckline, three-quarter-length sleeves, button trim on hem, hip-level piped pockets. Gathered patterned silk-chiffon mini skirt. Leather shoes with high heels and pointed toes. 3 1997. Red wool jersey single-breasted two-piece suit, collarless hip-length jacket with step opening and full-length sleeves with four-button trim, flared mini skirt with centre-front inverted pleat worn with a quilted leather belt and black silk T-shirt. Knee-length leather boots. 4 1996. Yellow suede mini dress with zip fastening from below V-shaped neckline to hip-level, with cut-away armholes, pockets set into curve of side-panel seams, top-stitched seams and edges. Yellow suede shoes with high stiletto heels and small bar straps above elongated pointed toes. 5 1997. Grey striped wool flannel two-piece suit, collarless hip-length jacket with buttoned flap-and-patch pockets, short sleeves with button cuff and tab, matching detail at back of neck above centre pleat, inset waist belt, ankle-length straight skirt with back slit to knee-level. Leather shoes with high heels and pointed toes. 6 1995. Two-piece blue checked wool suit, hip-length single-breasted jacket, high button fastening to under high collar, long sleeves gathered into wrist cuffs, fitted mid-calf-length trousers with deep turn-ups. Knitted wool sweater. Sandals with high thick heels and open toes.

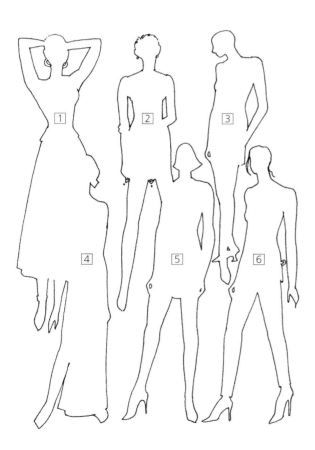

Evening Wear 1991–1997

1 1991. Strapless hip-length boned basque with multi-coloured embroidery and beaded decoration, worn over black velvet spotted cotton voile dress with high round neck, long tight sleeves and mid-calf-length gathered skirt. Black tights. Black suede shoes with wide ankle straps and pointed toes. 2 1993. Mini-length crochet black cotton dress with low neckline, double shoulder straps and fringed hemline. Black leather strap sandals with ankle straps and open toes. 3 1996. Mini-length silk-chiffon dress embroidered all over with silver sequins, low neckline and narrow rouleau shoulder straps, hip-level gilt double-chain belt with large clasp. Kid shoes with high shaped heels and gilt buckle above pointed toes.
4 1992. Full-length white silk-crepe dress with high round neckline, cut-away armholes and low back, semi-fitted bodice and flared skirt with split from ankle to thigh-level on one side. Gold kid sandals with ankle straps and open toes. 5 1995. Two-piece black lace evening outfit with scalloped edges, top cropped to under bust, mounted on flesh-coloured silk, low neckline and narrow shoulder straps decorated with red, orange and gold sequins, mini skirt in matching fabrics. Black leather sling-back shoes with high stiletto heels and narrow bar strap above pointed toes. 6 1997. Hip-length green and blue silk-panne velvet top with broad panel of lace over bust, matching hemline, rouleau shoulder straps and bow tie on one side of hip. Ankle-length skin-tight green stretch-fabric trousers. Black silk strap sandals with high straight heels, ankle straps and open toes.

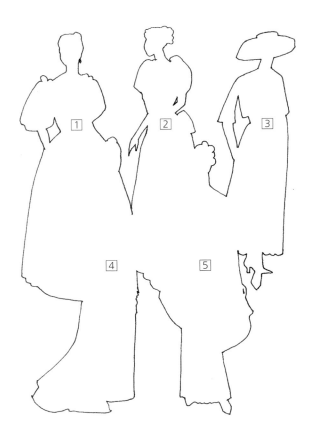

Bridal Wear 1991–1997

1 1991. Cream textured silk dress with fitted boned hip-length bodice cut into shaped panels and deep V-shape on centre front, low neckline with double curve, elbow-length gathered puff sleeves decorated with self-fabric flowers over each shoulder, full-length gathered skirt worn over stiffened petticoats. 2 1992. White silk dress with hip-length fitted bodice cut into shaped panels, self-covered button fastening down centre back from under V-shaped neckline to above large hip-level bow with long tails, decorated with multi-coloured floral embroidery matching heads of full-length leg-of-mutton sleeves, full gathered skirt with long back train. 3 1994. Ankle-length cream lace dress with bloused bodice above cream satin belt, lace and pearl motifs on belt and in centre of square neckline, elbow-length flared sleeves, open over skirt with curved edges, straight underskirt mounted over cream silk, neck and all hems finished with scalloped edge of lace. Large cream silk-covered hat with up-swept brim and large crown with wide pink satin band. White silk shoes with decorated tongue detail and pearl trim above pointed toes. 4 1996. Hip-length fitted and boned red silk-velvet bodice, cut in shaped panels with low sweetheart neckline and tight full-length sleeves. Full-length heavy cream silk-satin skirt, draped across front and over hips to form long, full back train. 5 1997. White pleated silk two-tier dress with off-the-shoulder neckline above two wide shoulder straps, semi-fitted knee-length bodice bloused over full-length skirt. White silk flower hair decoration. White silk shoes with pearl trim above pointed toes.

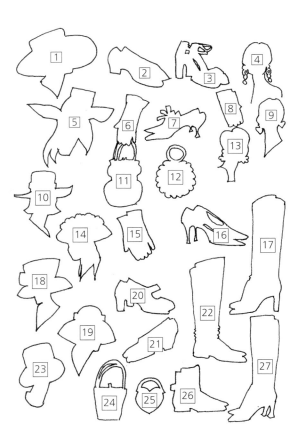

Accessories 1991–1997

1 1991. Felt hat, up-swept brim, flat-topped crown. 2 1991. Leather shoes, squat heels, low vamp, round toes. 3 1995. Suede shoes, open sides, ankle straps, straight high heels, cut-out detail, round toes. 4 1992. Shoulder-length pendant earrings set with coloured stones. 5 1992. Patterned stiff cotton hat, up-swept brim, tall crown. 6 1996. Leather gloves with quilted cuffs. 7 1993. Leather shoes, ribbon laces, stiletto heels, pointed toes. 8 1993. Leather gloves with square gilt stud trim. 9 1992. Pendant heart-shaped gilt earrings set with coloured stones. 10 1993. Leather hat, brim swept up on one side, tall crown, buckled band. 11 1995. Leather bag, mock buckled belt detail, rouleau handles. 12 1996. Knitted raffia bag, sequin trim, round handle. 13 1994. Clip-on pendant earrings set with coloured stones. 14 1995. Straw hat, wide turned-down brim, crown of silk roses. 15 1997. Leather gloves with mock zip fastenings. 16 1996. Coloured patent leather shoes, open sides, gold kid trim, stiletto heels, pointed toes. 17 1997. Knee-length leather boots, embroidered sides, high straight heels, pointed toes. 18 1994. Straw hat, turned-down brim, open turned-up crown, self-fabric bow trim on front. 19 1991. Straw hat, turned-down brim, small crown, stand-up band and gilt chain trim. 20 1997. Two-tone leather shoes, buckled bar strap, thick heels, round toes. 21 1996. Coloured patent leather shoes, flared heels, strap and buckle trim above round toes. 22 1996. Knee-length leather boots, ankle-level ruched detail, flat heels, pointed toes. 23 1996. Fabric hat, wide brim, fake fur lining, tall crown. 24 1995. Straw bucket-shaped bag with lid and two handles. 25 1996. Leather heart-shaped bag with gilt clasp. 26 1996. Leather ankle boots, buckled strap fastening, flat heels, round toes. 27 1994. Knee-length suede boots, high shaped heels and pointed toes.

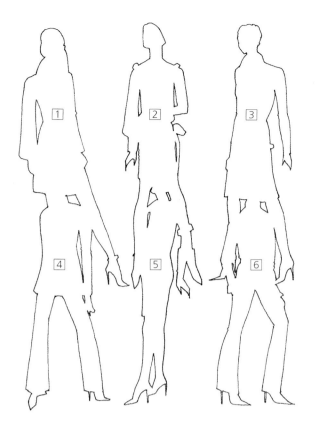

Couture Wear 1998–present day

1 Gucci 2000. Mini-length semi-fitted one-piece silk shift dress with an outsized 1970s geometric pattern, high round neckline, long sleeves gathered at wrist, headscarf in matching fabric. Leather shoes with ankle straps, high spike heels and elongated pointed toes. 2 Dolce & Gabbana 2001. Silk top gathered onto hip-level band with side bow fastening, V-shaped neckline, single sleeve gathered into wide wrist band, padded epaulettes on both shoulders in contrast colour, matching knee-length skirt with centre-front ruched seam. Lace fingerless gloves. Leather ankle boots with side-button fastening and pointed toes. 3 Dior 1998. Fine wool two-piece suit, fitted hip-length jacket with long sleeves, concealed fastening and wide shawl collar with edges fringed in contrast colour, matching edge of side split on knee-length skirt, knife pleats on opposite side. Leather shoes with high spike heels and elongated pointed toes. 4 Armani 1999. Two-piece fine wool jersey trouser suit, hip-length semi-fitted jacket with diagonal opening between button fastenings on shoulder and waist, long tight sleeves, wide trousers. Leather shoes with high spike heels and pointed toes. 5 Dolce & Gabbana 2006. Tight-fitting mini-length lace dress with python-skin front strap and button fastening, matching buckled belt and carriers, buttoned sleeve straps and buttoned flap-and-patch pockets. Long leather gloves. Python-skin shoes with ankle straps, high spike heels and open toes. 6 Valentino 2005. Satin blouse with long bow tie under wide collar, frilled edges to strap opening, long sleeves with wide frill on cuffs. Sleeveless double-breasted corded velvet waistcoat. Flared striped wool trousers with button trim on hip-level pockets, worn with leather hip-level belt. Leather boots with high spike heels and elongated pointed toes.

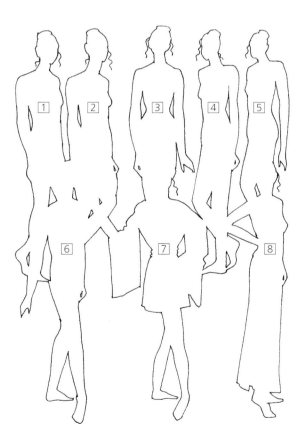

Underwear 1998–present day

1 1998. Pink elasticated fabric bra, underwired cups trimmed with lace, matching edges of adjustable shoulder straps and side edges and front of low-cut briefs. 2 1999. One-piece cream elasticated body with elasticated lace cups and side-front gussets above high-cut legs, adjustable shoulder straps, low-cut back. 3 2000. One-piece pink lace body incorporating contrast-colour bra with adjustable shoulder straps and linked suspenders, matching briefs with high-cut legs. 4 2000. Black elasticated fine mesh bra with underwired cups, adjustable shoulder straps and solid black appliqué foliate trim, matching briefs with high-cut legs. 5 2003. One-piece black elasticated fine-mesh body, solid black stretch-fabric underwired cups with straight-across neckline, matching shoulder straps, panel seams and edges of high-cut legs. 6 2005. Waist-length red stretch-satin corset with underwired, padded and black lace-trimmed cups, black satin adjustable shoulder straps, panel seams, sham front-laced fastening and suspenders, briefs with high-cut legs in matching fabrics. Black nylon stockings with lace tops. 7 2003. Thigh-length floral-patterned silk-satin kimono-style dressing gown, wrapover front with self-fabric tie belt, inside edges of hanging sleeves and neckline faced with plain contrast-colour silk satin. 8 2006. Ankle-length bias-cut silk-satin nightdress with edges of low neckline front and back piped with self-fabric, side-front lace panels inset at bust level, matching trim on knee-length slashed side seams.

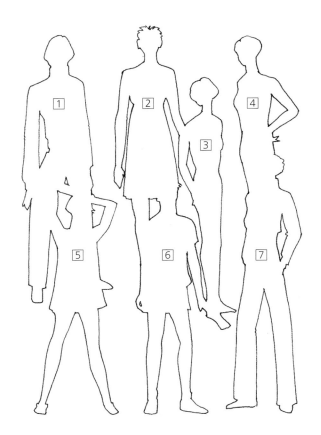

Leisure Wear 1998–present day

1 2000. Two-piece checked wool golfing trouser suit, single-breasted collarless cropped jacket with inset suede sleeves, matching covered buttons, waist band and edging trim, straight-cut trousers with piped pockets and self-fabric hip-level buckled belt. Polo-neck sweater. Lace-up leather golf shoes with flat heels. 2 1999. Mini-length three-colour knitted cotton tennis dress with low round neckline and narrow rouleau shoulder straps. Knitted cotton ankle socks and lace-up tennis shoes. 3 2005. Orange stretch-fabric bathing suit, backless bra top with narrow rouleau halter straps joined at side waist to thong in matching fabric. 4 2005. Green stretch-fabric bikini, crossover bra top with narrow rouleau halter and back fastenings, briefs in matching fabrics with narrow rouleau sides. 5 1998. Semi-fitted cotton sundress with multi-coloured 1970s-style print, underwired bra top with narrow rouleau shoulder straps and mini-length flared skirt. Brightly coloured plastic flip-flop sandals with daisy trim on toe posts. 6 2000. Two-piece white tennis outfit, semi-fitted hip-length knitted cotton top with V-shaped neckline and attached collar banded in contrast colour, matching short sleeves and trim on wrapover woven mini skirt. Knitted cotton ankle socks and lace-up tennis shoes with flat heels. 7 2006. Brushed cotton cropped jacket with zip fastening under high stand collar, raglan-style sleeves gathered into wrist cuffs, seams and edges decorated with top-stitching. Brushed cotton hipster trousers with adjustable drawstring band, piped side hip pockets and flared hems. Lace-up leather sports shoes with flat heels.

Day Wear 1998–2001

1 1998. Double-breasted ankle-length leather coat with large faux fur collar to waist-level, matching deep cuffs on long inset sleeves, hip-level flap pockets, top-stitched edges and seams. Leather boots with elongated pointed toes and high spike heels. 2 2000. Double-breasted knee-length denim coat with high collar and wide revers, top-stitched shaped yoke, matching buttoned decorative straps above wrist-level on long inset sleeves and vertical pockets set into panel seams. Straight-cut trousers in matching denim. Knitted wool sweater with high round neckline and long sleeves. Faux leopard-skin ankle boots with elongated pointed toes. 3 2001. Sleeveless knitted cotton cropped top with high round neckline. Knee-length denim skirt gathered under pin-tucked hip yoke with padded and quilted hemline. Wide leather hip belt with large decorative metal eyelets. Wide plastic bangle. Mesh tights. Denim ankle boots with side zip fastenings, elongated pointed toes with patent leather toecap, matching high spike heels. 4 1998. Semi-fitted ankle-length knitted wool sweater dress with low V-shaped neckline and long inset sleeves. Dark tights. Slip-on leather shoes with high tongues, pointed toes and low heels. 5 2000. Fine wool semi-fitted dress with draped polo neck, full-length inset sleeves gathered into a band, mini-length skirt ruched up on one side. Pale-coloured tights. Leather shoes with decorative diagonal straps, pointed toes and high spike heels. 6 2001. Knitted cotton fitted cropped top with high polo neck, single inset full-length sleeve on one side and cut-away armhole on the other. Straight-cut leather hipster trousers worn with wide leather belt, matching peaked cap, fingerless gloves and boots with elongated pointed toes and high spike heels.

Day Wear 2002–present day

1 2003. Lace-trimmed silk-satin bra worn over silk T-shirt with high round neck. Fitted waist-length cashmere cardigan with rouleau tie fastening, long sleeves with frilled cuffs, matching edges of neck and hemline. Transparent silk mesh knee-length skirt with fluted hem, worn over shorter silk underskirt. Leather hip belt with metal ring fastening. Leather shoes with ankle straps, open toes and platform soles. 2 2002. Fitted leather dress with side zip fastening from top of stand collar to hem of quilted mini skirt, raglan sleeves with zips from wrists to below elbow-level, top-stitched edges and seams. Knee-length leather boots with elongated pointed toes. 3 2004. Collarless knee-length knitted wool coat, edge-to-edge fastening with single loop and button, long sleeves and hip-level patch pockets. Knitted wool sweater with outsized polo collar and long sleeves. Mid-calf-length wool trousers. Knee-length suede boots with thick heels and pointed toes. 4 2005. Collarless patterned silk-crepe dress with short puff sleeves and ruched bodice above open midriff, matching ruched detail on front hipline of mid-calf-length skirt under narrow belt and clasp. Plastic necklace-collar. Shoes with wide crossed straps and blunt toes. 5 2005. Collarless denim jacket with large flap-and-patch pockets, long sleeves with stitched cuffs and single-breasted stud fastening, top-stitched edges and seams. Silk blouse with single-breasted strap opening and ruffle trim. Three-tier two-pattern silk hipster mini skirt worn with buckled leather belt. Leather mules with open toes, platform soles and high stacked heels. 6 2006. Cotton petticoat-dress with narrow shoulder straps, tiered skirt gathered from under bust, self-covered button trim on centre front, worn over patterned wool sweater with high neck and three-quarter-length sleeves. Boots with buckled straps on side at knee-level, blunt toes with toe caps and matching bar straps, platform soles and high thick heels.

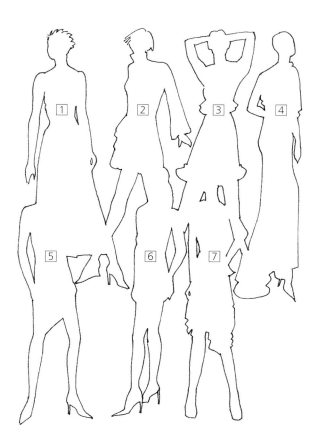

Evening Wear 1998–present day

1 1998. Ankle-length silk-crepe dress with all-over silver sequin embroidery, low draped neckline from narrow rouleau shoulder straps, flared skirt split on centre front from hem to mid-thigh. Knee-length satin boots with pointed toes and high spike heels. 2 2002. Unlined lace dress with high scalloped neckline, matching hems of long flared sleeves and mini-length skirt, worn over matching silk bra and briefs. Two-tone kid shoes with ankle straps, pointed toes and high wedge heels. 3 2006. Two-piece printed silk outfit, strapless top with wired cups and boned rib-length bodice, front fastening with self-covered buttons, edges frilled with lace-edged embroidered transparent silk, matching hem of flared mini-length skirt. 4 2003. Ankle-length bias-cut satin dress with short back train, low-cut back neckline with draped cowl over one shoulder, forming open-sleeve effect, narrow rouleau shoulder strap on opposite side, side button fastening to hip-level. Satin shoes with ankle straps, pointed toes and high spike heels. 5 1999. Sleeveless silk-crepe dress with asymmetric neckline embroidered on one side with large sequined star and radiating beams, matching motif on opposite side hip, short skirt with open hemline curved diagonally from mid-thigh to knee-level. Gold kid shoes with narrow bar straps, pointed toes and high spike heels. 6 2001. Leather bondage dress with all-over punched hole decoration, sleeveless bodice comprising interwoven crossed straps above open midriff, tight-fitting mini-length skirt. Leather shoes with ankle straps, elongated pointed toes and high spike heels. 7 2006. Chiffon dress with boned bodice open to waist on centre front, asymmetric drapery over one shoulder, matching layered multi-coloured skirts with uneven hemlines. Gold kid shoes with crossed straps, open toes and high platform soles.

Bridal Wear 1998–present day

1 1998. Strapless silk-satin princess-line dress with long back train, short transparent silk overblouse with off-the-shoulder neckline and short sleeves, hems fringed with pearl and crystal droplets, matching tiara headdress. 2 2001. Hip-length boned satin basque with self-fabric frills on edges of neck and hem, single shoulder strap trimmed with loops of ribbon and pearl strands. Ankle-length leather drainpipe trousers. Leather sandals with T-straps and blunt toes. 3 2006. Full-length silk dress with fitted hip-length bodice, single brightly coloured silk flower on centre front of low curved neckline, narrow rouleau shoulder straps, edges of bodice frilled with lace-trimmed self fabric, matching horizontal bands of trimming on flared skirt. 4 2005. Bias-cut silk-crepe dress with low back in-filled with a sequin-embroidered butterfly and draped with a cowl of silk chiffon matching trailing wings from each shoulder to hip-level, skirt cut in shaped panels from under curved hip yoke, long back train. Pearl and diamante butterfly hair ornament. 5 2000. Cotton-satin basque with low square neckline, short sleeves and centre-front zip fastening, ankle-length cotton broderie anglaise skirt cut into wide shaped panels. Diamante hair clips. Satin shoes with ankle straps, elongated pointed toes and high spike heels. 6 2006. Silk-chiffon dress, draped bodice criss-crossed from under bust to low hip-level with pearl and crystal-embroidered ribbon, matching shoulder straps above low curved neckline, layered pleated skirt. Fresh flower headdress, matching bouquet.

Accessories 1998–present day

1 1998. Felt hat, wide brim, tall crown, wool boa. 2 1999. Trilby hat, wide brim, tall crown, petersham band, wool scarf with fringed hem. 3 2000. Leather glove, ruched detail, button trim. 4 2000. Leather glove, punched holes under keyhole, strap and stud fastening. 5 2000. Denim shoulder bag with plastic clasp fastening. 6 2001. Denim peaked cap, brooch and badge trim, glitter scarf with fringed hem. 7 2003. Transparent plastic belt with punched hole pattern. 8 1998. Faux leopard-skin hat. 9 1999. Shiny plastic beret. 10 1998. Leather bag with double handles and shoulder strap. 11 2000. Knee-length two-tone leather boot, spike heel, pointed toe. 12 2000. Short suede boot, ruched side detail, stacked heel. 13 2001. Leather shoe, bar strap, thick heel, open-work detail above blunt toe. 14 2002. Embroidered shoe, kitten heel, pointed toe. 15 1998. Leather shoe, bar strap, combined sole and heel, blunt toe. 16 1999. Leather mule with jewelled bar straps. 17 2000. Leather ankle boot, high heel, pointed toe. 18 2002. Leather shoe, spike heel, elongated pointed toe. 19 2004. Leather mule, open toe, rope-covered wedge heel. 20 2003. Faux dalmatian-skin shoe, leather trim, matching kitten heel. 21 1998. Leather shoe, bar strap, elongated pointed toe. 22 1999. Beaded bag. 23 1999. Leather mule, cork sole and heel, blunt toe. 24 2000. Faux zebra-skin shoulder bag. 25 2003. Knee-length leather boot, bead trim, low heel, blunt toe. 26 2004. Short leather boot, fringed cuff, low heel, blunt toe. 27 1999. Leather shoe, ankle strap, spike heel, pointed toe. 28 1998. Ridged plastic bag with integral handle. 29 2000. Woven raffia bag with integral handle. 30 2001. Plastic belt. 31 2005. Leather mule, strap and buckle trim, thick high heel, platform sole. 32 2006. Leather bag, two handles, appliqué trim. 33 2000. High leather boot, side lacing, spike heel, pointed toe. 34 2001. Two-tone leather boot, spike heel, pointed toe. 35 2000. Leather clutch bag with appliqué suede flower trim. 36 2000. Leather sling-back shoe, squat heel, pointed toe, bow trim. 37 2001. Leather belt with silver clasp fastening. 38 2006. Belt with guitar-shaped buckle. 39 2005. Beaded bag. 40 2006. Knitted silk hat, silk scarf with bobble trim. 41 2006. Leather shoe, high heel, open sides and toe.

Chart of the Development of 20th-Century Fashion

1900   1904

Silhouette	S-shaped outline, small waist, flared skirt.
Bodice	Tight, worn over a boned corset, back fastening.
Neckline	High stand collars, low necklines infilled with lace.
Sleeves	Long tight inset, three-quarter-length, bishop-style.
Skirt	Ground-length, flared, fitted over hips, flat front, back train.
Fabric	Wool, serge, broadcloth, linen, cotton, silk.
Trimmings	Braid, ribbon, embroidered covered buttons, bows, tucks, flounces.
Colour	Dark muted, pale natural.
Accessories	Large hats, tight-fitting gloves, silk stockings, boots and shoes with pointed toes and louis heels, parasols.

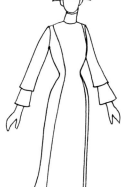

1905   1909

Silhouette	Shapely, high bust, waist higher towards 1909, flared skirt.
Bodice	Tight, worn over boned corset, front or back fastening.
Neckline	High stand collars, lace infills, some lower necklines.
Sleeves	Long, three-quarter-length, elbow-length with tight undersleeves.
Skirt	Ground-length, flared, fitted over hips, small train.
Fabric	Wool, linen, silk, cotton, lace.
Trimmings	Braid, ribbon, buttons, buckles, tassels, fringing.
Colour	Pale, subdued.
Accessories	Large hats, long gloves, small bags, silk stockings, shoes with pointed toes and louis heels.

1910   1914

Silhouette	Shapely, high round bust, high waist, narrow skirt.
Bodice	Fitted, worn over long-line corset, front or back fastening.
Neckline	High round, boat-shaped, square, neat collars.
Sleeves	Inset, long fitted, three-quarter-length, short dolman.
Skirt	Ankle-length, narrow, slightly flared, fitted hips.
Fabric	Linen, wool, silk, mixtures.
Trimmings	Braid, ribbon, embroidery, beading.
Colour	Subtle, pale, natural, bold combinations of light and dark.
Accessories	Large hats, some smaller hats, long gloves, small bags, silk stockings; shoes with pointed toes, bar straps and low louis heels; parasols, long-handled umbrellas.

1915   1919

Silhouette	Slim, high round bust, high waist, narrow skirt.
Bodice	Fitted, worn over long-line corset.
Neckline	High round, boat-shaped, square.
Sleeves	Long fitted, short dolman.
Skirt	Ankle-length, narrow; shorter from 1917.
Fabric	Silk, wool, crepe-de-chine, silk georgette, silk jersey.
Trimmings	Braid, ribbon, fur, monkey fur, fringing, embroidery, beading.
Colour	Bright, unusual colour combinations.
Accessories	Large hats with wide brims and crowns, muffs, long gloves, bags, silk stockings; shoes with pointed toes, bar straps and low louis heels; large parasols, long-handled umbrellas.

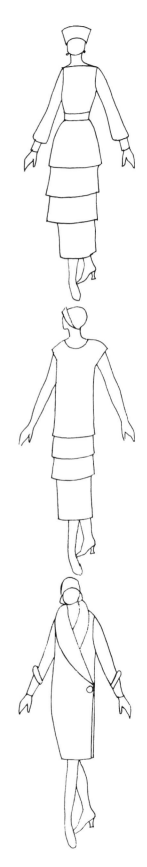

1920   1924

Silhouette	Elongated, shapeless, lower waistline, shorter skirt.
Bodice	Unfitted tube to low waist, over unboned corset.
Neckline	Various V-shapes, boat-shaped, low round.
Sleeves	Kimono, raglan, dolman, long inset gathered into cuffs.
Skirt	Ankle-, mid-calf- and below knee-length; straight, flared.
Fabric	Silk and wool jersey, crepe-de-chine, silk georgette.
Trimmings	Fur, embroidered ribbon, beaded and sequined embroidery.
Colour	Bright, emerald green, acid yellow, royal blue, purple, or pale and natural.
Accessories	Large hats with drooping brims, brimless cloches, short gloves, small bags with chain handles, lightweight shoes.

1925   1929

Silhouette	Long, shapeless, low waist, no bust, short skirt.
Bodice	Unfitted tube to hip-level.
Neckline	V-shaped, low round, cowl.
Sleeves	Kimono, raglan, dolman, some sleeveless models.
Skirt	From 1925: just below the knee; from 1929: longer or uneven hems, handkerchief points.
Fabric	Silk and wool jersey, crepe-de-chine, silk georgette, satin.
Trimmings	Fur, monkey fur, large buttons, all-over sequin embroidery.
Colour	Bright, pure, pale, subdued, dramatic combinations.
Accessories	Cloche hats, small bags, clutch bags, long glass bead necklaces and earrings, silk stockings, lightweight shoes.

1930 — 1934

Silhouette	Slim, narrow, longer skirts, natural waist; from 1933: wider shoulders.
Bodice	Semi-fitted, bias-cut, narrow belts.
Neckline	Low, cut away from neck, ties and scarves popular.
Sleeves	Inset, long fitted, bias-cut, inset panels, flared cuffs.
Skirt	Slim, clinging, intricate seaming, bias-cut; from 1934: mid-calf-length.
Fabrics	Silk and wool crepe, silk georgette, satin, panne velvet, organdie.
Trimmings	Top-stitching, contrast fabric insertions, large buttons.
Colour	Two-tone: black and white, brown and cream, navy and white.
Accessories	Small hats worn at an angle, gauntlet gloves, clutch bags, silk stockings, shoes with high heels.

1935 — 1939

Silhouette	Slender, small hips, natural waist, wide shoulders.
Bodice	Semi-fitted, natural waist, padded shoulders.
Neckline	High round, small neat collars, shoulderwide collars.
Sleeves	Long inset, short puff.
Skirt	Flared, straight with inverted pleat; from 1939: knee-length.
Fabric	Silk georgette, lightweight linen and wool, wool tweed.
Trimmings	Saddle stitching, contrast colour collars and cuffs, lace collars and cuffs.
Colour	Dark cream, mustard, grey, navy blue, brown, black.
Accessories	Small mannish hats, gauntlet gloves, clutch bags, shoulder bags, two-tone shoes with high thick heels.

1940 — 1944

Silhouette	Square shoulders, short skirts, heavy shoes.
Bodice	Fitted, with drapery, ruching or gathers; padded shoulders.
Neckline	High round, sweetheart, small collars.
Sleeves	Inset, short or long, puff.
Skirt	Knee-length, flared, straight, single pleats.
Fabric	Wool, cotton, linen, easy-care synthetics.
Trimmings	Limited buttons, contrast colour collars and cuffs, patch pockets.
Colour	Subdued, blue grey, bottle green, donkey brown.
Accessories	Tiny hats, large bags, shoes with high thick heels and some wooden soles.

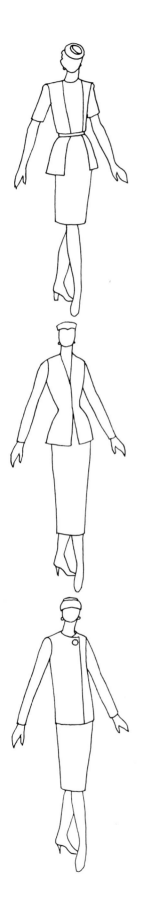

1945

<table>
<tr><td>Silhouette</td><td>As previous period to 1946; then shapely rounded bust, small waist, rounded shoulderline; from 1947: long narrow or full skirts.</td></tr>
<tr><td>Bodice</td><td>As previous period to 1946; from 1947: fitted small waist, sloping shoulders.</td></tr>
<tr><td>Neckline</td><td>High round, sweetheart; from 1947: grown-on collars.</td></tr>
<tr><td>Sleeves</td><td>As previous period to 1946; from 1947: dolman, raglan.</td></tr>
<tr><td>Skirt</td><td>Knee-length to 1946; from 1947: mid-calf and longer.</td></tr>
<tr><td>Fabric</td><td>As previous period to 1946; from 1947: silk taffeta, cotton, linen.</td></tr>
<tr><td>Trimmings</td><td>As previous period to 1946; from 1947: decorative buttons, piping, inset panels of contrast colour or fabric.</td></tr>
<tr><td>Colour</td><td>As previous period to 1946: from 1947: pale, pretty colours with white accessories.</td></tr>
<tr><td>Accessories</td><td>As previous period to 1946; from 1947: small hats, short gloves, small bags, costume jewelry, nylon stockings, shoes with high slender heels.</td></tr>
</table>

1950   1949

1950   1954

<table>
<tr><td>Silhouette</td><td>Curvacious, feminine, full bust, small waist, long skirt.</td></tr>
<tr><td>Bodice</td><td>Tight, fitted over lightly boned corset or waist cincher.</td></tr>
<tr><td>Neckline</td><td>Various V-shaped, boat-shaped, detachable collars.</td></tr>
<tr><td>Sleeves</td><td>Three-quarter-length dolman, raglan popular.</td></tr>
<tr><td>Skirt</td><td>Mid-calf-length, gathered, narrow.</td></tr>
<tr><td>Fabric</td><td>Fine wool, cotton, taffeta, nylon.</td></tr>
<tr><td>Trimmings</td><td>Outsized buttons on coats and suits.</td></tr>
<tr><td>Colour</td><td>Rich natural tones, some bright colours for evening.</td></tr>
<tr><td>Accessories</td><td>Small hats, long gloves, large bags, costume jewelry, nylon stockings, shoes with high slender heels.</td></tr>
</table>

1955   1959

<table>
<tr><td>Silhouette</td><td>Shapely, long, feminine, becoming straighter and shorter.</td></tr>
<tr><td>Bodice</td><td>Fitted, semi-fitted.</td></tr>
<tr><td>Neckline</td><td>High round, boat-shaped, collars standing away from neck.</td></tr>
<tr><td>Sleeves</td><td>Raglan, dolman, kimono; from 1956: some inset.</td></tr>
<tr><td>Skirt</td><td>Mid-calf-length, gathered, straight, pleated; from 1956: some flared.</td></tr>
<tr><td>Fabric</td><td>Cotton, wool, linen, rayon.</td></tr>
<tr><td>Trimmings</td><td>Braid, binding, leather buttons and trim.</td></tr>
<tr><td>Colour</td><td>Natural dye tones, subtle colours, sage green, burnt orange.</td></tr>
<tr><td>Accessories</td><td>Large pillboxes, short gloves, large bags, shoes with stiletto heels and pointed toes.</td></tr>
</table>

1960   1964

Silhouette	Easy, shift shape, shorter skirt.
Bodice	Semi-fitted, often cut in one with skirt (princess line).
Neckline	Low round, round, slashed, boat-shaped.
Sleeves	Inset, long or short, sleeveless popular.
Skirt	Straight, pleated, flared; rise to knee-length by 1964.
Fabric	Wool tweed, stiff cotton, linen mixed with rayon.
Trimmings	Braid, leather and suede, coloured top-stitching.
Colour	Subtle, often teamed with black.
Accessories	Large pillbox hats, short gloves, large bags, nylon tights, shoes with pointed toes and low stiletto heels.

1965   1969

Silhouette	Unfitted, flared shape, short to mini-length skirts.
Bodice	Semi-fitted creating flat chest.
Neckline	Round, cut away from the neck, collars set wide apart.
Sleeves	Inset, long or short, elbow-length with bias-cut frills.
Skirt	Short, mid-thigh-length (mini); from 1967: some ankle-length (maxi) coats over mini skirts.
Fabric	Wool, cotton or linen mixtures with man-made fabrics.
Trimmings	Braid, leather, top-stitching.
Colour	Clear, natural tones often teamed with bright colours or black.
Accessories	Berets, shoulder bags, shoes with round or square toes and low thick heels.

1970   1974

Silhouette	Flared mid-thigh-length (mini) or frilly ankle-length (maxi).
Bodice	Semi-fitted; from 1973: more fitted.
Neckline	Low round, V-shaped, polo necks popular.
Sleeves	Inset, shirt, short circular-cut.
Skirt	Mid-thigh-length (mini), knee-length to 1973, mid-calf-length (midi) and ankle-length.
Fabric	As previous period to 1973, some use of old and antique fabrics.
Trimmings	Braid, leather, top-stitching; from 1972: braid, ribbons, beads, feathers and fringing.
Colour	Bright, clear, pattern on pattern.
Accessories	Berets, shoulder bags, nylon tights, boots and shoes with high thick heels and platform soles.

1975 — 1979

Silhouette	Tall, slim, narrow shoulders, long and short skirts, heavy shoes.
Bodice	Fitted clinging, bloused full, natural waist; from 1976: widening shoulders.
Neckline	Shirt collars with long points, V-shaped necklines on blouses and sweaters.
Sleeves	Inset; long, short and sleeveless; some shoulder pads.
Skirt	Various lengths to 1977, knee-length popular to 1979.
Fabric	Wool jersey, printed washable synthetics, panne velvet.
Trimmings	Top-stitching, leather binding, piping, braid, ribbon.
Colour	Bright, clear, often teamed with black.
Accessories	Pull-on hats, peaked caps, shoulder bags, shoes and knee-length boots with high thick heels.

1980 — 1984

Silhouette	Mid-thigh-length (mini) skirts, tailored jackets with wide shoulders.
Bodice	Fitted, square shoulders.
Neckline	Low round, slashed, boat-shaped, tailored collars and revers.
Sleeves	Inset, dolman, raglan, kimono; all worn with pads.
Skirt	Short clinging mid-thigh-length (mini), some mid-calf-length (maxi).
Fabric	Wool and silk jersey, Lycra, fine cotton lawn.
Trimmings	Embroidery and appliqué.
Colour	Bright, vibrant, clashing colour schemes.
Accessories	Pull-on hats, berets, boaters, shoes with stiletto heels and pointed toes, flat pumps.

1985 — 1990

Silhouette	Wide padded shoulders, mid-thigh-length and shorter skirts.
Bodice	Fitted, body-hugging, no foundation garment.
Neckline	High round, slashed, deep V-shaped, tailored collars.
Sleeves	Inset, raglan, dolman, kimono; all worn with pads.
Skirt	Various, knee-length to upper-thigh-length, tight, clinging.
Fabric	Wool and silk jersey, Lycra, stretch satin, stretch velvet, linen.
Trimmings	Appliqué embroidery, beading, top-stitching, quilting.
Colour	Bright, electric, off-beat combinations.
Accessories	Pull-on hats, outsized jewelry, shoes with stiletto heels and pointed toes, flat pumps, ankle boots.

1991

Silhouette	Narrow shoulders, lean shape, short and long skirts, drainpipe trousers, very high heels.
Bodice	Fitted close to body, emphasis on bust, double-breasted fastenings.
Neckline	Low V-shaped, high round, shawl collars on jackets and coats.
Sleeves	Long, inset; no pads.
Skirt	Mini-length, ankle-length, figure-hugging.
Fabric	Woven and knitted wool, silk and cotton, stretch fabrics.
Trimmings	Machine embroidery, contrast-colour binding.
Colour	Clear, bright and shiny; subdued and muted; black, grey and navy blue.
Accessories	Knee-length boots and shoes with high spike heels and elongated pointed toes, small shoulder bags, chunky gilt jewelry.

1994

1995

Silhouette	Slender lean shape, narrow shoulders, long fitted jackets, bare midriffs, tight trousers, very high heels.
Bodice	Cropped tops, clinging, figure-hugging, sleeveless, cut-away armholes.
Neckline	High round or slashed.
Sleeves	Inset, long, tight.
Skirt	Mini-length and figure-hugging, gathered with hip yokes.
Fabric	Wool, man-made, transparent, various stretch fabrics.
Trimmings	Machine embroidery, top-stitching, faux fur.
Colour	Bright and clear; black, dark blue, dark brown and grey.
Accessories	Denim hats, peaked leather caps, shoes and ankle boots with pointed toes and high spike heels, hip belts, tiny shoulder bags.

2000

2001

Silhouette	Slender, curvaceous (especially evening wear), narrow shoulders and hips, layered, very high heels.
Bodice	Fitted, body-hugging, cropped tops, emphasis on bust.
Neckline	Very low or high round.
Sleeves	Long or short, long pushed up to elbow, frilled or buttoned cuffs.
Skirt	Various, mini-, knee- and ankle-length or multi-fabric in gathered tiers from hip yoke.
Fabric	Knitted wool silk and cotton, denim, faux fur, leather, various stretch fabrics.
Trimmings	Top-stitching, quilting, braid, leather and suede bindings, faux fur.
Colour	Bright, sharp, contrasting; black, dark blue, brown and grey.
Accessories	Shoes and boots with high spike heels and pointed toes or thick heels and platform soles, large bags, beaded bags, wool boas, long scarves.

Present Day

Concise Biographies of Couturiers and Designers

Amies, (Sir) Hardy (Edwin) 1909–2003 Born London, England. Amies began his fashion career at the firm of Lachasse, which he joined in 1934. In 1946 he opened his own house, specializing in classically tailored suits and dresses in tweed and wool. He was appointed dressmaker to the Queen in 1955. From the 1960s Amies was well known as a menswear designer.

Armani, Giorgio 1935– Born Piacenza, Italy. After working as a window dresser at the Milanese department store La Rinascente, Armani joined Cerruti in the early 1960s as a menswear designer. In the 1970s he worked as a freelance fashion consultant before establishing his own company in 1975. Armani is best known for his fine, uncluttered, tailored clothes for both men and women.

Balenciaga, Cristobal 1895–1972 Born Guetaria, Spain. Balenciaga learned dressmaking as a teenager and eventually owned three tailoring shops, in Madrid, Barcelona and San Sebastian. He moved to Paris in 1937, during the Spanish Civil War, and opened a couture house on avenue Georges V. The house closed in 1968. Balenciaga is best known for his severe, dramatic designs and for the purity and perfection of their construction.

Bates, John 1935– Born Northumberland, England. In the early 1950s, Bates joined the design team of Herbert Siddon in London. He later worked as a freelance fashion illustrator. In 1961 he joined the company Jean Varon, which became known for its young, daring designs, including London's skimpiest mini-dress. (It was for Jean Varon that Bates created the outfit on p. 185). In 1980 he opened under his own name. Bates is best known for glamorous evening wear and uncluttered day wear.

Beene, Geoffrey 1927–2004 Born Louisiana, USA. Beene studied at the Traphagen School of Fashion, New York, and at the Ecole de la Chambre Syndicale de la Haute Couture and the Académie Julian in Paris. From 1948 to 1958, he worked as a designer for several ready-to-wear companies, including Teal Traina. In 1963 he set up his own company on Seventh Avenue, New York. He designed for both men and women and was renowned for his superb craftsmanship and careful attention to detail.

Bergdorf Goodman New York department store specializing in ready-to-wear, Paris-inspired high fashion.

Callot Soeurs Couture house which began in Paris in 1895 as a shop selling ribbons and lingerie. It was set up by three sisters: Marie Callot Gerber, Marthe Callot Bertrand and Regina Callot Chantrelle. The eldest sister, Madame Gerber, was the chief designer. Callot Soeurs was best known for graceful day dresses, oriental-style gowns made from rich fabrics, and beaded chemises. It was the first house to use gold and silver lamé. Trimmings were also a feature of Callot Soeurs designs. In the late 1920s, Pierre Gerber (the son of Madame Gerber) took over the running of the house. It closed in 1937.

Cardin, Pierre 1922– Born Venice, Italy. At the age of fourteen, Cardin was apprenticed to a tailor. After World War II he worked in Paris for PAQUIN, Marcelle Chaumont, Schiaparelli and DIOR. He opened his own house in 1950 and his first ready-to-wear collection was presented in 1963. Initially known for simple, youthful couture, he later produced avant-garde designs in geometric forms influenced by Op Art and the 'space age'.

Chanel, Coco (Gabrielle Bonheur) 1883–1971 Born Saumur, France. Chanel began her fashion career in 1908 as a milliner in a small shop in Paris. Within a few years she had made her first dresses and achieved enough success to open boutiques in Deauville and Biarritz. Chanel's early designs were revolutionary: made of simple, cheap materials and often adapted from traditional menswear or from sportswear, they gave women unprecedented freedom of movement. She also encouraged the use of costume jewelry. She closed her house in 1939. After a period of exile in Switzerland, she returned to Paris in 1954 and eventually regained her former stature, mainly because of the popularity in the USA of the Chanel suit, the classic, timeless design for which she is still best known. The House of Chanel continues, with Karl LAGERFELD as designer.

Connolly, Sybil 1921–1998 Born Dublin, Ireland. Connolly trained at Bradley's dressmaking establishment in London in the late 1930s. In 1939 she returned to Dublin and joined the fashion house of Richard Alan as a designer. She founded Sybil Connolly Limited, Ireland's first couture house, in 1952. Connolly is best known for classic designs using fine pleated handkerchief linen, Irish tweeds and Carrickmacross lace.

Courrèges, André 1923– Born Pau, France. Courrèges worked with BALENCIAGA from 1950 until 1961, when he opened his own house. He is best known for the clean, spare, architectural shapes of his 1960s designs. His simple, well-tailored clothes, 'space-age' mini-dresses and slim hipster pants in white or pale colours were copied worldwide.

Creed, Charles 1909–1966 Born Paris, France. Creed studied tailoring and art in Vienna, learned weaving techniques at Linton Tweeds in Carlisle, England, and worked at BERGDORF GOODMAN in New York. In the mid-1930s he joined the family tailoring firm in Paris. In 1949 he opened his own couture house in London, which became known for its tailored suits and coats.

de la Renta, Oscar 1932– Born Santo Domingo, Dominican Republic. De la Renta studied art in the Dominican Republic and at the Academy of San Fernando in Madrid. He worked briefly as a sketcher for BALENCIAGA before moving to Paris in 1961 as assistant to Antonio del Castillo at LANVIN. In 1962 he moved to New York and spent two years as a designer at Elizabeth Arden. A year later he began designing for Jane Derby and on her death in 1965 took over the firm under his own name. He is best known for extravagant evening dresses and ball gowns.

Dior, Christian 1905–1957 Born Normandy, France. Dior worked in the 1930s as a freelance fashion artist for newspapers and magazines. He also sold fashion sketches to the milliner Agnès and to the couturier Robert Piguet, who hired Dior as a designer in 1938. In 1942 Dior joined LELONG, eventually leaving to form his own house. Dior showed his first collection under his own name in 1947. Called the 'Corolle' line, this collection was subsequently dubbed the New Look. With its ultra-feminine silhouette and extravagant use of fabric, it was an overwhelming success. Dior remained an influential couturier until his early death in 1957. The House of Dior continued with other designers, including Yves SAINT LAURENT and Marc Bohan.

Dolce & Gabbana Design partnership established in 1985. Domenico Dolce (b. 1958) and Stefano Gabbana (b. 1962) met at an atelier in Milan, Italy. They presented their first womenswear collection in 1986 to international acclaim. Four years later they showed their first menswear collection and opened their first boutique in Milan. The Dolce & Gabbana line is best known for its sensual and nostalgically glamorous designs.

Drécoll The House of Drécoll, originally founded in Vienna by Christopher Drécoll, opened in Paris in 1905 as a partnership between Drécoll and his chief designer Madame Besançon de Wagner. It was known for its elaborate afternoon and evening dresses. In the late 1920s the business passed into the hands of Madame Besançon de Wagner's daughter.

Fabiani, Alberto Born Tivoli, Italy. At eighteen, Fabiani began a three-year apprenticeship with a Parisian tailor. He returned to Italy to work in the family fashion house. In 1953 he married the designer SIMONETTA and in 1961 they opened a joint house in Paris. Fabiani eventually returned to Rome, where he continued designing until his retirement in 1974. He is best known for his tailored suits and dresses.

Fath, Jacques 1912–1954 Born Lafitte, France. Fath opened his Paris house in 1937. He was a popular designer in the USA, where, in the 1940s, he created ready-to-wear collections for the Seventh Avenue manufacturer Joseph Halpert. Fath is best known for slightly racy, glamorous evening wear.

Foale & Tuffin Design partnership established in 1962 and dissolved in 1972. Marion Foale (b. 1939) and Sally Tuffin (b. 1938) met when they were studying at Walthamstow College of Art and the Royal College of Art, London. They are best known for their trouser suits and lace dresses.

Goma, Michel 1932– Born Montpellier, France. Goma studied dressmaking and art before moving to Paris at the age of nineteen. He worked first as a freelance fashion sketcher and then, from 1950 to 1958, as a designer for Jeanne Lafaurie. In 1958 he bought out Lafaurie, renaming it Michel Goma. The house closed in 1963; Goma joined Jean PATOU the same year and remained there until 1973. He is best known for elegant, understated clothes.

Grès, Alix (Germaine Barton) 1899–1993 Born Paris, France. Grès learned her skills at Premet before beginning work on her own as a toile maker. She opened her own house in 1934 under the name Alix Barton (usually shortened to 'Alix'). The house closed in 1940, to be reopened after the war as Grès (the pseudonym of her painter-husband). Grès is best known for classically draped silk and wool jersey.

Gucci Founded in Florence, Italy, in 1921. Originally a small saddlery and leather goods company, the business expanded under the directorship of Guccio Gucci and opened its first boutique in Rome in 1938. The company achieved worldwide success with its much-imitated snaffled loafer, but by the 1980s was in decline. The ready-to-wear collection of 1995, designed by Tom Ford, resurrected the label, which has a reputation for sexy, sophisticated, luxury wear.

Hamnett, Katharine 1947– Born Kent, England. Hamnett studied Fashion Design at St Martin's College of Art, London, from 1965 to 1969. For the next ten years she worked as a freelance designer for companies in Britain, France, Italy and the USA. In 1979 she set up her own company. She is best known for cotton clothes, often based on workwear, and for T-shirts printed with anti-war and pro-environment slogans.

Hartnell, (Sir) Norman (Bishop) 1901–1979 Born London, England. In 1923 Hartnell worked for a short time with Lucile, before opening his own business later that year. He took his collection to Paris in 1927 and again in 1930. In 1938 he was appointed dressmaker to the British Royal Family. He is best known for his embroidered and beaded evening and ball gowns, and for his fine tailoring.

Heim, Jacques c. 1898–1967 Born Paris, France. Heim inherited the family furriers, for which he designed women's clothes. In the 1930s he opened his own house in the avenue Matignon. Ten years later he began to launch a chain of boutiques specializing in sportswear, for which he was best known. Heim was President of the Chambre Syndicale de la Couture Parisienne from 1958 to 1962.

Henri Early 20th-century French couturier, known in the 1930s for well-tailored active and spectator sportswear.

Kenzo (Kenzo Takada) 1940– Born Kyoto, Japan. Kenzo studied at the Bunka Gakuin fashion school in Tokyo. In 1965 he moved to Paris, where he produced freelance collections for various fashion houses and department stores. He opened his own shop, Jungle Jap, in 1970. The company name was later changed to Kenzo. He is best known for his inventive knitwear and his successful blending of traditional Japanese and Western ideas.

Klein, Calvin (Richard) 1942– Born New York, USA. Klein graduated from New York's Fashion Institute of Technology in 1962. He worked as a sketcher, a coat and suit designer, and as a copy boy for *Women's Wear Daily* before starting his own company in 1968. He is best known for the understated elegance of his designs.

Lacroix, Christian 1951– Born Arles (Bouches du Rhône), France. Lacroix studied History of Art at the Université Paul Valéry, Montpellier. In 1973 he moved to Paris and studied for a Master's Degree in 'Dress in 17th-Century French Painting' at the Institute of Art. In 1978 he became a stylist at Hermès and later worked for Guy Paulin before being appointed artistic director at Jean PATOU in 1981. In 1987 he opened his own couture house. Lacroix is known for his inventive and sophisticated use of colour, fabric and decoration, and for the dazzling variety of sources – from bullfighting, to everything English, to contemporary folklore – from which he produces his collections.

Lagerfeld, Karl (Otto) 1938– Born Hamburg, Germany. In 1956, at the age of eighteen, Lagerfeld was hired by Pierre Balmain after winning First Prize in the coat section of a competition sponsored by the International Wool Secretariat. In 1958 he joined Jean PATOU as artistic director and remained there until 1964, when he took a year off to complete his education. Lagerfeld worked as a freelance designer from 1965 to 1967 and then joined Fendi as a consultant designer. In 1983 he became design director of CHANEL. His first collection under his own name was shown in 1984. He is best known for sophisticated day and evening wear, with a strong emphasis on accessories.

Lanvin, Jeanne 1867–1946 Born Brittany, France. Lanvin began in Paris in the 1890s as a milliner and then added children's and women's clothes to her repertoire. By 1914 she was an established couturier with a youthful and elegant clientele. She is best known for her romantic, feminine dresses, known as *robes de style*. The House of Lanvin continued after her death; its designers have included Antonio del Castillo (creator of the suit on p. 129), Jules-François Crahay and Maryll Lanvin (wife of Jeanne Lanvin's great-nephew).

Lapidus, Ted (Edmond) 1929– Born Paris, France. After studying technology in Tokyo, Lapidus opened a boutique in Paris in the early 1950s. He is best known for his precise tailoring.

Laroche, Guy 1923–1989 Born La Rochelle, France. Laroche began his career as a milliner before joining Jean Dessès in 1950. Seven years later he opened his own house. He showed his first ready-to-wear collection in 1960. Laroche is best known for sophisticated, elegant clothes.

Lelong, Lucien 1889–1958 Born Paris, France. Lelong established his own house in 1918 and diversified into ready-to-wear in 1934. He was president of the Chambre Syndicale de la Couture Parisienne from 1937 to 1947 and was instrumental in keeping French fashion houses open during the war. He is best known for beautiful fabrics and fine workmanship.

Maison Rouff Fashion house established in Vienna in the 1880s, and in Paris in the early 20th century. PAQUIN trained there. In 1928 the house was taken over by DRÉCOLL's former director, Madame Besançon de Wagner, who subsequently designed under the name Maggy Rouff. Maison Rouff was best known for elaborate day wear.

Mattli, Giuseppi (Gustavo) 1907–1982 Born Locarno, Switzerland. Mattli trained at the House of Premet. In 1934 he opened in London under his own name. Though he stopped producing couture in 1955, he continued his ready-to-wear lines until the early 1970s. Mattli is best known for cocktail and evening wear.

Michael (Michael Donellan) Born Ireland. Donellan worked for many years with Lachasse, before establishing his own company, Michael of Carlos Place, in 1953. He closed at the end of the 1960s. Michael was best known for elegant, tailored clothes.

Molyneux, (Captain) Edward 1891–1974 Born London, England. Molyneux began his career as a freelance sketcher for newspapers and magazines. In 1911 he won a competition organized by Lucile, who later employed him in her London house. After serving as a captain in the British Army in World War I, he established his own house in Paris in 1919. Between 1925 and 1929 he opened branches in Monte Carlo, Cannes, Biarritz and London. Molyneux closed in 1950. He is best known for his conservative, tasteful clothes.

Montana, Claude 1949– Born Paris, France. Montana began his career in London in the 1960s as a designer of jewelry made of papier-mâché and rhinestones, which he sold in street markets. In 1972 he returned to Paris and began working for the leatherwear manufacturer MacDouglas. Montana showed his first collection under his own name in 1977. He is best known for his designs in leather.

Morton, Digby 1906–1983 Born Dublin, Ireland. Morton moved to London in 1928 and began working with Lachasse. In 1933 he opened his own house. In 1942 he was a founder member of the Incorporated Society of London Fashion Designers. His house closed in 1957. Morton is best known for well-tailored clothes, often in pale tweeds, and for elegant evening wear.

Mugler, Thierry 1948– Born Strasbourg, France. Mugler designed his first collection in 1971, under the name Café de Paris, and his first collection under his own name in 1973. He is best known for sexy, glamorous, highly theatrical clothes.

Ozbek, Rifat 1953– Born Istanbul, Turkey. Ozbek studied architecture and then fashion design at St Martin's School of Art, London. After graduating he worked as a designer in Italy for the ready-to-wear company Monsoon. In 1984 he established his own company, producing couture and ready-to-wear clothes that have become well known for their unconventional use of colour, ethnic inspiration and surface decoration.

Paquin ?–1936 Madame Paquin joined MAISON ROUFF as a house mannequin and then trained there before opening her own house in 1891. In 1900 she was selected to organize the Fashion Section of the Exposition Universelle in Paris. Her success before World War I was such that she opened branches in London, Madrid and Buenos Aires. Paquin retired as a designer in 1920 but the house did not close until 1956. She is best known for her lively yet tasteful designs. Her opulent, fur-trimmed walking suits became a signature of the house.

Patou, Jean 1880–1936 Born Normandy, France. After working in his uncle's fur business, Patou opened and closed two small dressmaking establishments of his own in Paris before founding Maison Parry in 1912. In 1914 he sold an entire collection to an American buyer. After serving in the army during World War I, Patou reopened under his own name in 1919. He is best known for spectator and active sportswear and for chic, wearable clothes. The House of Patou continued after his death with designers such as Karl LAGERFELD, Michel GOMA and Christian LACROIX.

Poiret, Paul 1879–1944 Born Paris, France. Poiret sold sketches to various houses before joining Doucet in 1896. Four years later he moved to WORTH, with whom he remained until he opened his own house in 1904. Poiret's greatest success was in the years 1904 to 1914. He introduced into fashion a looser, less restrained, less corseted look, and after 1909, under the influence of Bakst's designs for the Ballets Russes, produced an oriental line using exotic colours and shapes. In 1910 he created the notorious 'hobble skirt'. Poiret closed his house during World War I and though he reopened after the war he never regained his former status. He was forced to close his house in 1929.

Quant, Mary 1934– Born London, England. Quant studied at Goldsmith's College of Art, London. In 1955, with her husband-to-be Alexander Plunket-Greene and business partner Archie McNair, she opened the shop Bazaar in the King's Road, Chelsea, the first shop to sell cheap clothes aimed specifically at young people. Soon after, Quant began stocking clothes of her own design. She is best known for popularizing the mini-dress.

Redfern (House of) The house originated in the mid-1850s in Cowes on the Isle of Wight, where its founder, John Redfern, had developed a small drapery into a successful business selling sportswear. Branches were eventually opened in London, Paris, Edinburgh and New York. Ernest Arthur Redfern (1856–1947) managed the London and New York branches; Charles Poynter managed the Paris branch. In 1888 Redfern was appointed dressmaker to Queen Victoria. The houses closed in the 1920s. Redfern is best known in the early years for sportswear and the tailored suit and later for evening dresses of considerable theatrical elegance.

Ricci, Nina (Maria Nielli) 1883–1970 Born Turin, Italy. Beginning in her early teens, Ricci served a long apprenticeship with a Paris couturier before opening her own house in 1932. An immensely successful couturier, she was best known for sophisticated, elegant clothes in classic styles. She retired in 1945. Subsequent designers for the House of Ricci have included Jules-François Crahay and Gérard Pipart (who created the dress on p. 185).

Rykiel, Sonia 1930– Born Paris, France. Rykiel's first designs were maternity sweaters for herself. She then went on to design a range of sweaters which she sold in her husband's boutique, Laura. In the mid-1960s she opened her own company. She is known for her fluid, clinging designs, in jersey, suede, knitted wool and soft, knitted cotton.

Saint Laurent, Yves (Henri Donat Mathieu) 1936– Born Oran, Algeria. Saint Laurent studied in Paris. In 1953 he won First Prize in a competition sponsored by the International Wool Secretariat and was subsequently hired by Christian DIOR, with whom he worked until Dior's death in 1957. Saint Laurent then took over as art director of the Christian Dior Company, enjoying worldwide success with his first collection: the trapeze line. In 1961 he opened his own house, presenting his first collection under his own name in January 1962. In the 1960s Saint Laurent created a range of young and innovative designs for women, including the 'smoking' or 'tuxedo' jacket, velvet knickerbockers and the safari jacket. He is best known as a master of casual chic.

Simonetta (Duchesa Simonetta Colonna di Cesaro) 1922– Born Rome, Italy. In 1946 Simonetta opened a house in Rome under her married name, Simonetta Visconti. After her second marriage – in 1953, to designer Alberto FABIANI – she continued to work under the name Simonetta. In 1961 she and Fabiani opened a house together in Paris. Four years later Simonetta returned to Rome, where she continued as a designer for some years. She is best known for knitwear, and for structured, elegant clothes.

Soprani, Luciano 1946–1999 Born Reggiolo, Italy. In 1967 Soprani joined the ready-to-wear firm MaxMara and remained there for seven years before becoming a freelance designer in 1975. He designed for GUCCI, Helyette, Pims and Basile. In 1982 he presented his first collection under his own name. He is best known for strong colours and expert tailoring.

Stein & Blaine Early 20th-century U.S. firm. Stein & Blaine imported original Paris couture model gowns to be copied for the ready-to-wear market, as well as producing their own Paris-inspired high fashion.

Strassner English designer, popular during World War II. Strassner is best known for sportswear and leisure wear, as well as evening wear featuring contrasting colours at the back and front, and at the top and bottom.

Ungaro, Emanuel (Maffeolti) 1933– Born Aix-en-Provence, France. Ungaro trained as a tailor in the family business. In 1955 he joined BALENCIAGA in Paris, moving in 1961 to COURRÈGES. He opened his own business in 1965. Known initially for his crisp, tailored, 'space-age' clothes, he later softened his look, producing a more flowing line.

Valentino (Garavani) 1932– Born Voghera, Italy. At the age of seventeen Valentino moved to Paris and apprenticed with Jean Desses and Guy LAROCHE. In the early 1960s he established his own company in Rome. His first collection, shown in 1962, was hugely successful. He is best known for elegant, classic designs.

Vernon (House of) Late 19th-century/early 20th-century English ladies tailoring establishment. Best known for exquisitely cut and trimmed clothes.

Versace Founded in Milan, Italy, in 1978 by Gianni Versace (1946–1997), who studied architecture before beginning his career in fashion design at the age of 25. He achieved particular success with his knitwear and in the mid-1970s was hired by Complice. His first solo collections in 1978 were immediately successful and the company quickly expanded. After his untimely death, his sister Donatella became creative director. The house is best known for its sexy, exhibitionist, glamorous designs.

Westwood, Vivienne 1941– Born Derbyshire, England. Westwood trained as a primary school teacher. She began designing in 1971 in collaboration with her then-partner, Malcolm McLaren. Her first design was a pair of Lurex drainpipe trousers which were put on sale in their shop in Chelsea, along with fifties memorabilia. In 1976 Westwood and McLaren created their infamous 'Punkature', consisting of ripped T-shirts, bondage trousers, safety pins, etc. Their first fashion collection, 'Pirate', was presented in 1981. Since that time Westwood has become Britain's most influential designer, known for original and innovative cutting techniques and bold mixtures of colours and fabrics.

Worth, Charles Frederick 1825–1895 Born Lincolnshire, England. The House of Worth was founded in 1858. After Charles Frederick's death the firm was taken over by his sons, Jean-Philippe (1856–1926) and Gaston (1853–1924). Jean-Philippe was responsible mainly for design and Gaston for organization and administration. In the 1920s and 1930s the design passed into other hands. The house merged with PAQUIN in 1954 and closed in 1956. In the late 19th century the house was best known for its evening wear.

Sources for Fashion Since 1900

Anderson Black, J., and Madge Garland, *A History of Fashion*, 1975.

Battersby, Martin, *Art Deco Fashion*, 1974

Blum, Stella, *Everyday Fashions of the Twenties*, 1981.

Boucher, François, *A History of Costume in the West*, 1965.

Bradfield, Nancy, *Historical Costumes of England*, 1958.

—, *Costume in Detail*, 1968.

Brooke, Iris, *A History of English Costume*, 1937.

Buckley, V. C., *Good Times*, 1979.

Coleridge, Lady Georgina, *The Ladies Realm*, 1972.

Contini, Mila, *Fashion*, 1965.

De Courtais, Georgine, *Women's Headdresses and Hairstyles*, 1973.

Dorner, Jane, *Fashion in the Twenties and Thirties*, 1973.

—, *Fashion in the Forties and Fifties*, 1975.

Drake, Nicholas, *The Fifties in Vogue*, 1987.

Etherington-Smith, Meredith, *Patou*, 1983.

Ewing, Elizabeth, *Fur in Dress*, 1981.

—, *Dress and Undress: A History of Women's Underwear*, 1978.

Gallery of English Costume, *Weddings*, 1976.

Ginsburg, Madeleine, *Wedding Dress 1740–1970*, 1981.

—, *The Hat: Trends and Traditions*, 1990.

Hall-Duncan, Nancy, *The History of Fashion Photography*, 1979.

Hamilton-Hill, Margot, and Peter A. Bucknell, *The Evolution of Fashion 1066 to 1930*, 1967.

Hansen, Henny Harald, *Costume Cavalcade*, 1956.

Harrison, Michael, *The History of the Hat*, 1960.

Hermitage Museum, *The Art of Costume in Russia: 18th to the Early 20th Century*, 1979.

Hopkins, J. C., *The Twentieth-Century System of Ladies Garment Cutting*, 1902.

Howell, Georgina, *In Vogue: Six Decades of Fashion*, 1975.

Jarvis, Anthea, *Brides, Wedding Clothes and Customs 1850–1980*, 1983.

Kelsall, Freda, *How We Used to Live: 1936–1953*, 1981.

Kennett, Frances, *The Collector's Book of Twentieth-Century Fashion*, 1983.

Langley-Moore, Doris, *Fashion through Fashion Plates*, 1971.

Latour, Anny, *Kings of Fashion*, 1958.

Laver, James, *Costume*, 1963.

—, *A Concise History of Costume*, 1969.

Lee-Potter, Charlie, *Sportswear in Vogue*, 1984.

Lynham, Ruth, ed., *Paris Fashion: The Great Designers and Their Creations*, 1972.

Mulvagh, Jane, *Vogue: History of 20th Century Fashion*, 1988.

O'Hara, Georgina, *The Encyclopaedia of Fashion*, 1986.

Peacock, John, *Fashion Sketch Book 1920–1960*, 1977.

—, *Costume 1066–1966*, 1986.

—, *The Chronicle of Western Costume*, 1991.

Polhemus, Ted, and Lynn Proctor, *Fashion and Anti-Fashion: An Anthology of Clothing and Adornment*, 1978.

Pringle, Margaret, *Dance Little Ladies: The Day of the Debutante*, 1977.

Ribeiro, Aileen, *Dress and Morality*, 1986.

Robinson, Julian, *The Fine Art of Fashion: An Illustrated History*, 1989.

Saint Laurent, Cecil, *The History of Ladies Underwear*, 1968.

Silmon, Pedro, *The Bikini*, 1986.

Stevenson, Pauline, *Edwardian Fashion*, 1980.

Waugh, Norah, *Corsets and Crinolines*, 1954.

—, *The Cut of Women's Clothes 1600–1930*, 1968.

Wilcox, R. Turner, *The Mode in Costume*, 1942.

—, *Five Centuries of American Costume*, 1963.

—, *The Dictionary of Costume*, 1969.

Winter, Gordon, *A Country Camera, 1844–1914*, 1966.

—, *A Cockney Camera*, 1971.

—, *The Golden Years: 1903–1913*, 1975.

Yarwood, Doreen, *English Costume: From the Second Century to 1967*, 1952.